Library of Public Policy and Public Administration

Volume 15

Around the world there are challenges to the way we administer government. Some of these have to do with brute force that is backed by self-interest. However, there are those intrepid souls who think we are all better than this. This series of monographs and edited collections of original essays seeks to explore the very best way that governments can execute their sovereign duties within the sphere of ethically-based public policy that recognizes human rights and the autonomy of its citizens.

Proposals to the series can include policy questions that are nationally or internationally situated. For example, regional migration from victims of war, terrorism, police integrity, political corruption, the intersection between politics and public health, hunger, clean water and sanitation, global warming, treatment of the "other" nationally and internationally, and issues of distributive justice and human rights.

Proposals that discuss systemic changes in the structure of government solutions will also be considered. These include *corruption and anti-corruption, bribery, nepotism,* and *effective systems design.*

Series benchmark: 110,000-150,000 words. Special books can be somewhat longer.

More information about this series at http://www.springer.com/series/6234

Edward H. Spence

Media Corruption in the Age of Information

Springer

Edward H. Spence
Department of Philosophy
University of Sydney
Sydney, NSW, Australia

ISSN 1566-7669
Library of Public Policy and Public Administration
ISBN 978-3-030-61611-3 ISBN 978-3-030-61612-0 (eBook)
https://doi.org/10.1007/978-3-030-61612-0

This Springer imprint is published by the registered company Springer Nature Switzerland AG
The registered company address is: Gewerbestrasse 11, 6330 Cham, Switzerland

For The Sempiternal Muse

Contents

Chapter 1
Introduction

We shall not cease from exploration
And the end of all our exploring
Will be to arrive were we started
And the know place for the first time.

T.S. Eliot, from Little Gidding, *Four Quartets.*

1.1 Why a Book on Media Corruption?

The aim of this book is to introduce the topic of media corruption. The topic of media corruption is important in the age of information in which we now live and most of our daily activities including work, shopping, travel, banking, communication, learning and teaching, and play, are conducted informationally online, through the internet. For good or bad, we are now to an unprecedented extent, *informational beings* in possession of digital informational identities. We use these to communicate with other informational beings, globally. Information matters to us because information dominates all aspects of our lives. The need to know, communicate and share information with others is, therefore, a significant and crucial aspect of our lives as citizens. As the current Covid-19 pandemic has so painfully shown, we need and require information to be true or at least truthful (intended to be true), accurate, reliable, trustworthy, and credible. Information places upon us, in our capacity of producers, users, and disseminators of information, as individuals and collectively as groups, institutions and societies generally, both epistemic and ethical responsibilities in ensuring the accurate, truthful, reliable and trustworthy dissemination and communication of information on the World Wide Web. When those responsibilities are not only not complied with, out of ignorance or negligence, but worse intentionally infringed for personal interest or profit, the value of information like counterfeit currency is corrupted and is diminished, undermining trust and the common good of society.

E. H. Spence, *Media Corruption in the Age of Information*, Library of Public Policy and Public Administration 15, https://doi.org/10.1007/978-3-030-61612-0_1

This book examines and evaluates the impact of the corruption of information though misinformation and disinformation, as well as the corruption of media institutions whose informational practices are conducive and result in media corruption, and as the Cambridge Analytica case illustrates, the corruption of the democratic system itself. The main objective of this book is to show why media corruption matters and matters crucially in the age of information and why we should take it much more seriously than we have up to now. Other forms of corruption, such as political, financial and sports corruption, and corruption within the church are taken seriously, as of course they should. Talking metaphorically, given the global reach of information through the World Wide Web, media corruption has become, in an age dominated by the platformization of information by the Information Technology companies, such as Facebook and Google, a global pandemic problem. That problem and its global epistemic, ethical and eudaimonic impact on society will be explored in Chaps. 3 and 4.

Having explained briefly why a book on media corruption is required, this introductory chapter will offer an explanation of media corruption through its relation to other better known forms of corruption, such as political, corporate, financial, sports and police corruption and corruption in the clergy, as well as provide an outline of the main features of each chapter.

Corruption is pervasive, diverse, and present in almost all areas of society. There is corporate corruption. From the "greed is good" heyday of the 1980s that encompassed the rise and fall of corporate high-flyers such as Alan Bond[1] and Christopher Skase,[2] right through to the 2000s and the spectacular collapses of Enron[3] and WorldCom in the U.S. and HIH Insurance in Australia, corruption seems to continue unabated. The financial and human costs of corruption have been enormous. Billions of dollars have been lost to both the corporations and the shareholders – in the case of Enron, employees who had invested most of their life savings in that company, lost everything. Reputations have been destroyed, lives turned upside down, and a number of the heads of corporations have been imprisoned. Enron chief financial officer Andrew Fastow, WorldCom chief executive Bernard Ebbers and HIH's Rodney Adler and Bradley Cooper have all landed in jail. Nick Leeson, a Singapore based employee of the United Kingdom based merchant bank Barings, virtually destroyed that enterprise by hiding details of unsuccessful deals in temporary internal accounts that he had the authority to operate. His purpose was to boost

[1] For details about Alan Bond's heroic status and then fall from grace after jailed for corruption see ABC News https://www.abc.net.au/news/2015-06-05/alan-bond-10-things-you-need-to-know/6520736. Accessed April 3, 2020.

[2] For details of the collapse of Christopher Skases's $1.8 billion business empire through corruption see https://www.nzherald.co.nz/world/news/article.cfm?c_id=2&objectid=206714. Accessed April 3, 2020.

[3] For a detail account of Enron and its collapse through corruption see Miller, Seumas, Roberts, Peter, and Spence, Edward, (2005) *Corruption and Anti-Corruption: An Applied Philosophical Approach*, pages, 34–37.

his standing within the bank by appearing to generate earnings that were not there. Leeson was convicted and served a jail sentence in Singapore.

There is police corruption. In Australia, officers were brought before the Royal Commission to investigate corruption in the New South Wales Police Service in the mid-1990s on charges of taking bribes, dealing in drugs, organizing bank robberies, and selling child pornography. Some of these officers were sent to prison to be among the criminals they once used to pursue. In the United States of America in the 1970s one of the most celebrated cops in modern history, Frank Serpico, went public to expose police corruption in the New York Police Department. However, it was not until the *New York Times* published a front-page story on Serpico that Mayor John Lindsay appointed the Knapp Commission to investigate. The role of investigative journalism in exposing corruption with the help of whistleblowers, such as Frank Serpico, will be examined in Chap. 6.

Watergate is an example of political corruption on a grand scale. It forced the resignation of President Richard Nixon and launched the careers of two virtually unknown journalists from *Washington Post*, Carl Bernstein, and Bob Woodward. There is judicial corruption as in the case exposed by the *Chicago Tribune* in 1999, which reported several cases of men sentenced to death in Illinois State who had been beaten by police officers into confessing crimes they had not committed. Worse, they were defended by incompetent lawyers that led to the men's convictions on questionable evidence. As a result of that exposure, the governor of Illinois suspended all executions in that State. In 2016, Eddie Obeid, an influential politician and 'power broker' of the Labor Party of New South Wales in Australia, was jailed for 5 years after the Supreme Court of New South Wales found him guilty of misconduct in public office.

There is corruption in sport none bigger than the uncovering of corruption in the bidding process that had won the 2002 Winter Olympics for Salt Lake City. Olympic athletes and sports administrators have been suspended and their careers ruined when athletes tested positive for illicit performance- enhancing drugs. Following Italy's victory in the World Cup final in 2006, several A-League clubs in that country were relegated to the B-League because of match-fixing. On the eve of the allegations of corruption going public, the manager of Juventus one of the most celebrated and successful clubs not only in Italy but worldwide, tried to commit suicide. He survived and was not charged for corruption as the reason for his suicide remained unclear and thought to be related to depression over a medical condition and the fate of his club, rather than corruption (McMahon 2006).

There is corruption in the Church involving several reported cases of priests and ministers sexually abusing children in their care. One examined in this book involved the exposure of sexual abuse in the Catholic Archdiocese of Boston by the *Boston Globe* in 2002. In 2020, Cardinal George Pell, the highest-ranking Catholic cleric in Australia, once touted to become the first Australian Pope, was jailed in 2019 for 6 years after being charged in court for sexually abusing children (Cooper 2020). However, on a recent court appeal in April 2020, he was found not guilty and released from prison.

Corruption is everywhere. Metaphorically speaking, it could be compared in its ubiquity to humanity's legendary fall from grace after expelled from the Garden of Eden. How did we end up in this sorry state? Corruption is not a new phenomenon. It has been with us a long time, at least since Plato's time, who first alerted us to its attraction and destructive immoral influence and impact. For as we shall see throughout this book, corruption is first and foremost, *a moral problem*. Given the ability of individuals or corporations to use their *power* when they have the *opportunity* and *disposition* to do so under conditions of *concealment* that promises immunity from detection and punishment, in dereliction and *abuse of their fiduciary duty of trust* to others, for their own *self-gain*, it will continue for a long time yet. The terms in italics in the preceding lines highlight the general characteristics present and common to all types of institutional and personal corruption, including media corruption that is the main topic of this book.

Plato recognized the problem and the pull of corruption in his celebrated "Myth of Gyges" in *The Republic*. He refers to it as the "highest reach of injustice, being deemed just when you are not". He labels this "the most perfect injustice"[4] and asks what possible reason would someone like Gyges have for not being unjust or immoral (and analogously "corrupt" as explained and illustrated in this book) if they think it is in their self-interest and gain and there is a good chance, they might get away with it through concealment.

Just like Gyges, corrupt police officers, corrupt corporate magnates, corrupt priests and church ministers, corrupt politicians and members of the judicial system, corrupt athletes, corrupt sports administrators and academics, and as we shall examine in this book, corrupt media professionals and media institutions, as well as corrupt practices by the Big Tech companies, such as Facebook and Google, among others, all have one thing in common: secretly and covertly they abuse their fiduciary duty of trust to the public for self-gain under conditions approaching those of perfect injustice – they appear just and honourable, when in truth they are not. And just like Gyges, who as the King is obliged to use his authority and office for the public good, all who engage in corruption use their authority and office to abuse the interests of those they are meant to serve and protect – the people who put their trust in them. Under the pretext that they are law abiding and ethical, corrupt people and institutions everywhere engage as Glaucon tells us, in Plato's *Republic*, in "perfect injustice".

You may think it is just as well that we can depend on the media, in the form of the fourth Estate, especially investigative journalism, to expose and report on all forms of corruption whenever and wherever it takes place. After all, we only know of corruption, when we see it, hear of it, and read it as news in the media. It is the role of the media and journalism specifically to inform the public on matters of public interest, matters that impact on our individual and collective freedoms and wellbeing (Spence 2008, 2017), and apart from pandemics and wars, none have a bigger impact on society than corruption. And it is because of that role that the

[4] *The Republic*, Book 2, p. 361.

freedom of the press even if not enshrined in the constitution, as in the United States of America, is sacrosanct in democracies across the world. It is the corner stone of democracy itself. In an age heralded as the age of information, the media's freedom to inform the public on matters of public interest truthfully, because the public has a right to know, as the Covid-19 pandemic has currently demonstrated, is both necessary and crucial.

What happens then when it turns out that this sacred cow, the media, is unbeknown to the public, engaging in corruption – not only in isolated instances of corruption but systemic corruption that undermines our institutions and the whole democratic system? Who can we trust if we cannot trust the media to tell us the truth and not lie to us? Who is watching the watchers? Although the media exposes all other forms of corruption, its own corruption remains for the most part unidentified and unknown. Even when identified, instances of media corruption are usually described by the generic term of "unethical" practices or merely practices not complying with "best practice" or "codes of ethics" but rarely if ever are they labelled as instances of *media corruption*. In the age of information, when information has become the most valuable commodity in the world; *weaponised* by politicians in the form of propaganda and fake news; *monetized* by the Big Tech companies, such as Facebook and Google, two of the most financially successful corporate entities worldwide, made affluent simply for selling users' data to advertisers and other information brokers for profit, without the users' informed consent, as in the Cambridge Analytica scandal of 2016; it is time to look more closely and critically into some of the unethical practices of the media, which on closer examination appear to have all the characterizing features of corruption, as well as meet both the necessary and sufficient conditions of corruption generally.

1.2 What Is Corruption?

Although in defining corruption both by its characterising features and conditions will be analysed and illustrated in detail in Chaps. 3 and 4, it would be useful to summarise them here, in outline:

1.2.1 The Characterising Features of Corruption

The six features that characterize corruption generally, including media corruption, as highlighted above in the context of Plato's Myth of Gyges, are: the *possession of power*, *disposition* to exercise that power, *opportunity* to exercise that power, *invisibility* or concealment, *self-regarding gain*, and a pre-existing *fiduciary duty of trust*.

Possession of power is the ability or capacity to act in a manner capable of bringing about a certain intended desired outcome; a *disposition to exercise that power* is the possession of a predisposition, pro-attitude or willingness to purposefully exercise that power; *opportunity* is having the opportunity, either presented to oneself or engineered by oneself, to engage in some activity for which one has the power and the predisposition in which to engage; *invisibility* or *concealment* is the ability or quality an agent has for keeping the motives and the identity of the agency of his actions invisible, concealed, or hidden from the gaze of others; *Self-regarding gain* is any gain, not necessarily financial, that accrues to the agent personally or to a group of which he is a member, as a result of his or the group's actions; *fiduciary duty of trust* is a socially pre-established and widely acknowledged fiduciary relationship of trust that exists between the corrupt person or corrupt group and the person or group of persons who are wronged or harmed in some way by the corrupt person's or the corrupt group's actions. With regard to the condition of invisibility, while the actions themselves would be visible at least with regard to their effects and consequences, the identity of their agency is for the most part, invisible. Or at least the corrupt agent's intention is to keep his agency invisible or concealed.

Many of the characterizing features of corruption are present and accompany nearly all acts of corruption. For without power, one cannot commit a corrupt act. Possessing power is not enough; one must have the disposition to exercise that power willingly. Similarly, through lack of opportunity, one cannot engage in corrupt activity, even when one has both the power and the disposition to act corruptly. Invisibility seems to also be a characterizing feature of corruption that is usually, if not always, present in instances of corrupt activity.

Invisibility seems to be at least instrumentally desirable-, for without invisibility, one might not be able to evade detection, which is essential to escape possible social disapproval and punitive retribution from others or the state. Like Glaucon's perfectly unjust person, perfectly corrupt persons maintain an outward appearance of probity, justice, and morality, while carrying out their corrupt deeds in secret. In this way they maximize their self-regarding gain, which can accrue to them personally or to a group to which they belong or cause to which they are committed, with little or no instrumental cost to themselves, their group, or their cause. A socially pre-established and widely acknowledged fiduciary relationship of trust is also a necessary characterizing feature of corruption that must be present in all types of corruption, especially institutional corruption. The fiduciary relationship can be articulated in political, professional, educational, social, or the duties relating to the institutional role of the clergy or the media. Thus, for example, a priest or minister of religion, or teacher who sexually abuses children in his or her care is acting corruptly, even though there might not be any financial gain, as the self-regarding gain as a feature of corruption need not be financial but any gain that accrues to a person of group engaging in corruption.

1.2.2 The Necessary and Sufficient Conditions of Corruption

As in the case of the aforementioned characterizing features of corruption, it would also be useful to outline the necessary and sufficient conditions of corruption, with regard to corruption generally and as they specifically apply to media corruption (Miller 2018; Spence et al. 2011).

1. An instance of institutional corruption is an instance in which an action or joint action or set of actions performed by an agent or set of agents undermines or has a tendency to undermine or contribute to the undermining of a legitimate institutional role, process, goal(s) or purpose(s) (understood as a collective good) of that institution and/or an effect of the despoiling of the moral character of an institutional role occupant (s), qua role occupant of that institution. This is the *Institutional Actor Condition*.
2. An action or set of actions is corrupt only if it corrupts something or someone. This constitutes the *Cause and Effect Condition*.
3. An action or set of actions is corrupt only if the role occupant(s) who performs that action(s) intended it or foresaw the corrupting effects of that action(s) – or at the very least, could and should have foreseen the corrupting effects – or could have reasonably avoided the action(s). This is the *Moral Responsibility Condition*.

A common trait of institutional corruption that is not, however, a *necessary condition,* is its predominantly *systemic* nature. It is not a necessary condition for even if the corruption as illustrated by the Cambridge Analytica case that will be examined in Chap. 5 was a one-off case, it would still count as corruption because of its high societal impact and wide unethical repercussions and damage to public trust.

Another general feature of corruption is that all forms of corruption are immoral, though not all forms of immorality constitute corruption. So, although a burglar who breaks into your house to steal has committed an illegal act, he has not acted corruptly. Corruption requires a pre-exiting fiduciary duty of trust that renders the act corrupt though the act may not be illegal. Many forms of corruption, such as political bribery, are illegal, though some, like fabricating stories in journalism and advertorials, are not (Spence 2008; Spence et al. 2011). Corruption as understood and explained in this chapter and in more detail in Chaps. 3 and 4, is therefore fundamentally a moral problem.

1.3 Why Care About Media Corruption?

Apart from the aforementioned reasons, there are at least five other good reasons why we should be concerned and care about corruption in the media:

First, some practices by the media constitute corruption and should be recognized and described as such. Merely labelling such practices as unethical, does not capture the full moral seriousness of those practices, especially in the case of *institutional corruption*, nor does it allow for their proper *governance* and *regulation* and if warranted, prosecution under appropriate laws as in the case of other forms of corruption.

Second, media corruption like other forms of institutional corruption not only harms us individually, but also harms us collectively as a society by undermining the institutions that comprise and are necessary for our shared democratic system. A system that at least in principle is for the common good and, if not always in practice, is designed to protect and advance our individual and collective freedom and wellbeing as citizens.

Third, media corruption unlike other forms of corruption affects us all. We may, as individuals, not suffer personal and direct harm by corporate or police corruption. By contrast, insofar as we all rely on the dissemination of accurate and reliable information by the media to make informed choices and decisions on issues such as health, sport, elections, investments, war, and education, the corruption of information through disinformation in the form of fake news, deep fake videos, 'alternative facts', unsubstantiated conspiracy theories, as well as advertisements and public relations media releases masquerading as journalistic news or editorial comment, can have far-reaching harmful consequences and repercussions for all of us, and society at large, especially in the case of Tech Media corruption a topic we shall examine in Chap. 5.

Fourth, media corruption corrupts the source of the one thing we all rely on and need: Accurate, truthful, and reliable, trustworthy information. Information about our shared beliefs and more importantly, our ethical principles and values as citizens. The corruption of information by the media is no less serious than the pollution of our sources of clean water and air. In the current information age, information communicated through our shared global infosphere, just like water and air in the biosphere, is vital to our survival as civilized citizens. Media corruption corrupts and undermines our ability to function properly as citizens by corrupting the necessary condition for successful citizenry – accurate and reliable information. It is no surprise that dictators, oligarchs, and political leaders who see themselves to be above and beyond the law and ethical principles and values, try to muffle the media, in some cases, though imprisonment and the murder of journalists.

Finally, unless we can stem the flow of media corruption, we will end- up like the prisoners in Plato's *Allegory of the Cave*:[5] mistaking the shadows that the media create for our consumption, for reality. Worse still, we might not be able to discern the truth from the lies. Discerning and educated perception, based on accurate and reliable information, will be replaced, as in George Orwell's novel *1984*, with orchestrated and systemic mass deception.

At a time when increasingly the media is becoming more commercialized, when profits compete with the public interest, when cross-media laws allow the concentration of media ownership in the hands of fewer and fewer powerful moguls with

[5] See Appendix 2.

political and profit interests that override the public good, the need for more accurate and reliable information becomes more not less. As well, in a situation like the present pandemic, when political leaders in some democratic counties, by omission or commission, fail to provide truthful, reliable and trustworthy information, and moreover hinder trustworthy media and experts in the field from doing so, that could prove catastrophic.

Recognizing, documenting, and reporting media corruption will allow society to become less complacent, less tolerant, and more vigilant and resistant to its presence. It will also allow for its governance and minimization if not eradication, through appropriate regulatory measures as in the case of other forms of corruption. Further still, it will encourage the renaissance of a more vigorous and robust investigative journalism that is aware and expository of *media corruption* as it is of other forms of corruption. Chap. 6 will examine how investigative journalists, over a span of more than 70 years is still alive and well, and active in exposing and reporting on corruption and holding the corrupt, to account.

1.4 The Structure of the Book

This book will offer a comprehensive conceptual and applied philosophical analysis of media corruption, which is essential in assessing both the depth and breadth of media corruption and its nefarious and harmful impact on democracy and society.

Starting with the conceptual and philosophical analysis of corruption in general, the book will use and apply a *normative model of media corruption* that I developed specifically for application to the media (Spence 2008, 2017). Methodologically, I will utilize that model to first *identify* and *analyse* the phenomenon and practice of media corruption and then *evaluate* both epistemically and ethically, major *types* of corruption that arise regularly and systemically in the media. Key historical *case studies* discussed in relevant chapters in the book, provide a practical *illustration and contextualization* of the major types of media corruption.

The case studies analysed and evaluated in this book, given their frequency, are not meant to be exhaustive. Nor can they be. They are intended to provide practical examples that illustrate not individual specific tokens of issues, but *general types* of issues that constitute media corruption. Such general types of media corruption, as, for example, advertorials and cash-for-comment, have occurred and continue to occur regularly, across the global media over a span of many years. The illustrative case studies are, therefore, primarily indented to exhibit the *universal* and *global* nature of key types of media corruption, which occur regularly and systematically, across time and space. For example, one of the key types of media corruption identified, analysed, and normatively evaluated in Chap. 5 of this book, is *Tech Media corruption*, referred to as media corruption of the *sixth Estate* to differentiate it from corruption in the traditional legacy media of the fourth and fifth Estates.

In addition to identifying, analysing, and ethically evaluating the major types of corruption in the media, the book will also provide a diagnostic analysis of media corruption in terms of its possible causes and contexts. One major cause and context to be explored is the increasing commercialization and platformization of the media though the *monetization* of information. Indeed, one of the aims of the book is to enquire and analyse how and in what ways, in the new digital age of information, the commercial and market interests of media organizations and corporations are undermining and in some instances corrupting both the process and product of the communication of information to the public. That enquiry will importantly include the platformization of the media by the Big Tech companies, such as Facebook and Google, which for all intents and purposes, this book will identify as essentially *media companies* comprising the *sixth Estate*[6] and subject to the same rules and principles as other traditional media companies of the of the fourth and fifth Estates that comprise both the legacy media as well as the social media.

Another cause and context of media corruption to be explored in terms of the epistemology and ethics of information, is the selling of information as just another consumer commodity on the market, which is both epistemically and ethically problematic. And in the case of "cash-for-comment", "advertorials" and "media release journalism" practices, as well as misinformation in the form of fake news and deep fake videos, for example, may also prove conducive and constitute media corruption.

A close conceptual analysis of the notions of information and persuasion will be conducted to determine some of the theoretical and practical inherent inconsistencies that underlie those two concepts. The book will investigate how these inherent inconsistencies when allowed to covertly converge or be blurred, undermine the integrity of the media communication processes and products and moreover, are conducive to the corruption of the information communicated and the media institution by which it is communicated.

Closely related to the convergence of information and persuasion practices within the media, is the conflict of professional roles which can also be conducive to corruption. In the case of media release journalism, for example, where journalists reproduce press or media releases as news or editorial comment, without independent corroboration of content or disclosure as to their source, the roles of journalism and that of public relations give rise to a conflict of interest through a convergence of their inherently conflicting roles that is conducive to corruption. Advertorials are another example of a conflict of interest that arises from the blurring and convergence of the inherently conflicting roles of journalism, on the one hand, and advertising on the other. Advertorials are a phenomenon that facilitate the commercial self-interests of advertisers in selling products. They do so by trading on the legitimacy that attaches to public news and information services usually associated with legacy journalism, not normally engaged in advertising. This blurring of the distinction between an advertisement and objective reporting effectively masks the conflict of interest that arises when advertisers masquerade as

[6]The sixth Estate is a neologism used specifically in this book to describe the media practices of the Tech Companies such as Facebook and Google, which essentially, are operating as media companies.

disseminators of information, or objective reporters or commentators, acting in the public interest. Such practices are conducive to and invariably result in media corruption.

One of the aims of the book is to show that the 'unholy alliance' between journalism on the one hand and advertising and public relations on the other, is one of the major and pervasive causes of corruption within the media. The same problem manifests itself in some of the key practices of Big Tech media companies, such as Facebook and Google, which aided by their business models and opaque algorithms, collect and sell users' information to advertisers and other information brokers for vast profits, often without the users' knowledge or consent.

Another major objective of the book is to examine whether a rejuvenated investigative journalism offers an effective way of combating corruption through its long-standing exposure and reporting of corruption, including media corruption. Insofar as most of the exposures of corruption generally, and media corruption specifically, comes to us through the media, and particularly through investigative journalists, the media seems the obvious place to start an inquiry into potential practical and effective anti-corruption measures against corruption generally, and media corruption specifically. Although the media exposes corruption within the media, it does not identify it as such. At best, it is a retrospective piecemeal exercise that does not address the underlying fundamental causes of media corruption. The systematic conceptualisation, identification, evaluation and classification of the different types of corruption that arise in the media, both in the legacy media of the fourth Estate and the social digital media of the fifth Estate as well as in the sixth Estate, as illustrated by Facebook's part in the Cambridge Analytica scandal in 2016, will assist in a more accurate and systematic exposure of media corruption and its reduction if not elimination, through prospective anti-corruption remedies and policies, including government regulation. These should include at the very least, a re-assessment of media education in combating media corruption.

Finally, the book will examine the concept and practice of regulation and whether it provides effective ethical if not legal regulation over the media. If the market constrains on the media are such that the media's ability to communicate reliable and credible information to the public comes into doubt, then more regulation of the media may be required. Opposed to that suggestion, considerations of censorship and freedom of the press come into play. Theoretically, however, insofar as the media's freedom of communication of information to the public is based on the public's right to receive such information, then the media's freedom is constrained and overridden by the public interest. And the argument can be put forward that the public interest opposes information that is tainted by commercial and other interests, which when it results in misinformation, is not in the public interest or for the common good of society.

A major concern explored in this book is whether the corruption of the media, as the central conduit of public information, is contributing to the corruption of our collective civic values and our ability as citizens to participate and contribute effectively in our shared democratic way of life. Insofar as this is the information age, and information is constitutive of our social, political, and financial institutions and our relationships with those institutions; and moreover, information has become *constitutive of us as informational beings*, is media corruption corrupting our societies? Especially, when it is conducted systematically, as we shall examine in Chap. 5, through the platformization and monetization of information and the media by the Big Tech companies such as Facebook and Google, identified in this book as essentially media companies of the sixth Estate, bound by the same ethical principles and values as the media companies of the fourth and fifth Estates.

1.5 Chapter Outline

Chapter 2 – The Normative Structure of Information: Beginning with a simple definition of the concept of *information* as "the communication of instructive knowledge" the concept of *knowledge* in turn will be defined as "justified true belief". Using this traditional epistemological definition of knowledge, the chapter develops a *normative* account of information as it relates to the media. Insofar as information is a type of knowledge it must comply with the epistemic conditions of justification and truth. And insofar as the media's professional role is to provide information to the public on matters of public interest, that the public has a right to know, then the media is in principle committed to provide information that is both justified and true in accordance with widely recognized and accepted epistemic criteria, such as objectivity, independence, reliability and credibility of the sources that generate the information. The epistemology of information, in turn, commits the media to certain ethical principles and values, such as truthfulness, honesty, trustworthiness, and fairness, including justice, which requires the equal distribution of the informational goods to all citizens. Thus, information has an inherent normative structure that commits the media to both epistemic and ethical responsibilities and those normative responsibilities being necessary, are mandatory and cannot be avoided.

Chapter 3 – Characteristics, Causes and Contexts of Corruption: This chapter provides a general philosophical account of corruption that applies to all forms of corruption, such as political, financial, corruption in the clergy, sports corruption, police corruption and media corruption, which demonstrates why such practices are not only unethical but also corrupt. Such practices are of greater concern as they have the tendency not only to cause harm to individual persons or groups of persons but also cause harm to the institutional structure of the democratic system itself. Insofar as this is the case, the harm that is caused by corruption and especially media corruption, affects every citizen. However, like the proverbial fifth-phalanx, media corruption is not always apparent and when apparent is not understood as media corruption as other forms of corruption are, such as political, police, financial or sports corruption. As in Plato's Myth of Gyges (*Republic* Book II)[7] that will be

[7] See Appendix 1.

examined in this chapter, the media, when acting corruptly, merely "appears just, when it is not".

Chapter 4 – Media Corruption: This chapter identifies and examines the presence of corruption as it is manifested, specifically in the media. As in the case of the general account of corruption examined in Chap. 3, this chapter also examines media corruption by reference to Plato's Myth of Gyges as this has contemporary significance and relevance in explaining corruption generally and specifically as it applies to the media. The chapter uses a *model of media corruption* that shares the same characterizing features of the general account of corruption that is examined in Chap. 3 but designed specifically and developed for application to the phenomenon and practice of corruption in the media (Spence 2008, 2017). As well, the chapter identifies and categorizes the different *types* of media corruption, the ways in which these are caused, and the contexts in which they are manifested in current physical and online media environments and practices.

Chapter 5 – Tech Media Corruption in the Age of Information: Choosing *Facebook* as the specific example of what is referred to in this chapter as the *6th Estate*, in order to distinguish it conceptually from the fourth and fifth Estates, the primary objective of this chapter is to examine if digital information created, disseminated, curated, and mediated increasingly via Facebook and Google, is also subject to the same normative principles, both epistemic and ethical, as the fourth and fifth Estates. Having established that Facebook and analogously Google, operate as essentially *media companies*, the chapter demonstrates that Facebook and Google are also subject to the same epistemic and ethical principles and values, as well as professional requirements that other media companies of the fourth and fifth Estates, are. The chapter then examines if Facebook's role in the Cambridge Analytica case not only violated the fundamental normative principles and requirements to which all media companies are subject, but moreover, its actions constituted media corruption.

Chapter 6 – Investigative Journalism: We know of the key cases of media corruption and corruption referred to in this book, because they were first exposed and reported through the media, and specifically investigative journalists working in conjunction with whistleblowers and citizen journalists of the fourth and fifth Estates. Using the metaphorical analogy of Socrates, as the first investigative journalist, the ancient Greek philosopher that features in Plato's dialogues, including *The Republic*, the chapter demonstrates the crucial importance that investigative journalism still plays in exposing and reporting worldwide corruption as illustrated by the *Panama Papers* case and the *Cambridge Analytica* controversy, analyzed in that chapter. The chapter also examines how the symbiotic relationship between the fourth and fifth Estates work effectively together in conjunction to expose and report on global corruption.

Chapter 7 – Public Policy and Regulative Change to Combat Media Corruption: This chapter examines the systemic changes in policy and legislation as well as issues of self-regulation and government regulation needed in combating corruption and media corruption specifically in the Big Tech companies such as Facebook and

Google. As well, it explores anti-corruption solutions and policies needed in effectively responding to the challenge of media corruption in the age of information.

The role of investigative journalists in the exposure of corruption is revisited to illustrate the ongoing significance of investigative journalism in the regulation of corruption and media corruption specifically. The chapter then argues for a clear public articulation of public ethical principles and values through an examination of their historical rational justification and motivation, on the basis of several contemporary ethical theories. The chapter then examines the necessary normative alignment of public ethical principles and values with government regulation comprising both retrospective regulation through penalties, such as fines, as well as prospective regulation through external and independent audits of the Big Tech companies by the government and its associated agencies. As well, the chapter argues for the inculcation of public ethical principles and values within the corporate structures of the Big Tech companies, through education and training programs.

Epilogue – from Knowledge to Wisdom in the Age of Information: Finally, by way of summing up as well as looking forward to the future, this epilogue introduces the notion of *wisdom.* As a *meta-type of knowledge*, knowing how to understand and use information upon reflection and with good judgement for the benefit of oneself and the common good of society, wisdom can provide practical "know-how" for applying information to improve our lives and that of others. It is also a *reflective virtue* in the form of practical prudence, which can teach us how to create and use information to live good and meaningful lives in the infosphere – lives that are capable of leading to self-fulfilment, wellbeing, eudemonia, or happiness, for us and others, and generally for the common good of society at large. What wisdom requires is that we learn the husbandry of information. How to reflect upon it, how to understand it, how to control it so it does not control us, how to judge its implications, so we can foresee its consequences, whether they are good or bad, for us and others. And how to use it in ways that enhance our well-being, as individuals and collectively as a society, as well as promote and protect our rights to freedom, privacy, security, and autonomy, for the common good of society and the global well-being of humanity.

References

Cooper, Adam. 2020. More alleged victims of George Pell to have abuse claims aired on ABC. *The Sydney Morning Herald and The Age*, April 2, 2020. https://www.smh.com.au/national/new-allegations-of-child-sexual-abuse-by-pell-emerge-20200402-p54gbs.html. Accessed 2 Apr 2020.

McMahon, Barbara. 2006. Italian football in shock as Juventus manager tries to kill himself on eve of corruption hearings. *The Guardian*, June 28, 2006.

Miller, Seumas. 2018. *Corruption. Stanford Encyclopedia of Philosophy*, ed. Edward N. Zalta. (Winter 2018 Edition).

Miller, Seumas, Peter Roberts, and Edward Spence. 2005. *Corruption and Anti-Corruption: An Applied Philosophical Approach*. Upper Saddle River: Pearson/Prentice Hall.

Plato. 1952. *The Republic*, *The Dialogues of Plato*. Trans. Benjamin Jowett, Book II: 359–361. Chicago: Encyclopedia Britannica Inc.

Spence, Edward. 2008. Corruption in the Media. *International Journal of Applied Philosophy* 22 (2 Fall): 231–241.

———. 2017. Corruption in the Media. In *The Handbook of Business and Corruption: Cross-Sectoral Experiences*, ed. Michael S. Aßländer and Sarah Hudson, 453–480. Bingley: Emerald Group Publishing.

Spence, Edward, Andrew Alexandra, Aaron Quinn, and Anne Dunn. 2011. *Media, Markets and Morals*. Oxford: Wiley- Blackwell.

Chapter 2
The Tree of Knowledge: The Normative Structure of Information

"Verifiability helps establish credibility". (Fuller 1996, p. 40)

2.1 Introduction

Beginning with the initial premise that the internet has a global character, this chapter explains that a process for a *normative* evaluation of digital information on the internet necessitates an evaluative media model that is itself universal and global in character.[1] The process has to be able to transcend cultural borders so as to be able to objectively evaluate the quality of information that is in its essence, borderless and global. By cultural borders, I mean all types of borders, including geographical, national, ethnic, religious, gender, political, and lifestyle.

Throughout this chapter and the book the term *normative* will be used as a general term that collectively defines those epistemic principles that prescribe and guide what can be believed and known on the basis of justifiable evidence (epistemic norms) as well as those ethical principles that prescribe and guide ethical behavior (ethical norms).

This chapter will show that information has a dual normative structure that commits all disseminators of information to both *epistemic* and *ethical* norms that are in principle universal and thus global in application. Based on this dual normative characterization of information, the chapter will demonstrate that: information and, specifically, digital information on the internet, as a process and product of communication, has an inherent normative structure that commits its producers, disseminators, communicators, and users, everyone in fact that deals with information, to certain mandatory epistemological and ethical commitments; and that the negligent or purposeful abuse of information in violation of those commitments is also a

[1] I agree, therefore, with Gorniak-Kocikowska's claim that because of its global nature "computer ethics has to be regarded as global ethics" (1996).

E. H. Spence, *Media Corruption in the Age of Information*, Library of Public Policy and Public Administration 15, https://doi.org/10.1007/978-3-030-61612-0_2

violation of universal rights to freedom and wellbeing, to which all agents are entitled by virtue of being informational agents.[2] I refer to the above argument as the *Dual Obligation Information Theory (DOIT)* (Spence 2009). The Dual Obligation Information Theory (DOIT) was designed specifically for the purpose of providing an information-communication normative model that applies universally and globally. For the normative principles applicable to the internet, being a global network, requires a normative model that has universal theoretical justification in virtue of the inherent normative structure of information, as well as global practical applicability, which the DOIT model reveals and justifies.

Any theoretical model for the critical evaluation of the cultural quality of information generally and of digital information specifically – particularly as it concerns the *creation*, *production*, *storage*, *search, communication*, *consumption,* and *multiple uses* of information both offline and online (collectively referred to as the dissemination of information) – has to be able to address the problem that there are many cultural varieties and differences, not always compatible or consistent, that exist both within and among nations. Cultural relativism, and more critically moral relativism, threatens from every corner. How does one propose – let alone provide – a theoretical (and practical) model for the evaluation of information that can address the problem of cultural and moral relativism?

Given the global reach and scope of the World Wide Web, which now reaches and affects every part of the world, any theoretical model that seeks to not merely describe the cultural quality of digital information but *evaluate* it, at least in its epistemic and ethical manifestations, must itself be global in its application and scope. It must be able to evaluate digital information on the basis of universal principles that most if not all reasonable individuals, irrespective of their cultural differences and affiliations, can accept and, more importantly, must accept on the basis of their shared minimal rationality, which is necessary for all human communication. Communication cannot proceed let alone succeed if no one observed, for example, the rational principle of non-contradiction (that "A" and "not A" cannot both be true at the same time and in the same respect).

The abuse of information through, for example, misinformation practices, constitutes both a violation of the epistemic and ethical commitments to which the normative inherent structure of information, *as a process and product of communication* gives rise, as well as a violation of universal rights to which all agents and specifically informational agents are entitled.

[2] By "agent" understand any person engaged in any purposive activity, such as taking a walk, searching the internet, writing an essay, or disseminating information etc.

2.2 The Normative Structure of Information

The Dual Obligation Information Theory (DOIT) model is based on a minimal semantic definition of information: Following Luciano Floridi, information is defined here as "well-formed meaningful data that is truthful" (Floridi 2005), and following Fred Dretske, information is further defined as "an objective commodity capable of yielding knowledge" (Dretske 1999, 44–45; 86); knowledge in turn is defined as "information-caused belief."

What is necessary for both information and knowledge is truth. Information without truth is not strictly speaking information but either *misinformation* (the unintentional dissemination of well-formed and meaningful false data) or *disinformation* (the intentional dissemination of false "information").

Of course, journalists and media practitioners generally cannot always *know* with certainty whether the information they disseminate is true. However, they should have a reasonable justified belief, responsive to at least some minimal objective and independent verification capable of sustaining that belief; namely, that the information disseminated is probably true. This consideration satisfies the absolute minimal condition of *truthfulness*. That is, disseminators of information with journalistic intent must at least ensure that to the best of the journalist's knowledge the information they are disseminating is probably true, if and when they are unable to know with absolute certainty that it is true.

One could make the case, for example, that the dissemination of "information" by journalists concerning the claim that Iraq possessed weapons of mass destruction before the start of the war in Iraq was not based on a reasonable justified belief capable of yielding knowledge. Insofar as this was the case, the dissemination was misinformation at best, disinformation at worst. This was not a "reasonable justified belief" for journalists to hold because the evidence for the claim that Iraq had weapons of mass destruction was at best inconclusive. It was, moreover, uncorroborated by independent and credible sources. The information of those sources ultimately became known to be misinformation largely based on the overarching aim of the Pentagon of bringing about "régime change" in Iraq.

A central claim of this chapter is that all informational processes comprising the dissemination of information commit all rational agents to both epistemic and ethical conduct. The role of the media generally as disseminators and communicators of information commits it to ethical norms in a twofold manner simply because the Dual Obligation Information Theory (DOIT) model comprises two main parts that together demonstrate that information as *communicative action* is *doubly normative*. The argument for DOIT is as follows:

(A) Information has an inherent normative structure that commits its producers, communicators, mediators and users, everyone in fact that communicates and deals with information, to certain mandatory epistemic and ethical commitments. For if information is a type of knowledge (it must be capable of yielding knowledge, one must be able to learn from it) it must comply with the epistemic conditions of knowledge, specifically, that of truth and justification. And if the dissemination of information is based on the justified and rightful expectation among its disseminators, and especially its users, that such information should meet the minimal condition of truth or at least truthfulness, then the disseminators of information are committed to certain widely recognized and accepted epistemic criteria. Those epistemic criteria comprise in the main, objectivity as well as the independence, reliability, accuracy, and trustworthiness of the *sources* that generate the information. The epistemology of information, in turn, commits its disseminators to certain ethical principles and values, such as honesty, sincerity, truthfulness, trustworthiness and reliability (also epistemological values), and fairness, including justice, which requires the equal distribution of the informational goods to all citizens. Hence, in terms of its modes of dissemination and communication, information has an intrinsic normative structure that commits everyone involved in its creation, production, search, communication, mediation and consumption to epistemic and ethical norms and these norms being intrinsic to the normative structure of information are rationally unavoidable and thus not merely optional.

(B) The negligent or purposeful abuse of information in violation of the epistemic and ethical commitments to which its inherent normative structure gives rise is also a violation of universal rights – specifically, universal rights to freedom and wellbeing to which all informational agents are entitled by virtue of simply being agents (Gewirth 1978, 1996)[3] and in particular *informational agents* that

[3]The universal entitlement to universal rights to freedom and wellbeing by all human agents is based on the Argument for the Principle of Generic Consistency (PGC) by the American philosopher Alan Gewirth. For a detailed discussion and defense of that argument see Spence (2006); Beyleveld (1991) and Gewirth (1978, 1996, 1998). In brief, Gewirth's main thesis is that every rational agent, in virtue of engaging in purposive action, is logically committed to accept a supreme moral principle, the Principle of Generic Consistency. The basis of his thesis is found in his doctrine that action has a normative structure, and because of this structure every rational agent, just in virtue of being an agent, is committed to certain necessary prudential and moral constraints. Gewirth undertakes to prove his claim that every agent, *qua* agent, is committed to certain prudential and moral constraints in virtue of the normative structure of action in three main stages. First, he undertakes to show that by virtue of engaging in voluntary and purposive action, every agent makes certain implicitly evaluative judgments about the goodness of his purposes, and hence about the necessary goodness of his freedom and wellbeing, which are the necessary conditions for the fulfillment of his purposes. Secondly, he undertakes to show that by virtue of the necessary goodness which an agent attaches to his freedom and wellbeing, the agent implicitly claims that he has rights to these. At this stage of the argument, these rights being merely self-regarding are only prudential rights. Thirdly, Gewirth undertakes to show that every agent must claim these rights in virtue of the sufficient reason that he is a *prospective purposive agent* (PPA) who has purposes he wants to fulfill. Furthermore, every agent must accept that since he has rights to his freedom and wellbeing for the sufficient reason that he is a PPA, he is logically committed, on pain of self-contradiction, to also accept the rational generalization that all PPAs have rights to freedom and wellbeing. At this third stage of the argument these rights being not only self-regarding but also other-regarding, are now moral rights. The conclusion of Gewirth's argument for the PGC is in fact a generalized statement for the PGC, namely, that all PPAs have universal rights to their freedom and wellbeing. A full and detailed defense of the argument for the PGC against all the major objections raised against it by various philosophers can be found in Spence (2006) chapters 1–3; Beyleveld (1991); and Gewirth (1978).

routinely engage in *informational action* (Spence 2009, 2011; Spence et al. 2011, Chapter 2; and Elliott and Spence 2018, Chapter 5).

The goal of this second part of the argument for DOIT is to show that in addition to committing its disseminators to unavoidable epistemological and ethical standards by virtue of the *inherent normative structure of information*, information qua *communicative action* (the *purposive action of communicating* information to others) commits its disseminators to respect for peoples' rights to freedom and wellbeing, by virtue of the *inherent normative structure of action* (specifically, *communicative action*, the action of communicating information), (Spence 2009, 2011; Spence et al. 2011; Elliott and Spence 2018). That is, information must not be disseminated in ways that violate peoples' fundamental rights to freedom and wellbeing, individually or collectively, or undermine their capacity for self-fulfillment (Negative Rights) when they engage, as they routinely do, in informational action by means of communication; that is, engage in the dissemination and communication of information both as transmitters and receivers or, as in the case of Facebook, in its role of a media company, as mediators. Facebook's and Google's role as *media companies* bound by epistemic and ethical responsibilities that all media companies are, will be examined in Chap. 5.

In addition, information must as far as possible be disseminated in ways that secure and promote peoples' generic rights and capacity for self-fulfillment (Positive Rights)[4] when those rights cannot be secured or promoted by the individuals themselves and can be so secured and promoted at no comparable cost to its disseminators.

Therefore, the abuse of information through, for example, misinformation or disinformation practices, as well as *fake news* constitutes (a) a violation of the epistemic and ethical commitments to which the inherent normative structure of *information* itself gives rise and (b) a violation of universal rights to freedom and wellbeing that the inherent normative structure of *action* gives rise and to which all agents and specifically informational agents, are entitled. Echoing Umberto Eco's claim in *The Open Work* (1989: 66) that with regard to human beings, *information theory becomes communication theory* – this chapter shows that the demonstrated dual normative structure of information in terms of its own inherent normative structure, as well as the universal rights of informational agents to which information as *informational action* in the form of communication, gives rise, confirms and supports Eco's claim. Moreover, the ethical and epistemic commitment that binds the media in this twofold manner is universal and global.

Conceived as the fourth Estate, this places a significant and important responsibility on disseminators of information in their capacity as journalists. For example,

---

[4] For Gewirth's argument for the justification of universal *positive rights* see Gewirth, Alan (1996) *The Community of Rights*. Chicago: University of Chicago Press; Beyleveld, Deryck (1991*) The Dialectical Necessity of Morality; An Analysis and Defense of Alan Gewirth's Argument to the Principle of Generic Consistency*. Chicago: University of Chicago Press; and Spence, Edward (2006) *Ethics Within Reason: A Neo-Gewithian Approach* (2006). Maryland: Lexington Books (a division of Rowman and Littlefield, USA), Chapter 3.

media release journalism (Simmons and Spence 2006, 167–181), in which some news sites misleadingly and deceptively present as objective and independently produced information that is actually given to them by public relations professionals, without disclosure that these so called "news stories" are produced to meet the needs of clients with private interests rather than the public interest. They are deceptive because they are designed to mislead users to believe that a 'news story' is produced by journalists and written to promote the public interest rather than the interests of the public relations consultants and their clients. Moreover, these practices, as we shall examine in Chap. 4, constitute media corruption, for they are conducive to the corruption of the informational processes and products that are essential for informing citizens on matters of public interest in an objective, truthful, and fair manner.

If the deception involves collusion by PR professionals, journalists, and government representatives, in that they are all aware that they are intentionally misleading citizens, as some of the cases examined in Chap. 4 illustrate, this violates all citizens' rights to freedom and wellbeing collectively by undermining the democratic process itself. Democracy requires truthful, fair, and objective production and dissemination of information on matters of public interest. It is partly for that reason that media control is sought and exercised by totalitarian regimes that do not want their citizens to be well informed.

In response to the claim that information must be true or at least truthful, and that intentional misinformation violates informational agents' rights to freedom and wellbeing, one could raise the objection that in some rare cases, deception might be conducive to the informational agents' freedom and wellbeing and, thus, be a justified exception. Investigative journalists sometimes use deceptive means to investigate, uncover, and expose government, corporate, or police corruption. This is justified if they have no other means of gathering data for matters of significant public interest, such as for example, government or police corruption, and if they are willing to explain and justify to their audiences and the subjects of their investigation why they used such deceptive techniques. A successful argument will rest on their ability to show that deception was required to defend and promote the collective rights to freedom and wellbeing of all citizens to be informed on matters of public interest and for which they had a right to know. A case in point, was the 1970s *Washington Post* reporting on what is known as Watergate. There, some undercover deception by the *Washington Post* journalists was necessary in uncovering and exposing the Watergate political scandal that resulted in the uncovering of corruption in the U.S. executive branch of government and the resignation of President Nixon.

2.3 The Attitudinal Modes of Information

Information can also be evaluated regarding informational practices by reference to its *Attitudinal Modes*. In this chapter, I propose at least the following attitudinal modes of (in)formation:

Formation: production, dissemination or use of information to form plans of action in accordance with one's purposes or goals. Since *formation,* constitutes purposive action, it can be directly evaluated by reference to the PGC that locates ethics in purposive agency. Formation can result in at least *deformation* or *reformation*:

Deformation: The intentional or negligent misuse or abuse of information though unjustified access, production, dissemination, or communication. E.g., corruption of information through unethical media practices such as *media release journalism, invasion of privacy, unjustified censorship*, etc. Insofar as deformation undermines the inherent normative structure of information, it is *internally* ethically objectionable. Insofar as it violates the rights to freedom and wellbeing of others, it is also *externally* ethically objectionable. As we shall see in the examination of Facebook's role in the Cambridge Analytica scandal in Chap. 5, its actions constituted *deformation* as well as media corruption.

Reformation (reactive or proactive): Acts or systemic practices of deformation exposed and corrected by remedial information action. E.g., anti-corruption action through exposure of corruption by investigative journalists; corrections to information posted in Wikipedia. Insofar as reformation secures and promotes the normative structure of information and secures the informational agents' rights to freedom and wellbeing, it is ethically commendable, both internally and externally.

Transformation: Information that results in fundamental or transcendent change that benefits people both individually and collectively. For example, the Copernican Revolution that replaced the Ptolemaic cosmology with that of Copernicus and Galileo; the ethical transformation recommended by Plato and Aristotle and the Hellenistic philosophers, the Epicureans, and the Stoics; and the Internet. Insofar as information in its transformative mode contributes to the personal and or collective wellbeing and self-fulfilment of individuals then it is ethically commendable. To the extent that a good life should at least be capable of leading to self-fulfilment, especially self-fulfilment as capacity-fulfilment (making the best of oneself as a human-being)[5] then *wisdom* can be thought of as a type of meta-information: acquisition of knowledge of how best to create, communicate and use information so as to render oneself and others capable of achieving capacity-fulfilment – being the best one can become qua human-being both as an individual and as a member of ones' community, locally and globally (Hui and Spence 2016; Spence 2011, 2013).

[5] See Alan Gewirth's notion of self-fulfilment as *capacity fulfilment* in A. Gewirth. *Self-fulfillment*. Princeton NJ, Princeton University Press, 1998.

2.4 Information as Communication

In *The Open Work* (1989, p. 66) Umberto Eco makes a very interesting and pertinent comment to the present concerns of this chapter. He claims that,

> It would indeed be possible to show that the mathematical concept of information cannot be applied to the poetic message, or to any other message, because information (qua entropy and coexistence of *all* possibilities) is a characteristic of the *source* of messages: the moment this initial equiprobability is filtered, there is selection and therefore order, and therefore meaning. The objection is perfectly correct if we consider information theory only as a complex of mathematical rules used to measure the transmission of bits from a source to a receiver. But the moment the transmission concerns *information among human beings* [added emphasis] information theory becomes a theory of communication, and we need to establish whether concepts borrowed from a technique used to quantify information (that is, a technique concerned with the physical exchange of signals considered independently from the meaning they convey) can be applied to human communication.

Given the space constraints of this chapter, I am not able to offer but the briefest analysis of Eco's insightful and promising comment. Eco's comment is insightful and promising because it points in the same conceptual analytical direction of the present Chapter. That is to say, it clearly articulates what this Chapter implicitly suggests that with regard to *information among human beings*, *information theory becomes a theory of communication*. As a point of departure from Eco's penetrating comment, the present Chapter further and with some novelty argues moreover that information theory as a theory of communication commits its disseminators to certain epistemic and ethical norms by virtue of its dual normative structure: First, because being a teleological orientated activity in its own right that *aims* at truth or truthfulness (has as its *telos* or *goal* truth or truthfulness), information as communication, has an inherent normative structure that universally commits all its disseminators to both epistemic and ethical normative standards; and secondly, information as a form of communication among informational agents universally commits all informational agents to the respect of the rights of freedom and wellbeing of all informational agents. This as we saw above requires that information must not be abused and misrepresented in the form of different types of misinformation in ways that violate those rights. Such purposeful misinformation constitutes under certain conditions, a form of media corruption, a topic examined in Chap. 4: the corruption of information as a process and product of communication (Spence 2008). Another insightful and pertinent comment by Umberto Eco that seems to anticipate our analysis and normative evaluation of information in terms of its *attitudinal modes* is the following (Eco 1989, pp. 70–71):

> …Questions of information become *questions of communication*, and our attention must shift from the message itself, qua objective system of possible information, to the relationship between the message and receiver – a relationship in which the receiver's interpretation constitutes the effective value of the information. ….This, in turn, means that it may be necessary to add a psychological point of view to the structural analysis of certain communication phenomena….To consider the psychological aspect of the phenomenon merely means that we recognize that the message cannot have any meaning, at least for-

mally speaking, unless it is interpreted in relation to *a particular situation* (a psychological situation) that is also, by extension, historical, social, anthropological, etc.

The *psychological shift* in information that Eco refers to in the above passage is nicely captured by our analysis and the evaluation of information in terms of its attitudinal modes, namely, *formation, deformation, reformation and transformation* that draws attention to the psychological, social, professional and other attitudes that informational agents adopt in their informational and communicative interactions and transactions with each other. Such attitudinal stances with regard to information as communication involving human beings as both transmitters and receivers of informational messages have also important ontological implications. As in the case of Dr. Faustus, for example, or the repentant thief at Christ's crucifixion, we become in a sense *informational being*: that is to say, we become through our informational practices and psychological, social, and professional attitudes to information, potentially at least, *formed, deformed, reformed, and transformed* informational beings. This is, of course, a complex matter that requires further analysis and comment that the present constraints of space do not allow in this Chapter.

2.5 Global Information Ethics: Cultural Relativism Without Moral Relativism

This section will expand upon an earlier claim by arguing that the DOIT model overcomes the problem of *moral relativism* while remaining responsive and sensitive to a varied and robust international *cultural relativism* that is undeniably present throughout the world. However, cultural relativism by no means necessitates or supports claims or calls to moral relativism. Moreover, cultural relativism even of the most varied and robust kind is theoretically at least consistent and compatible with the DOIT model.

This is at least for the following reasons. First, the kind of universalism that the DOIT model supports is neither *ethnocentric* nor *dogmatic*. The ethical universalism argued for in this chapter does not equate nor is it supportive of cultural homogeneity or uniformity. *Universality* is not the same as *uniformity*. The former, unlike the latter, is compatible with cultural variety and difference. It is a mistake to think that universality imposes uniformity. Insofar as the arguments adduced in this chapter in favor of both the inherent normativity of information, as a process and product of communication, and the universal rights to freedom and wellbeing to which it gives rise by virtue of Alan Gewirth's *Principle of Generic Consistency* (Gewirth 1978) are rationally sound and thus theoretically at least persuasive for all minimally rational agents, then they are universally applicable.

Let us first consider the inherent normativity of information per se, as a process and product of communication. That normativity, being inherent to information itself, cannot be affected by the contingencies of the variety and difference between cultures. For insofar as information as a process and product of communication must of logical necessity be true or truthful, the epistemic and ethical commitments to which that necessity gives rise are universally applicable to all informational agents, irrespective of their other legitimate cultural differences. Apart from some specific cases alluded to above with regard to investigative journalists, for example, misinformation by way of negligent or purposeful deception can never be justified, whether it takes place in the West or in the East. Interestingly but not unexpectedly, the notion of truth and/or its associated cognate concepts such as honesty, objectivity, etc., features in most codes of media ethics across the world. According to the International Federation of Journalists, for example, *respect for truth and for the right of the public to truth is the first duty of the journalist (IFJ).* Of course, how and the degree by which people choose to *respond* to such deception from within their own particular cultural perspectives might vary from culture to culture. This, however, does not in any way diminish the ethical wrongness of misinformation. Good investigative journalism that seeks the truth, whether conducted in Russia, Africa, Asia, Europe or the United States, transcends cultural and national borders. It is for that reason that in less-democratic states, investigative journalists are both feared and persecuted, in some cases fatally.

In addition, since the universal rights to freedom and wellbeing of informational agents are based and derived from a rationally sound argument, namely, the argument to the Principle of Genetic Consistency, then they too are universally applicable. This universality is also conceptually consistent and practically compatible with cultural variety and difference. This is so because how people choose to interpret the degree of relevance of purposive freedom and wellbeing in their own lives, over and above the minimally necessary conditions for action, may undoubtedly vary from culture to culture with regard to specific cultural and social practices within those diverse cultures. That some minimal freedom and wellbeing is necessary for all purposive action remains, however, true and by logical consequence, gives rise to universal rights. The *content* of those rights remains universal notwithstanding that the cultural *context* in which those rights are expressed, exercised, or withheld, may indeed vary from culture to culture. The DOIT model, because it is universal, applies to all modes of information, analog as well as digital, regardless of the different contexts in which information is produced, used, and expressed.

2.6 Media Convergence of the Fourth Estate and Fifth Estate

Traditionally, at least in Western democracies, legacy news organizations have been viewed, as the Fourth Estate: An important and essential organization for safeguarding basic rights of citizens, such as freedom of speech, and the right of citizens to be informed and heard on matters of public interest. Historically, the media and journalism in particular have exercised the role of protecting and promoting those basic rights. This has been done through the dissemination of essential information to the public on matters of public interest that safeguarded those rights and the democratic system in which those rights have traditionally been in principle enshrined (Elliott and Spence 2018, 105).

However, technological advances in the digitalization of information and its global dissemination through the use of emerging information and communication technologies have profoundly and fundamentally changed the way in which information is now sourced and communicated. Digital media including social media, now available through the internet, Twitter, smart phones, and social networks, such as Facebook, Google and YouTube, are having a profound impact on the social life and democratic processes and practices of societies.

The fundamental role of journalism as stipulated in its Australian Media Entertainment and Arts Alliance code of ethics (MEAA), and echoed by its equivalents in the United States, the EU and elsewhere, is to disseminate information to the public on matters of public interest truthfully, reliably, fairly, and in a trustworthy manner, for the ultimate purpose of supporting and promoting a democratic way of life as an important and fundamental public good (at least in principle, if not always in practice). How has the role of journalism, as the fourth Estate, changed in the virtual world? To answer that question, we need to assess both the internal and external impacts. *Internally,* the impact is in the way that journalists of the fourth Estate use digital media in sourcing and disseminating information through digital media technologies, such as Twitter, Google or Facebook, for example; and *externally,* in the way nonprofessional communicators of the fifth Estate, such as bloggers, influencers, and new media networks, such as WikiLeaks until recently used to, and currently *Technology Platforms* such as Facebook and Google, are disseminating information to the public. As we shall examine in detail in Chap. 5, Facebook's role in the *Cambridge Analytica* case, had a significant epistemic, ethical and eudaimonic harmful impact on society and democracy itself, resulting, in media corruption.

Since the dissemination of information can both benefit and harm us as individuals and collectively, as a society, we need to examine the wider implications and consequences of that impact on the quality of information and its communication as well as the life of individual citizens and collectively as a society affected by that impact. Is that impact good or bad in terms of how it affects our basic rights as citizens to freedom and wellbeing? For example, is the use of Twitter by journalists and other media practitioners an appropriate technology for communicating court proceedings in real time? Should jurors, who may see themselves as "citizen journalists," be allowed to access online information on defendants during a trial? Should they be allowed to "report" on the case after the fact? Should citizen journalists and bloggers such as Julian Assange be considered journalists, and if so, should they be allowed to disseminate information to the public in that role? If they are journalists, do they then have the right to the confidentiality of their sources and the protection of shield laws that protect all journalists?[6]

---

[6] This is an important and pertinent question at present (April 2020) as Julian Assange is appearing before a UK Court to challenge extradition charges brought against him by the US Government. Perhaps foreseeing such a future scenario, a group of my media ethics students in the School of

In order to answer those *practical* questions, we first need to ask the *theoretical* question how the impact of the convergence of the fourth and fifth Estates[7] can be reliably and objectively determined and normatively evaluated. Given the global reach of digital information through the affordance of the internet and other Information Technology companies, including *digital platforms* such as Facebook, and Google, the importance of providing an answer to that question has both national and international implications. As we shall examine in Chap. 5, determining the underlying media role of digital platforms, such as that of Facebook and Google, for example, has crucial normative implications for the ethical, epistemic and eudaimonic responsibilities of those information and communication technology platforms; especially, in determining whether some of Facebook's *media* practices, as illustrated in the Cambridge Analytica case, constituted institutional media corruption.

2.7 The Normative Impact of Media Convergence: Four Illustrative Cases

What follows is an analysis of some key historical case studies essential for providing a diachronic perspective on the convergence of the fourth and fifth Estates and a clearer understanding of its normative informational implications, as well as the ongoing convergence initiated by media platforms, such as Facebook and Google, referred to in this book as the sixth Estate, a topic we will examine in greater detail in Chaps. 5 and 7. The diachronic approach to the analysis of the historical illustrative cases examined in this chapter as well as throughout this book, is purposely designed to provide a deeper understanding of how the media has evolved and been

---

Communication and Creative Industries at *Charles Sturt University* in Australia, presented a play they wrote and performed in class for one of their group assignments in 2017. The title of the play was *The Trial of Julian Assange*. Using various ethical theories and arguments we canvased in lectures, such as Utilitarianism, Social Contract theories, and Ethical Rationalist and Human Rights theories, such as those of Alan Gewirth (1978, 1996), for example, the defense team defended Julia Assange successfully against the charges brough against him by the US government prosecutor.

[7] Traditionally the Four Estates were understood to include, the government, the clergy, the public and the press in the form of the legacy media whose role was to hold the other three estates to account for the public good. In the advent of the Internet and the World Wide Web where anyone with access to the Internet can disseminate and communicate information to the public, nationally and internationally, the fifth Estate is a more recent addition that includes the social media, mediated digitally via Tweeter, Facebook, Google and other information technologies. The relevance and significance of the fourth and fifth Estates especially through their symbiotic convergence i.e., the *Convergent Media*, is that they act as a monitoring and accountability measure to hold the other two governing estates, that of government and clergy to account. For example, it has been the Convergent Media, including Wiki Leaks, that has exposed the misdemeanors and corruption of governments and clergy (police corruption and corruption of the clergy in the form of sexual abuse are two out of many examples).

transformed by the far-reaching changes that have taken place during a period of digitization and platformization. The diachronic approach adopted in this book is important for demonstrating that however technologies of the dissemination of information have changed, and will in future change, the fundamental normative principles and values that underlie the communication of information have not; they apply equally, as the application of Dual Obligation Information Theory (DOIT) illustrates, to both the digital media and the analog media that preceded it, as well as the *convergent media* of the fourth and fifth Estates, and as we shall see in Chap. 5, the sixth Estate comprising the *Technology Platforms* such as those of Facebook and Google.

Case Study 2.1: The Omnipresent Witness

The verbal abuse was recorded by a student of Athena Middle School on his mobile telephone and later posted to YouTube. The video shows Karen Huff Klein trying to ignore the verbal abuse to which she is being subjected, which included insults and threats.

The case of Karen Huff Klein[8] that was published and broadcast in the world-wide media, both offline and online, is a paradigmatic example of the *convergence* of new and old media. A digital media user videoed a public event, which he then uploaded to YouTube; the video then went viral on the internet; the story was then picked up and published worldwide as a news story that ran in virtual and physical-world publications. This is an illustrative case of what is described in this chapter as media convergence – the convergence of digital media and corporate media in the dissemination of information to the public.

Case Study 2.2: The Wikileaker

Another key case involving a whistleblower is that of Chelsea (formerly Bradley) Manning[9] the twenty-four-year-old U.S. Army intelligence analyst who stands accused of releasing the Collateral Murder[10] as well as other classified documents to WikiLeaks. The video shows unarmed civilians and two Reuters journalists being killed by a U.S. Apache helicopter crew in Iraq. It received wide publicity in the mainstream media. This case demonstrates how news media in the virtual and physical worlds increasingly use content generated by digital media users and from media-activist sources, such as WikiLeaks, to inform the public.

Case Study 2.3: The NSA Leaker

Edward Snowden, a former U.S. National Security Agency (NSA) contractor, now lives in Russia after fleeing the United States having revealed extensive internet and phone surveillance by U.S. intelligence. He is charged with theft of government property, unauthorized communication of national defense information and willful communication of classified communications intelligence. His leaks have led to

---

[8] For more information see Karen Huff Klein. https://en.wikipedia.org/wiki/Bus_monitor_bullying_video.

[9] For more information see Chelsea (formerly Bradley) Manning.

[10] For more information see Collateral Murder. https://collateralmurder.wikileaks.org/.

revelations that the U.S. intelligence systematically seized and gathered vast amounts of phone and web data of citizens under the NSA program Prism, https://www.bbc.com/news/world-us-canada-22837100 (BBC News, 16 December, 2013).

The three case studies examined so far clearly illustrate the symbiotic convergence of the legacy fourth Estate and the fifth Estate represented by citizen journalists, bloggers, and whistleblowers. As the three cases illustrate, together the fourth and fifth Estates working together in tandem provide important information to citizens on matters of public interest, and moreover, as we shall examine further in this book, their role in investigative journalism is an important and crucial measure for the exposure and reporting of corruption, including media corruption. In addition, the analysis of the three cases show how the normative impact of the convergent media can be assessed on the basis of the DOIT by demonstrating how the convergent media of the fourth and fifth Estates acted in accordance with the epistemic and ethical responsibilities for disseminating information in accordance with the requirements of DOIT, for the common good of society by informing the public on matters of public interest truthfully that the public had a right to know.

Case Study 2.4: Fiction as Fact

The Gay Girl in Damascus[11] case refers to an online blog, supposedly written by a lesbian young woman named Amina Arraf living in Damascus, that purported to give minute-by-minute reporting on the Syrian conflict. The blog was in fact a hoax written by Tom MacMaster, at the time a graduate student from the University of Edinburgh. The photos of "Amina Arraf" proved to be those of a Croatian young woman living in the United Kingdom with no relation to Syria or the fictional "Amina Arraf." It attracted wide publicity from around the world, which led to its publication by the mainstream international media.

The application of DOIT to this case study, by contrast, clearly demonstrates the violation of both the epistemic and ethical responsibilities for disseminating information to the public. First, the information, which turned out to be disinformation, was false, what we now refer to as *fake news*, therefore violating the epistemic component of DOIT that requires the communication of information to be true or at least truthful. Second, the theft of the Croatian woman's digital identity and use of her photos to create the fictional character of Amina Arraf violated her rights to freedom and wellbeing. Publication also violated the rights of the many recipients of Tom MacMaster's disinformation, who were misled and deceived by his hoax, in violation of the ethical component of DOIT. As we shall examine further in Chap. 4, MacMaster's disinformation also constituted a type of personal media corruption as his disinformation and deception was carried out under the assumed fake role of a blogger or citizen journalist; an abuse and violation of that media role that resulted in media corruption. Recall that according to DOIT anyone who disseminates digital information is normatively responsible for the dissemination of that information. Arguably, therefore, the dissemination of disinformation by MacMaster under

[11] For more information see "Gay Girl in Damascus". https://en.wikipedia.org/wiki/A_Gay_Girl_In_Damascus.

the assumed role of a 'citizen journalist' was not only a violation of the normative requirements of DOIT but moreover, as we shall examine in Chap. 4, constituted personal media corruption. This case illustrates that *fake news* and disinformation is not a new phenomenon. It is an ongoing problem that has been present in the mass media for at least the last 20 years and continues to the present in a new form expressed through social media by the affordance of the Tech Media platforms such as Facebook, Google and You Tube. That topic, referred to in this book as media corruption in the *sixth Estate*, will be investigated in greater detail in Chap. 5.

2.8 The New Journalists of the Fifth Estate?

Whistleblowers and leakers are traditionally seen as enemies by the holders of state secrets. Acting by stealth, as in Chelsea Manning's case, or openly, as in the case of Daniel Ellsberg (who leaked the Pentagon Papers, a secret dossier of documents on the conduct of the U.S. political and military operations in Vietnam from 1945–1967, to the *New York Times* and other news organizations), they claim to act on moral conscience by undertaking to make public for the common good what the state wants concealed. Manning, Assange, Snowden and Ellsberg leaked information to the press that they believed that the public had a right to know. We shall examine in more detail in Chap. 6 the important and crucial role investigative journalists and whistleblowers play in exposing and reporting corruption to the public; be it political, financial, or media corruption, which as in some key cases, as we shall examine in Chap. 7, can motivate and lead to government regulation.

In his article "Who is a Journalist," Jay Black wrote, "Broad-based citizen and web-based journalism augments the knowledge base and is making a persuasive case for enjoyment of the status, rights, and protections formerly enjoyed only by the elite media." He correctly points out, "Now is not the time to argue for a narrow definition of journalism" (Black 2010, 112).

He concludes that "the issue of who is a journalist should not center on where one works but on how one works" (Black 2010, 114). Black's wider definition of who is a journalist, correctly highlights a major issue of journalism ethics raised by Christopher Meyers in the introduction to his edited book on that topic (Meyers 2010). Meyers argues that epistemic credence and trust is at the center of who and what a journalist is or at least ought to be in principle – not just in name and style but more fundamentally and crucially, in substance. I concur with both Black's wide definition of what constitutes a journalist and Myers's claim above concerning epistemic credence and trust. For what matters with regard to the dissemination of information both in the case where the dissemination is by a professional journalist of a major newspaper, such as the UK *Guardian* or the *New York Times*, for example, or by a "web-based journalist" or "citizen journalist" writing a blog on the internet, is whether the information is credible and reliable with regard to truth and trust, especially on matter of public interest.

Insofar as Julian Assange, for example, has been disseminating information on his WikiLeaks website that is true, credible, reliable, and trustworthy, and moreover information that is of public interest he can be, as he himself claims to be, a journalist – a journalist of the fifth estate. In this chapter as we saw earlier, the fifth estate is loosely defined as the estate comprising all the world-denizens operating in cyberspace that, as individuals or groups, disseminate information on matters of public interest to the world at large and who are doing so with journalistic intent, understood in this book more broadly as the intent of their information being truthful, reliable and trustworthy, in keeping with the normative requirements of DOIT. And who do so, without fear or favor.

Citizen journalists, such as Daphne Caruana the Maltese blogger-journalist who was murdered for her part in the *Panama Papers* investigation of corruption in Malta, that led to the resignation of the Maltese Prime Minister Joseph Muscat in January 2020 (see Chap. 6) and whistleblowers such as Julian Assange and Edward Snowden, among many others, provide an invaluable service in the best tradition of investigative journalism, but without the commercial constraints that unfortunately sometimes at least undermine, restrict, or even muzzle good investigative journalism, or worse still, lead to the kind of gross ethical and legal abuses evident in the News Corporation's *News of the World* phone-hacking case, a case examined in Chap. 6.

A symbiotic relationship has developed between the journalists of the legacy and digital media – and some journalists operate in both. When done correctly in accordance with the epistemic and ethical principles of DOIT, as in the case of the information leaked by Chelsea Manning on the *Collateral Murder* video and publicized by WikiLeaks and the mainstream media, that symbiotic relationship augments the quality and quantity of information disseminated to the public on matters of public interest and enhances the substance and scope of deliberative democracy. However, when false information or false sourcing is provided, as in the case of the *Gay Girl in Damascus,* the disinformation undermines the public interest and casts doubt on what one can accept as true or dismiss as false on the internet. This is a major challenge for journalists but also for everyone who disseminates information on the internet. Ultimately, it comes down to a question of trust in the truthfulness and reliability of the information disseminated.

Lee Wilkins correctly argues that in addition to their traditional role of informing the public, journalists, but I would also add, communicators of public information generally, should also seek to mitigate harm to the public. To do so, she says, the definition of news should not only include what actually happens but also what might happen. As Wilkins eloquently puts it, "preventing harm becomes the predominant ethical obligation" of journalists (2010, 313). Journalists, she argues, should become "mitigation watchdogs," anticipating and mitigating harm to the public. Wilkins's argument for "mitigation reporting" sits well with the position of this book, that a global ethics requires not only a negative duty of not causing harm but also a positive duty of offering others positive assistance and promoting their welfare when we can (Spence 2007).

The argument that journalists should act as "mitigation watchdogs" adds further value and justification to the role that citizen journalists, leakers and whistleblowers, such as Chelsea Manning and Daniel Ellsberg, play in the worldwide dissemination of information to the public, with the helping hand of legacy media journalists, as in the case of Daniel Ellsberg, and equally as citizen journalists such as Julian Assange, in the case of Bradley Manning. The only thing we have to fear from true information that is of public interest is that its concealment by governments and the military can lead to far greater harm than its publication. Specifically, when the information concealed is in the public interest and for the interest of supporting and promoting a healthy and robust deliberative and participatory democracy.

2.9 Conclusion

Beginning with the initial premise that as the internet has a global character, this chapter argued that the normative evaluation of digital information on the internet necessitates an evaluative model that is itself universal and global in character.

The chapter then proceeded to show that information has a dual normative structure that commits all disseminators of information to both universal epistemic and ethical norms. Based on the dual normative structure of information the chapter presented an argument for the Dual Obligation Information Theory (DOIT) that demonstrates that (1) information, both analog and digital, has an inherent normative structure that commits its disseminators to certain mandatory epistemic and ethical commitments; and (2) that informational agents have universal rights to freedom and wellbeing that renders the negligent or purposeful abuse of information in violation of the epistemic and ethical commitments to which it inherently gives rise, objectionable.

Using Umberto Eco's insightful comments that with regard to information among human beings, information theory becomes a theory of communication, the chapter confirmed Eco's claim that information theory among human beings becomes indeed a theory of communication. It does so by demonstrating that when information becomes communication, as it must with regard to informational practices among human agents, it unavoidably and universally gives rise to both epistemic and ethical commitments.

Furthermore, and echoing Eco's notion of a *psychological shift* in information, the chapter explored how information when it becomes communication, acquires a further *normative ontological character* by means of its attitudinal modes. That is to say, informational agents become through their attitudinal modes of informational and communication practices *informational beings* of a certain type that can be evaluated both epistemically and ethically on a broad *scale of good to bad* (Socrates being informationally *good* and Faustus being informationally *bad*).

Finally, the chapter analyzed and assessed the normative societal impact of the *convergent media* comprising the fourth Estate of the legacy media and fifth Estate of the new digital media of bloggers, tweeters, citizen journalists, as well as all communicators of information on the interment that disseminate information with journalistic internet, on the basis of the Dual Obligation Information Theory (DOIT) that applies equally to both the fourth and fifth Estates of the convergent media.

References

Beyleveld, Deryck. 1991. *The Dialectical Necessity of Morality: An Analysis and Defense of Alan Gewirth's Argument to the Principle of Generic Consistency*. Chicago: University of Chicago Press.

Black, Jay. 2010. Who Is a Journalist? In *Journalism Ethics: A Philosophical Approach*, ed. C. Meyers, 103–116. New York: Oxford University Press.

Dretske, Fred. 1999. *Knowledge and the Flow of Information*. Stanford: CSLI Publications.

Eco, Umberto. 1989. *The Open Work*. Trans. Anna Cancogni. Cambridge, MA: Harvard University Press.

Elliott, Deni, and Edward Spence. 2018. *Ethics for a Digital Era*. Oxford: Wiley-Blackwell.

Floridi, Luciano. 2005. Is Semantic Information Meaningful Data? *Philosophy and Phenomenological Research* 70 (2).

Fuller, Jack. 1996. *News Values: Ideas for an Information Age*. Chicago: Chicago University Press.

Gewirth, Alan. 1978. *Reason and Morality*. Chicago: University of Chicago Press.

———. 1996. *The Community of Rights*. Chicago: University of Chicago Press.

———. 1998. *Self-Fulfillment*. Princeton: Princeton University Press.

Gorniak-Kocikowska, Krystyna. 1996. The Computer Revolution and the Problem of Global Ethics. *Science and Engineering Ethics*, April 1996.

Hui, Jin, and Edward Spence. 2016. Internet Addiction and Wellbeing: Daoist and Stoic Reflections. *Dao: A Journal of Contemporary Philosophy*. Springer.

International Federation of Journalists. 1986. *Declaration of Principles on the Conduct of Journalists*. Accessed January 23, 2009. https://www.ifj.org/who/rules-and-policy/global-charter-of-ethics-for-journalists.html. Accessed 1 April 2020.

Meyers, Christopher. 2010. *Journalism Ethics: A Philosophical Approach*. New York: Oxford University Press.

Simmons, Peter, and Edward Spence. 2006. The Practice and Ethics of Media Release Journalism. *Australian Journalism Review* 28 (1): 167–181.

Spence, Edward. 2006. *Ethics Within Reason: A Neo-Gewirthian Approach*. Lanham: Lexington Books (a division of Rowman and Littlefield).

———. 2007. Positive Rights and the Cosmopolitan Community: Right-Centred Foundations for Global Ethics. *Journal of Global Ethics* 3 (02).

———. 2008. Media Corruption. *International Journal of Applied Philosophy* 22 (2 – Fall): 231–241.

———. 2009. A Universal Model for the Normative Evaluation of Internet Information. *Ethics and Information Technology* 11 (4): 243–253.

———. 2011. Information, Knowledge and Wisdom: Groundwork for the Normative Evaluation of Digital Information and Its Relation to the Good Life. *Ethics and Information Technology* 13 (3): 261–275.

———. 2013. Wisdom and Wellbeing in a Technological Age. *Synesis: A Journal of Science, Technology, Ethics, and Policy* 4: T:16–T:20.

Spence, Edward, Andrew Alexandra, Aaron Quinn, and Anne Dunn. 2011. *Media, Markets and Morals*. Oxford: Wiley- Blackwell.

Chapter 3
The Serpent's Lair – Characteristics, Causes and Contexts of Corruption

To waste his whole Creation, or possess
All as our own, and drive as we were driven
The puny habitants, or if not drive,
Seduce them to our party....

From John Milton, Paradise Lost Book II.

3.1 Introduction

Taking its departure from an applied philosophical model of corruption first developed by Miller, Roberts, and Spence (2005) the chapter will provide, using conceptual and applied philosophical analysis, an explanation of the nature, and causes of corruption generally, but also specifically as it relates to the media (Spence 2008, 2017). It will be argued that the same features that characterize corruption generally are also present in certain media practices identified and analysed under the different types of media corruption in Chap. 4.

This chapter demonstrates why such practices are not only unethical but also corrupt. Such practices are of greater concern as they have the tendency not only to cause harm to individual persons or groups of persons but also cause harm to the institutional structure of the democratic system itself. Insofar as this is the case, the harm that is caused by corruption and especially media corruption, affects every citizen. However, like the proverbial fifth-phalanx, media corruption is not always apparent and when apparent is not understood as media corruption as other forms of corruption are, such as political, police, financial or sports corruption. As in Plato's Myth of Gyges (*Republic* Book II)[1] examined later in this chapter, the media, merely "appears just, when it is not". Moreover, unlike certain financial instances of corruption as exemplified by the spectacular collapses of Enron in 2001 and WorldCom

[1] For a detailed account of the Myth of Gyges in Plato's *Republic*, see Appendix 1.

E. H. Spence, *Media Corruption in the Age of Information*, Library of Public Policy and Public Administration 15, https://doi.org/10.1007/978-3-030-61612-0_3

in 2002, and unlike political corruption as exemplified by the Watergate scandal the led to the resignation of the U.S. President Richard Nixon in 1974, media corruption is all pervasive and systemic. Often it goes unnoticed and unpunished. In Chap. 4, we will examine some more recent examples of media corruption as illustrated in the *News of the World* scandal in the UK in 2006–2011 and the Cambridge Analytica controversy involving Facebook in 2016–2018, whose effects and repercussions still resonate in 2020.

Corruption generally is pervasive, diverse, and present in almost all areas of society. From the "greed is good" heyday of the 1980s that encompassed the rise and fall of corporate high-flyers such as Christopher Skase, right through to the 2000s and the spectacular collapses of Enron and WorldCom in the U.S. and HIH Insurance in Australia,[2] corruption seems to continue unabated.

The financial and human costs of corruption have been enormous. Billions of dollars have been lost to both the corporations themselves and the shareholders – in the case of Enron, employees who had invested most of their life savings in that company lost everything. Reputations have been destroyed, lives turned upside down, and several heads of corporations have been imprisoned. Enron chief financial officer Andrew Fastow, WorldCom chief executive Bernard Ebbers and HIH's Rodney Adler and Bradley Cooper all landed in jail.

Typical cases of corruption involve the breach of a socially, professionally, or institutionally pre-established fiduciary relationship of trust between the corrupt agents and their victims. This is in keeping with one of the traditional dictionary definitions of "corruption", namely: "the changing from the naturally sound condition"; or "the turning from a sound into an unsound impure condition"; or "the perversion of anything from an original state of purity".

Plato was perhaps the first to recognize both the problem and the pull of corruption. In his celebrated "Myth of Gyges" in *The Republic* (Book 2) he poses the problem and attraction of corruption through a rhetorical question, which I paraphrase:

> "Why not act corruptly, when you can do so for profit or glory, if you can remain undetected and so immune from public accountability and punishment? Better to merely pretend that you are moral but act immorally or corruptly when you can do so without being detected." Plato calls this "a perfect injustice – appearing just when you are not".

The following is a brief exposition of that myth as related by Glaucon to Socrates in Book 2 of Plato's *Republic*.

[2] HIH Insurance was one of Australia's largest insurance companies that was placed into liquidation in 2001. Its collapse considered to be one of the largest in Australia's corporate history, was the result of corruption and fraud resulting in the imprisonment of a number of its members of management.

3.2 The Ring of Gyges

Once upon a time a certain shepherd from Lydia named Gyges whilst tending to his sheep found a ring which he put on his finger. Gyges soon discovered that by turning the ring on his finger he could make himself invisible. A few days later he went to the palace with a delegation of shepherds to see the King. Then by making himself invisible, he seduced the Queen, killed the King, and assumed total power by becoming himself the new King. Glaucon continues the story by asking us to imagine an ordinary person who like Gyges has the ability through a possession of a similar magical ring to render himself invisible thus allowing that person the opportunity to act unethically at will with total impunity.

Through the words of Glaucon, Plato asks us to consider what possible reason would a Gyges-like person have for acting ethically towards others if he had the ability to act unethically under a cloak of invisibility that allows the agency of his unethical conduct to remain invisible and hidden from others? For his ability to render the agency of his corrupt deeds invisible, will in turn provide him with total impunity from the social disapproval and/or punishment or other punitive repercussions for his unethical conduct that is ordinarily reciprocated from others or the state. Moreover, under the cloak of invisibility, the corrupt agent would be able to act corruptly whilst maintaining an appearance of ethical probity and rectitude.

Glaucon, Socrates' interlocutor in Book 2 of Plato's *Republic*, refers to this possibility as the "highest reach of injustice, being deemed just when you are not". He labels this "the most perfect injustice" (Plato 1952a, b). Given such a possibility, what possible reason then would someone like Gyges have for not being corrupt but being non-corrupt and moral instead? Especially, if we assume that the latter option was known to the agent to be to his personal disadvantage and personal instrumental loss? As Glaucon says to Socrates, one would be mad to be moral under those circumstances. Better to be immoral and corrupt if it is to your gain or advantage and simply appear to be moral and non-corrupt. Following Glaucon, I will refer to this proposition as the condition of "*perfect injustice*". The question of "why be moral" under Gygean conditions of perfect injustice is referred to in the ethics literature as the "*authoritative question of morality*" (Gewirth 1978, p. 3). The philosophical debate as to whether a compelling answer can be given to that question is still ongoing. Though we will not pursue that debate here we will, however, consider the kind of answer that Socrates might offer and indeed it is the kind of answer pursued by Plato in the *Republic*.

Plato, through the character of Socrates, argues that neither absolute power nor invisibility exempts anyone from acting ethically towards others. Apart from harming others through one's unethical conduct, Plato claims that in acting unethically one also harms oneself. He argues that unethical conduct is self-defeating for it *corrupts the character* of the person that acts unethically and causes internal disharmony that prevents the perpetrator of immoral deeds from being truly happy. Plato believes that behaving ethically provides the best means of living a good and happy life and it is only through ignorance that people act unethically since everyone wants to be happy. Plato identifies happiness with virtuous activity and the possession of an ethical character which together are necessary for internal harmony and integrity both for the individual citizen as well as the State. In parallel fashion, Plato also argues that corporate or institutional injustice can create disharmony and conflict within the State that can ultimately threaten civil authority and the very stability of the State itself. Hopefully, our discussion will prove more than a footnote to Plato. We will return to Plato later for further discussion of some of these issues.

3.3 The Characterizing Features of Corruption

Five features that emerge from the discussion of the Myth of Gyges by Glaucon in Plato's *Republic*, that seem, at least initially, to characterize corruption generally, are the *possession of power*, a *disposition* or *motivation* to exercise that power, an *opportunity* to exercise that power, *invisibility* or *concealment*, and *self-regarding gain*. I will define *power* as the possession of the ability or capacity to act in a manner capable of bringing about a certain intended desired outcome. A *disposition to exercise that power*, as the possession of a predisposition, pro-attitude, motivation, or willingness to purposefully exercise that power. *Opportunity*, as having the opportunity, either presented to oneself or engineered by oneself, to engage in some activity for which one's has the power and the predisposition to engage in. *Invisibility* or *concealment*, as the ability or quality an agent has for keeping the motives and the identity of the agency of his actions invisible, concealed or hidden from the gaze of others. In some special circumstances, the condition of invisibility can be self-directed. Directed, that is, towards the agent himself. Under these special circumstances, let us refer to them as circumstances of *self-deception*, the corrupt agent through specious rationalizations or through plain ignorance, deludes oneself in thinking that his actions or his motives or both, are not corrupt. Moreover, that his actions or motives involved in those corrupt activities are ethically appropriate. Some instances of "conflicts of interest", as we shall examine in Chap. 5 regarding Facebook's part in the Cambridge Analytica case, fall into this category of corruption. *Self-regarding gain* is any gain, not necessarily financial, which accrues to the agent personally or to a group of which his is a member, as a result of his or the group's actions. Regarding, the condition of invisibility, whilst the actions themselves may not be and need not be invisible, for in many cases they would be visible at least in regard to their effects and consequences, the identity of their agency will be invisible. Or at least the corrupt agent's intention will be to keep the identity of the agency of his corrupt activity invisible.

We will see, pending further investigation, that these five characterizing features of corruption, usually if not always, are present and accompany acts of corruption. For without power, understood as the ability to act in a manner capable of bringing about a certain intended desired outcome, one cannot commit a corrupt act. Without a disposition to exercise that power willingly, the possession of power to engage in corrupt activities may not be exercised. Similarly, through lack of opportunity one cannot engage in corrupt activity even when one has both the power and the disposition to act corruptly.

At this juncture, it would be useful to distinguish between, *gratuitous*, one-off aberrant instances of corruption, from *systematic* ones. For I think we will be willing to grant that someone who acts corruptly on one occasion only but is not disposed to do so at other times under similar circumstances may not really be corrupt though his action might be deemed to be corrupt. That is, gratuitous, one-off aberrant corrupt action does not constitute a corrupt *character* because the agent of that action may have acted out of character – he is not normally disposed to act that way.

This distinction between non-habitual or non-dispositional immoral behavior, and habitual or dispositional immoral behavior, is also recognized by Plato. In the *Myth of Er* in Plato's *Republic* (10.614–10.621), for example, he describes how the souls of non-habitual sinners are given several chances to reform whereas the souls of recalcitrant habitual sinners are cast straight into the depths of Tartarus. In the Christian religion we also come across the distinction between the character of the sinner and the sin itself. We are told that although God hates the sin, He nevertheless loves the sinner. Of course, it is possible that non-habitual acts of corruption can over a period of time corrupt the character and turn non-dispositional acts of corruption into a dispositional corrupt character. Practice unfortunately does not only make perfect it can also make imperfect. Habituation applies to both good and bad alike. That is why Plato insists, through the words of Socrates, that in acting unethically, we not only harm others, but equally and more importantly, risk of harming ourselves by corrupting our characters.

The distinction between a corrupt character and a corrupt action is crucially important for *compliance*. Briefly, if self-regulation is a primary factor in regulating corruption and encouraging compliance with ethical rules and principles in professional practice, at least in some professions such as journalism and accounting, for example, then to the extent that an ethical character is an important contributing factor to professional self-regulation, an ethical character is also of importance to regulating corruption, at least within some self-regulated professions. As we shall in Chap. 5 in our discussion of the Cambridge Analytica case, self-regulation of corruption, media corruption in that particular case, is not enough. For a major cause conducive to corruption, at least in the Cambridge Analytica case, is Facebook's business model that underlies it, rendering the corruption systemic and requiring government regulation to ensure compliance. We shall examine compliance by government regulation in Chap. 7.

Invisibility seems to also be a characterizing feature of corruption that is usually, if not always, present in instances of corrupt activity. Invisibility seems to be at least instrumentally desirable,[3] for without invisibility one might not be able to evade

[3] By "instrumentally desirable" understand the kind of practical prudence attributable to an instrumentally rational agent intending to act corruptly in an environment in which corruption is either illegal or if not illegal at least generally considered unethical. In such an environment it would be a desirable requirement of instrumental rational agency that the agent intending to engage in corrupt activity should take the required measures to keep the agency of his corrupt actions invisible

detection thus escaping possible social disapproval and punitive retribution from others or the State. Even for a Gyges-like person, keeping the identity of the agency of his immoral acts hidden, lest he invokes social disapproval, which may eventually undermine his power to rule and invite retribution from those he harms through his unethical conduct, would be prudent. Like Glaucon's perfectly unjust person, the perfectly corrupt person is one who maintains an outward appearance of probity, justice, and morality, whilst carrying out his corrupt deeds in secret. In this way he maximizes his self-regarding gain, which can either accrue to him personally or to a group to which he belongs or cause to which he is committed, with little or no instrumental cost to himself, his group or his cause;[4] at least in terms of avoiding social disapproval and/or punitive retribution from others or the State. Invisibility, therefore, seems to be a characterizing feature of corruption, at least for instrumentally rational agents. For it would be self-defeating for those agents to engage in corrupt activities openly and transparently since that would minimize, not maximize their means of achieving their corrupt goals at little or no ethical or legal cost to themselves.[5]

3.4 An Objection Against the Argument That Invisibility Is a Regular and Characterizing Feature of Corruption

One objection against the claim that invisibility is a characterizing feature of corruption is that as a matter of fact people sometimes engage in corruption openly and transparently.[6] Whether or not corrupt agents do actually flaunt their corruption

---

or concealed. For not to do so, could prove self-defeating and therefore instrumentally irrational. We will consider certain exceptions to the instrumental desirability of the invisibility condition, below. An underlined presupposition to our argument is that the agent addressed throughout this chapter is an instrumentally rational agent.

[4]The *self-regarding gain* need not be merely a *self-directed* gain accruing to the corrupt agent himself. Thus, the perceived gain from the corrupt activities of some of President Nixon's associates in the Watergate affair was self-regarding, in the sense that it benefited the Republican Party of which they were members, but not self-directed in the sense that it benefited or was intended to benefit those associates personally.

[5]Unless of course the corrupt agent is seeking exposure. By hoping that his corrupt deeds would be discovered and exposed, the agent might perhaps be seeking atonement for his corrupt deeds through exposure and subsequent punishment. Under these psychological circumstances, the instrumentally rational agent's non-avoidance of concealment for his corrupt agency is not self-defeating as its goal is maximized through the means used to bring about his eventual exposure and punishment.

[6]This objection was raised by at least two respondents at a reading of an earlier paper on which this chapter is based. In response to my challenge to provide specific instances of open and transparent corruption that flouted the condition of concealment or invisibility, those respondents were unable to do so. My charitable interpretation of their objection is that it is conceivable even if actual cases cannot be readily cited that under certain relevant circumstances, open and transparent corruption is possible and thus invisibility is not a characterizing feature of a corrupt agency; at least not

openly is a matter of further empirical investigation. However, what is more directly relevant to the question concerning the claim that invisibility is a characterizing feature of corruption is whether it is *conceivable* that an agent can act corruptly without the instrumental desirability of concealing the agency of his corrupt deeds. This possibility can be examined under at least three different scenarios.

3.4.1 The Corrupt Agent Does Not Meet the Presupposed Condition of Minimal Instrumental Rationality

To the extent that the corrupt agent is not minimally instrumentally rational, it is questionable whether that agent can be considered corrupt. He may be deemed foolish or reckless perhaps, but not necessarily corrupt; his action no doubt would be corrupt, but not his character. For it would be self-defeating and therefore irrational to act corruptly openly and transparently under conditions of perfect injustice other than under circumstances of omnipotence (see footnote 5). Reckless perhaps, for if the agent is instrumentally rational, why would he openly and transparently act corruptly if in doing so he risks undermining his self-interest with no compensating benefit? Unless of course the reckless agent fits the category of the agent who seeks atonement and thus deliberately exposes his corrupt agency to invite self-perceived justification for retribution and punishment for his corrupt deeds. In this special psychological case, which was canvassed earlier, the agent's instrumental rationality, through setting a higher value on atonement over corruption is, from the agent's own perspective, instrumentally rational. For the agent is using the most effective

always. It will be recalled that the characterizing features of corruption discussed above, including that of invisibility, relate not to the actions but to the agency of the corrupt individual, group or institution. The actions of the corrupt agent and their consequences can and often, if not always, will be visible and transparent. By contrast, assuming instrumental rationality in the decision-making process, the agency of the corrupt individual, group or institution, cannot be visible or transparent; with perhaps the one exception where the corrupt agent deems himself to be so powerful that he considers himself to be immune from any punitive repercussions from others. Under those circumstances, the corrupt agent may still be deemed to be instrumentally rational. For insofar as his total power over others provides him with total immunity from any punitive repercussions, there is no pressing instrumental reason for that agent to conceal or render invisible the corruption of his agency. I will henceforth refer to this possibility as the condition of "omnipotence". One could say that power is inversely proportional to invisibility. That is, the more powerful the corrupt agent is, the less of an instrumental reason he has for rendering his corrupt agency invisible. By contrast, the least powerful the corrupt agent is, the more of an instrumental reason he has in concealing the corruption of his agency. However, even under conditions approaching "omnipotence", one could argue that invisibility would overall be an instrumentally rational choice, as someone so powerful may stand to lose a lot, if he was found to be corrupt and as a result lost his power that sustained his corrupt conduct.

means to achieve his goal of atonement through exposure and ensuing punishment.[7]

Another possibility for failing to conceal the agency of one's corrupt actions is that of an agent who overestimates his ability to conceal the agency of his corrupt actions. Although intending to render the agency of his corrupt deeds invisible, the agent fails either through overconfidence of his own ability to do so or through an epistemological failure in assessing all the relevant facts for successful concealment. There is thus an epistemological indeterminacy that undercuts both the agent's own ability, as well as the agent's knowledge of the relevant facts, for achieving successful concealment. Hence, the instrumental desirability that renders invisibility a characterizing feature of corruption applies primarily to the agent's intention of keeping the agency of his corrupt actions invisible rather that the agent's success in achieving invisibility for his corrupt agency in practice.

The fact that the corrupt activities of corrupt agents are sometimes exposed indicates that the corrupt agent's attempts to conceal the agency of his corruption are not always successful, even when the corrupt agent intended them to be so. It is for that reason that one of the primary functions of auditing internal controls as a compliance measure within a corporation, for example, is to render the invisibility of corruption difficult to initiate and maintain. Measures of transparency and accountability are precisely a compliance anti-corruption requirement because invisibility is a characterizing feature of corruption. We shall examine in Chap. 7 that transparency and accountability as anti-corruption measures that provide independent oversight, are absent in certain 'black box' technology corporate environments such as those of Google and Facebook, among others. As we shall see, this raises crucial questions as to whether some of these 'black box' practices might constitute corruption or at least be conducive to corruption.

In sum, if, as I have argued, it is self-defeating for instrumentally rational non-omnipotent agents to act corruptly in a visible and transparent manner, then agents who are not instrumentally rational cannot be deemed corrupt, though their actions may constitute corruption. For the whole point of acting corruptly under a cloak of invisibility when conditions of perfect injustice obtain, is to gain impunity for one's corrupt deeds, not invite retribution. Thus, agents who do not meet the minimal condition of instrumental rationality cannot be deemed corrupt. They can be deemed foolish perhaps, but not corrupt. Although the fool's actions may be described as corrupt, the agency of the fool cannot. The fool's character is exempt from a charge of corruption. To the extent that fools fail the minimal condition of instrumental rationality, they should not be deemed corrupt even when they sometimes succeed

[7] It is an open question, one that we do not have the space to pursue here, whether a reckless agent who takes no precautions in concealing the agency of his corrupt actions under circumstances where he is able to do so and in the absence of omnipotence, can still be considered instrumentally rational. Because of the self-defeating aspect of reckless behavior, especially where the consequences can be punitively costly. I will treat reckless disregard of taking proper precautions for concealing the agency of one's corrupt actions as an instance of instrumental irrationality.

in engaging in corrupt activities. This is just a general point about culpability. Namely, that ethical responsibility is directly proportional to culpability.

3.4.2 The Corrupt Agent Operates in a Hobbesian State of Nature

In a Hobbesian State of Nature (HSN), one can openly be corrupt with social, ethical and legal impunity, because there are no legal or moral restrictions on anyone. In such a State of Nature there is as Thomas Hobbes tells us, "a war of everyone against everyone" (*bellum omnium contra omnes*) (Hobbes 1651: chapter 14) that ultimately benefits no one as no one can operate effectively in maximizing one's self-interest. Under these circumstances the condition of invisibility becomes redundant since the social, legal and ethical constraints that render invisibility instrumentally desirable in normal circumstances, become themselves invisible by their absence. In such a state, an agent would not need to keep the agency of his corrupt deeds invisible from others. For in such a state, the normal laws of retributive justice and normative ethical principles of social disapproval and legal or social repercussions would not apply. So, there would be no instrumental advantage for a corrupt agent to conceal the agency of his corrupt deeds from others. In such a Hobbesian State of Nature environment, there would in fact be no corruption as there would be no legal or moral laws and institutions or professions to corrupt as corruption presupposes an existing legal and ethical background against which acts of corruption can be determined as corrupt. It would be an environment where lawless anarchy prevails.

In short, global visibility and transparency of lawless and unethical practices by everyone in an HSN environment eliminates the instrumental desirability for maintaining the agency of one's corrupt or unethical actions, invisible. By contrast, under those conditions it may be instrumentally advantageous to render the agency of one's corrupt actions visible and transparent to others. It's a kind of an inverse social contract, an "unsocial contract" one could say: "Keep out of my way because I am as bad if not worse, than you are – whatever you can do to me, I can do worse to you." It is perhaps this kind of inverse social contract that operates in the criminal underworld.

From an instrumentally rational perspective only those who can render themselves *invincible* but not necessarily invisible stand to benefit in a Hobbesian State of Nature. However, invincibility outside a hypothetical HSN or actual states resembling an HSN, as for example the criminal underworld, is not, in normal circumstances, a practical option; for in the case of ordinary social human interaction, it might not always guarantee cooperation or submission from others. Only omnipotence can guarantee that, but though hypothetically possible, omnipotence is not practically feasible for mere mortals. We will examine again the notion of 'near-omnipotence' later in this book in the case of Tech Giants such as Google and

Facebook that operate without transparency, accountability and oversight in 'black box' cooperate environments, which allow them to engage in illegal and unethical practices, and as we shall see in Chap. 5, some of which are conducive to corruption – in short, the corruption of our democratic institutions and democracy itself.

3.4.3 *Institutionalized and Systemic Corruption*

Another practical scenario, resembling to some extent an HSN, is institutionalized corruption. Possible examples of this type of corruption are political and economic regimes in some Asian, African, and South American countries as well as some ex-communist Eastern European countries. The assumption is that under institutionalized corruption, the practice of both systematic and gratuitous corruption is openly and generally acknowledged by the citizens of those countries. One could say that it is an open secret.

Though corruption may be openly and generally acknowledged in those countries, not everyone is involved in corrupt activity. For even if everybody has the inclination not everyone has the necessary power to engage in corrupt activity. Though typically in states where institutionalized corruption is widespread, individuals partake in corruption not only as agents but also as subjects. A taxi-driver, for example, who bribes a police officer to let him off on an actual or tramped-up traffic infringement, is a subject of corruption though unlike the police officer, not an agent of corruption.

An important factor about institutionalized corruption, however, is that although its practice is widely known and acknowledged on the streets, it is never officially acknowledged by the corrupt governments of those states. On the contrary, those governments will deny that widespread institutionalized corruption is rife in their states. To do so would deny them the instrumental benefits that invisibility confers on corrupt agents under conditions of perfect injustice. Moreover, to admit to institutionalized corruption and by extension their own possible involvement in corruption would incur the hefty cost of loss of trust and confidence in conducting international trade with those states. Further still, the official admission to institutionalized corruption, which is otherwise widely known and acknowledged on the streets, might run the potential and substantial risk of having valuable financial subsidies and foreign aid to those states cut-off at the source.

So again, invisibility is instrumentally desirable for maintaining a veneer of external respectability and probity whilst keeping the agency of the corrupt agents concealed. From a global, if not from a local perspective, it does not pay to wash one's dirty laundry in public. So even when *local* invisibility is absent within a state that engages in institutionalized and systemic corruption, *global* invisibility is still a required and instrumentally desirable feature of corruption. *Transparency International* is an organization dedicated to the exposure and reporting of corruption internationally. Their activities are precisely required because the agents of corruption are typically invisible either locally or globally. Thus invisibility, at least globally if not locally, is a characterizing feature of institutionalized and systemic corruption.

In sum, the above three scenarios help explain how the objection that invisibility is not a regular and characterizing feature of corruption, as it is normally understood, can be answered. Except for fools (understood as instrumentally irrational agents), cases resembling a Hobbesian State of Nature, as well as cases of institutionalized corruption, which may tolerate some local but not global visibility and transparency, corruption under the cloak of invisibility is still the most effective instrumental policy. Under normal circumstances, for normal instrumentally rational agents, invisibility is, therefore, a characterizing and regular feature of corruption.

3.5 A Further Essential Characterizing Feature of Corruption

If all the above features are regular features that normally accompany typical cases of corruption, they are nevertheless not sufficient in characterizing corruption. They are not sufficient for if they were, a house burglar or a professional bank robber would be deemed corrupt. However, though immoral, the actions of the house burglar and bank robber are not what we would normally describe as corrupt. The missing sufficient condition is a *socially pre-established fiduciary relationship of trust* between the corrupt person or group and the person or persons or group who are harmed in some way by the corrupt person's or the corrupt group's actions. The reason why house burglars or bank robbers are not deemed corrupt is because there is an absence of a prior fiduciary relationship of trust between the burglar and the bank robber on the one hand, and those who are harmed by their actions on the other; namely, the household owners, the banks and their customers. By contrast, typical cases of corruption and its sub-species fraud, involve a breach of a socially pre-established fiduciary relationship of trust between the corrupt agents and their victims, namely, those wronged by the corrupt agents' actions. The addition of the condition of a fiduciary duty of trust is in keeping with one of the traditional dictionary definitions of "corruption", namely, "the changing from the naturally sound condition" or "the turning from a sound into an unsound impure condition" or " the perversion of anything from an original state of purity".[8] The fiduciary relationship can be articulated in political, professional, social or familial terms.

Notice that if we were to remove the need for trust, whether it is familial, social, professional, or political, we would revert to a Hobbesian State of Nature. Interestingly, however, corruption involves a *halfway house* comprising actions that fall into a Hobbesian Sate of Nature and the agents of those actions, which operate unethically in a clandestine manner within a contractually Hobbesian social and moral society. It is a case of having your civic cake and eating it too. Thus typically,

[8] See the Shorter Oxford Dictionary.

a corrupt person avoids the ethical obligations of contractual and fiduciary relationships of trust based on trust by operating under conditions approaching those of perfect injustice. He does so by committing his corrupt deeds under a cloak of invisibility that allows him to avoid the social disapproval and retribution of socially recognized unethical and illegal conduct, whilst at the same time securing the social approbation of recognized ethical conduct by wearing the dissembling mask of morality; at least in the negative sense of not appearing to be conducting himself immorally. At this juncture one may ask the pertinent question whether some of the Big Tech companies such as Facebook and Google are not similarly operating in a Hobbesian *halfway house* in a "black box" corporate environment (Pasquale 2015) afforded to them by the opaqueness and non-accountability of their algorithmic systems and business models that appear to primarily benefit their financial interests over those of society. We shall return to that question in Chap. 5.

Typically, some of the most corrupt people in various societies at various times go to great lengths and spare no cost of conspicuous consumption to maintain an outward façade of probity and respectability. Corrupt dictators, Mafia bosses, and directors of various corporations engaging in corrupt activities will attempt to appear respectable by sending their children to the best private schools, living in the best neighborhoods and engaging in religious services, whilst engaging in corruption. The paradox of "perfect injustice" is that those who are the most corrupt want to appear as the least corrupt. Moreover, they want to appear morally and legally "respectable". In some forms of financial corruption, they use the products of their corrupt activities to clothe themselves in a veneer of respectability. To use a metaphor, "they launder their image by laundering money". This observation is in keeping with an aspect of Robert Merton's "means-ends" theory of corruption (Lipset and Lenz 2000). His theory suggests that there is a close relationship between achievement motivation and corruption, where the former is measured in terms of economic success. Thus, cultures that stress economic success as an important goal for achieving social status and recognition but nevertheless restrict access to opportunities will have high levels of corruption. As a result, people from those cultures, who realize that they have little or no access to opportunity, will seek to succeed by unconventional corrupt means.[9]

[9]Mentor's hypothesis seems to have been confirmed by the cross–national 1990–1993 World Values Survey which indicated a close correlation between achievement motivation and corruption in the less affluent countries. This may help explain, at least in the past, how organized corruption by criminal organizations like the Mafia exhibited a close relationship between achievement motivation and corruption. See Seymour M. Lipset and Gabriel S. Lenz, "Corruption, Culture, and Markets" in *Culture Matters*, 2000, pp. 116–118.

3.6 The Necessary and Sufficient Conditions of Corruption

Having examined corruption phenomenologically in terms of its characterizing features and prior to proceeding to examine its general taxonomy and the different types of media corruption in Chap. 4, it would be useful to first provide a general theoretical and formal account of corruption in terms of its necessary and sufficient conditions, especially with regard to institutional corruption, that would be the main focus of this book (Miller 2018; Spence et al. 2011):

1. An instance of institutional corruption is an instance in which an action or joint action or set of actions performed by an agent or set of agents undermines or has a tendency to undermine or contribute to the undermining of a legitimate institutional role, process, goal(s) or purpose(s) (understood as a collective good) of that institution and/or an effect of the despoiling of the moral character of an institutional role occupant(s), qua role occupant of that institution. This is the *Institutional Actor Condition*.
2. An action or set of actions is corrupt only if it corrupts something or someone. This constitutes the *Cause and Effect Condition*.
3. An action or set of actions is corrupt only if the role occupant(s) who performs that action(s) intended it or foresaw the corrupting effects of that action(s) – or at the very least, could and should have foreseen the corrupting effects – or could have reasonably avoided the action(s). This is the *Moral Responsibility Condition*.

A common trait of institutional corruption that is not, however, a *necessary condition,* is its predominantly *systemic* nature. It is not a necessary condition for even if the corruption as illustrated by the Cambridge Analytica case, we shall examine in Chap. 5 was a one-off instance, it would still count as corruption because of its high impact and wide unethical repercussions and damage to public trust.

Another general feature of corruption is that all forms of corruption are immoral, though not all forms of immorality constitute corruption. So, although a burglar who breaks into your house to steal, has committed an illegal act, he has not acted corruptly. Corruption usually requires a pre-exiting fiduciary duty of trust that renders the act corrupt though the act may not be illegal. Many forms of corruption, such as political bribery, are illegal, though some, like fabricating stories in journalism and advertorials, as we shall examine in Chap. 4, are not (Spence 2008; Spence et al. 2011). Corruption as understood and explained in this chapter is therefore fundamentally a moral problem (Spence et al. 2011; Miller 2018). This is further illustrated by the close conceptual connection between corruption and unethical conduct as illustrated by the types of media corruption in Chap. 4, on the basis of the Dual Obligation Information Theory (DOIT).

3.7 Taxonomy of Corruption

Having determined the essential characterizing features of corruption and its necessary and sufficient conditions, the following is a general *taxonomy of corruption.*

3.7.1 Systematic and Gratuitous Corruption

To begin with, corruption, as mentioned earlier, can be gratuitous or systematic. Systematic corruption is all things been equal, more ethically problematic than gratuitous corruption because of the greater potential harm it can cause to individuals, institutions, communities, societies or states. The harm that systematic corruption causes, as in some forms of advertising, for example, which subverts and perverts human values and principles, by associating them systematically with consumer products can be, like the corruption itself that causes it, visible but not readily transparent (Spence 2014, 2018). Like the early onset of cancer, it harms without the harm being transparent to the subject being harmed. This type of visible but non-transparent systematic corruption is the most pernicious form of corruption because its cause (agency) and consequences (harm) remain for the most part and for many people concealed. It is the enemy from within; the fifth-phalanx of corruption. It is difficult to discern and more difficult to control and correct. As we shall examine in Chap. 5, this visible but not transparent type of systemic corruption might also upon closer examination and reflection be understood to apply to *tech media corruption* as illustrated in Facebook's part in the Cambridge Analytica case. Though appearing to be ethically wrong it is not readily understood as a type of media corruption.

Some forms of unethical collusion between Journalism and Public Relations practices in the form of *media- release journalism* (Simmons and Spence 2006) also fall into this category of media corruption. Combined with their substantial power and influence, their capacity to harm is equally substantial and wide, both locally and globally. Thus, from a perspective of compliance, one would expect that media corruption would have one of the highest regulation priority rankings. The fact that it does not is further confirmation of both the substantial power of the media as well as the high degree of non-transparency of its forms of corruption. If we add to that the fact that compliance in the Media is primarily self-regulatory, we can see why the Media is able to get away with corrupt practices that in other professional areas, such as the police, for example, will not be tolerated. I shall return to the question of self-regulation in section (7) of this chapter. The topic of regulation, especially with regard to the tech media companies, such as Facebook and Google, will also be explored in detail in Chap. 7.

3.7.2 Actions and Actors

A further distinction that cuts across the distinction between systematic and gratuitous corruption, is the distinction between *actions* of corruption and corrupt *characters*. As mentioned earlier, corrupt actions alone do not determine a corrupt character. An agent can act corruptly gratuitously but not be corrupt because he is not normally disposed to act that way and hence though his actions may qualify as corrupt, his character need not. What determines whether one has a corrupt character is a disposition to act corruptly under repeated or repeatable similar circumstances.

By and large, systematic corruption can be attributed to corrupt characters whereas gratuitous acts of corruption by contrast, especially if they are one-off aberrant instances of corruption, would normally not. However, it is possible that gratuitous acts of corruption could still be attributed to corrupt characters. Though disposed to act corruptly under repeatable similar circumstances, a corrupt agent had, let us say, only the one life-time opportunity to engage in corruption. By parity of argument, it is at least conceivable that an agent has a corrupt character, in the sense that he is disposed under certain circumstances to act corruptly, even if he never acts corruptly because he never gets the opportunity.

Similarly, an agent involved in systematic corruption may not have a corrupt character notwithstanding his involvement in systematic corrupt activity. He is, let us say, a fallen angel who has fallen from grace into corruption without ever having the disposition for corruption. The example of the corrupt agent who avoids invisibility for his corrupt agency in seeking atonement for his corrupt activities is a hypothetical case in point.

This asymmetry between corrupt actions and corrupt actors finds resonance in the Christian concept of repentance and absolution at the 11th hour, as powerfully illustrated by Jesus' forgiveness of the repentant thief at his crucifixion. If there is no logical necessary connection between corrupt deeds and corrupt characters, then forgiving the uncorrupt character whilst condemning the corrupt deeds, makes perfect moral sense.

3.7.3 Constitutive and Regulative Corruption

A further distinction is that of *constitutive* and *regulative* corruption.[10] Constitutive corruption is corruption that involves the violation of rules or principles that constitute the activity that the violation corrupts. The activity itself is constituted by the rules and its existence is logically dependent on those rules. Regulative corruption on the other hand is corruption of rules that involves the violation of rules that regulate a pre-existing activity, an activity whose existence is independent of the rules.

[10] I borrow these terms from John Searle, see John Searle (1969), and Arthurs Isak Applbaum (1999).

Examples of constitutive corruption are amongst others, some forms of police, media, academic and medical and health care corruption. Examples of regulative corruption are amongst others, forms of advertising, public relations, and corporate corruption. The case of a police officer taking a bribe is an instance of constitutive corruption because the role of a police officer is constituted by the rules of upholding the law and supporting the criminal justice system that the corrupt activity of the police officer violates. That is, breaking the law and subverting the criminal justice system. The case of a bank clerk that embezzles money from the bank for which he works is a form of regulative corruption because the rule of not stealing from one's employer is logically independent from the pre-existing financial activity of banking.

Overall, instances of constitutive corruption are ethically more problematic and generally more harmful than instances of regulative corruption. Combined with systematic corruption, *constitutive systematic corruption* is the most ethically problematic and harmful because it potentially undermines the very foundations of the professional activity whose constitutive rules the corruption violates. Criminal Justice, Medical and Health Care, Political, Police and Journalism corruption when systematic, undermine not only the foundations of those professional and government institutions but more importantly undermine the foundations of democracy and the state itself. Take journalism for example. Because Journalism has as the Fourth Estate traditionally operated as society's watchdog in keeping the public informed about political and other institutional corruption, corruption within journalism itself in the form of media corruption, especially when systematic, can be particularly pernicious. It is for this reason that a fall in journalistic standards in objective and independent reporting is a matter of deep concern for it can undermine the ethical standards of society. For if the guardians themselves become corrupted, who will guard society from corruption?

Plato's parallel notion of individual and institutional corruption[11] that corrodes both the individual and the state is pertinent with regard to constitutive systematic corruption; for it does not only corrupt the individuals who participate in the corrupt activities, but equally and more seriously corrupts the professional, social and political institutions and by extension the whole state. Such extensive constitutive systematic corruption if unchecked can result in a Hobbesian State of Nature. As we will see in Chap. 5, insofar as Facebook is a media company with regard to its role of mediating and curating the information and communication of its users, it could be argued that its role in the Cambridge Analytica case was a type of constitutive systematic corruption: systemic, due to its underlying business model that is conducive to corruption and constitutive, because its professional role seems to be, upon closer reflection, that of a media company.

[11] Plato of course doesn't specifically use the term "corruption" but "injustice". However, to the extent that corruption is a form of injustice we can by analogy apply Plato's notion of parallelism between individual and institutional justice to the phenomenon of corruption.

3.7.4 Individual and Group Corruption

A final distinction we can make is that between individual and group corruption. As the terms suggest, *individual* corruption is corruption that is primarily carried out by individual agents working on their own. *Group* corruption by contrast, is corruption carried out by a group of individuals working together within a pre-existing social, political, familial, professional, or other institutional structure. Thus, an individual employee embezzling money from his bank employer is an instance of individual corruption. Laundering money by a criminal organization like the Mafia or the Chinese Triads is, by contrast, an instance of group corruption. Individual and group corruption can either be gratuitous or systematic, constitutive or regulative. Thus, the Watergate Affair can be described as an instance of gratuitous constitutive group corruption. By contrast, some typical cases of ongoing and regular police corruption can best be described as systematic constitutive group corruption. To be sure, both political and police corruption can take the form of either individual or group corruption. Thus, an individual police officer taking the occasional bribe from speeding motorists may count as an instance of gratuitous constitutive individual corruption. As one would expect, systematic constitutive group corruption is the most ethically problematic as its consequences can be the most harmful both for those directly wronged and indirectly for the whole of society whose ethical foundations could be undermined and threatened by this type of corruption if it remains unchecked, uncorrected and unregulated.

One important aspect of systematic group corruption is its relation to culture. There has recently been a growing literature on that relation. A recent exposition of the relationship between corruption and culture in the wider context of the notion of "trust" is Francis Fukuyama's book, *Trust* (1996). In "Corruption, Culture, and Markets" the authors of that article (Lipset and Lenz 2000), refer to this relationship through Edward Banfield's work on "amoral familism", a notion which Fukuyama also discusses in his book. According to Banfield, corruption is to a large measure an expression of particularism – the perceived obligation to help and give resources to members of one's family above all but also to friends and members of groups to which one belongs. This solidarity primarily with the family but also with other groups with one is closely associated, can produce a self-interested culture which is hostile to the outsider who is not a member. An expression of this is of course nepotism. According to Banfield, "in a society of amoral families, no one will further the interest of the group or community except as it to his private advantage to do so." As there is little or no loyalty to the larger community or acceptance of norms of behavior that require support of others, amoral familism can and does give rise to corruption. An extreme form of amoral familism is the Mafia (Lipset and Lenz 2000). Although Banfield's research concerns specifically the people of Southern Italy, Fukuyama in his book makes similar observations about other cultures, such as the Chinese for example. This is confirmed by Lipset and Lenz who add that Asian nations, which are known for their strong familial ties rank amongst the more corrupt according to Transparency International's Corruption Perceptions Index (CPI).

According to the CPI, familism and corruption relate strongly. The concept of amoral familism can be extended to some close-knit professional groups such as the police, where references to police corruption have often been related to perceptions of "police solidarity" and a "police culture". As we shall see in Chap. 6, 'police culture' is what Frank Serpico the whistleblower, was confronted with. It almost cost him his life, when he exposed police corruption within the New York police force in the 1960s–1970s.

Combined with group systematic corruption, a culture of familism can produce serious forms of corruption as the CPI indicates. Moreover, when combined with constitutive forms of corruption as in police corruption for example, the results can ethically be very harmful for society indeed. Furthermore, forms of group corruption either constitutive (police) or regulative (the Mafia), which are culturally and familially driven, are very deeply entrenched and thus much more difficult to correct than other forms of corruption. The *invisibility* of these forms of corruption is particularly dense and is further exacerbated by a wall of silence from its participants. When those two forms of corruption are combined through collusion, they are extremely harmful. An infamous example of corruption by collusion took place in Sydney, Australia, in the 1970s and 1980s. It involved the relationship between a police detective Roger Rogerson and a notorious criminal Neddy Smith. Roger Rogerson and his police colleagues were accused and charged for giving Smith and his gang the "green light" to commit crimes, including armed bank robberies without police interference. Both Rogerson and Smith were sent to prison for their crimes. Such types of corruption by collusion are historically not uncommon and often involve politicians, the police and members of organized crime. In the media, as we shall examine in Chap. 4, they involve corruption by collusion between journalists, advertisers and public relations consultants, through misinforming and misleading citizens and consumers in presenting paid-for comment in the form of *advertorials*, as news or independent editorial comment.

It is interesting to observe, moreover, that in these familial- based forms of corruption, it is the 'fiduciary relationship' that is motivating the corrupt practices. Unlike other forms of corruption where it is the violation of the fiduciary relationship that engenders the corruption, in familial corruption it is the reverse – it is the adherence to a misplaced fiduciary duty of trust that drives the corruption. This asymmetry can be explained if we take the role that fiduciary duty plays in familial forms of corruption to be a misplacement of solidarity and loyalty. Namely, that the particularistic fiduciary duty of trust to family, friends, or professional colleagues or affiliated members of other groups, becomes ethically misplaced and thus wrong when it is aimed and supports unethical practices that unjustly harm others outside those groups. In other words, fiduciary duty of trust cannot be used as a means to pursue unethical and corrupt practices. This indicates the requirement for universal as opposed to particularistic models of morality, as demonstrated, for example, by the Dual Obligation Information Theory (DOIT) that we examined in Chap. 2. The particularistic oriented communications by certain groups on social media that disseminate disinformation in support of their causes and beliefs are of concern when they engage in digital communications on their social networks that support unethical actions, practices and policies that undermine the universal ethical principles and values, which have traditionally provided the foundations of civil society and the democratic state. Is it for that reason that fake news on social media platforms such as Facebook and Google via YouTube, are of particular concern when they influence elections as illustrated in the Cambridge Analytica case, a topic involving media corruption that we shall investigate in Chap. 5.

3.8 The Corrosion of Character

It would appear then that as long as the corrupt person ensures the agency of his corrupt deeds remains undetected, he could reap the gains of immoral conduct with no moral or instrumental cost to himself. Let us understand moral cost here as measured solely in terms of social disapproval and social repercussions in the form of punishment from others or the State. Moreover, if the corrupt person can maintain a semblance of moral conduct, he could pass himself off as a person of moral probity. As we saw earlier, Glaucon refers to this possibility as the "highest reach of injustice being just deemed just when you are not".[12]

Although under Gygean conditions of perfect injustice one could in theory and possibly in practice avoid detection and thus act corruptly with impunity, one could not, however, remain totally *immune* from moral jeopardy. I want to suggest that the moral cost to a Gyges-like character operating corruptly under conditions of perfect injustice might be one of emotional and cognitive dissonance. For on the assumption that a Gyges-like character is minimally rational and subject to the human sensibilities and sentiments of a normal socialised person, he might be liable to experience the inner psychological stress and strain caused by emotional and cognitive dissonance; a dissonance, between his real corrupt motives and actions on the one hand, and his false and merely apparent moral reputation on the other. Like Macbeth, he would be liable to inner conflict and the loss of inner peace. The double-life of Dr. Jackyl and Mr. Hide is no life for one who at least has some of the cognitive and affective sensibilities and social sensitivities of normal socialised persons, unless one can successfully engage in self-deception about one's corrupt agency or corrupt actions. Self-deception, however, may not always be practically feasible for all agents who engage in corruption.

If I am right, *impunity* from acting immorally does not guarantee *immunity* from moral jeopardy in the form of inner conflict and the loss of inner peace. The story of Dr. Faustus who sold his soul to the devil in exchange of infinite knowledge, is a case in point. If honesty is the best policy because it generates trust and trust is the necessary fabric for the social tapestry of social inter-relations and interactions, *integrity* of character is the indemnity against the moral jeopardy of inner conflict that might be caused by emotional and cognitive dissonance. It is for this reason that

[12] Plato *Republic*, Book 2, p. 361.

integrity is morally important. It has the dual function of protecting a person from psychological dissonance, as well as providing personal motivation for avoiding corrupt conduct, even under favourable Gygean conditions of perfect injustice.

Plato is right to make integrity of character the glue that bonds individual self-regarding prudential integrity with social other-regarding morality. The underlying factor is avoidance of harm and generation of good not only to others but also for oneself. Our moral social inter-relation with each other is closely related to our moral intra-relation to our own individual characters and thus renders ethical conduct both socially as well as personally beneficial and desirable. By harming others through corrupt conduct, we can at least potentially harm ourselves precisely because of the close relation between social external morality, on the one hand, and individual internal morality, instantiated through integrity of character, on the other. According to the Stoic philosophers this relation is intrinsic because of our metaphysical inter-relation of belonging to the one same unitary rational cosmic reality. But I will not argue here whether the Stoics were right or not. It suffices for our present purposes that the relation between social morality and personal morality is close, even if it is not intrinsic.

An interesting question that arises at this juncture is this: Can the professional thief or professional hired killer have integrity and thus not be deemed corrupt by virtue that their actions accord with their professional and fiduciary duties? For unlike the corrupt police officer, whose corrupt actions are in direct conflict with his professional duties as a representative of the justice system and upholder of the law, and by extension morality, no such conflict exists in the case of a professional thief or professional killer. On the contrary their illegal and immoral actions are in keeping with their professional roles. Does this mean that although professional thieves and hired killers are immoral, they are nevertheless not corrupt? Our analysis above would suggest that this in fact is the case. And indeed, it is the case. This difference between on the one hand corrupt and immoral actions, and on the other merely immoral but not corrupt actions help explain the difference between say a bank robbery performed by a professional bank robber and a bribe taken by a police officer or an academic. Though both are unethical practices, only the latter practices are corrupt. For it is only in the latter but not the former case that a professional or fiduciary duty of trust pre-exists between the wrongdoers and those wronged by the wrongdoers' actions.

In conclusion of this section, although one can quite possibly act corruptly with impunity under conditions of perfect injustice, one might not be able to remain totally immune from the moral jeopardy of having one's character corrupted. The possible loss is one of inner peace and harmony through cognitive and emotional dissonance resulting from a potential loss of personal integrity as well as the psychological harm one might suffer through feelings of guilt and remorse, both about oneself and others. Moreover, the very attractive instrumental benefit of acting corruptly under conditions of perfect injustice is undercut and compromised by an unattractive potential loss of peace of mind resulting from a possible cognitive and emotional dissonance.

3.9 The Instrumental Rationality of Corruption

The problem with corruption is that it is rational – at least instrumentally rational. If you can maximize your self-seeking ends at a minimum or no cost to yourself, under conditions of more or less perfect injustice, then as Glaucon says to Socrates you would be mad not to act corruptly if it is to your advantage to do so, and moreover, you can get away with it (Plato, *The Republic* Book 2). It is the instrumental rationality of corruption and unethical conduct generally under conditions approaching perfect injustice that renders the authoritative question of morality "why be moral" of paramount significance to ethics and particularly, applied ethics. For unless we can provide very good if not entirely compelling reasons why one ought to act morally and therefore not corruptly in every instance, instrumental rationality, that in the absence of moral ends favors primarily self-regarding interest over morality, will hold sway over peoples' motives and consequent actions.

As both Aristotle and Plato argued, ethics must not only guide us as to the choice of means, but equally and more importantly it should also offer practical guidance with regard to the ends that we individually and collectively pursue.[13] For without the ethical guidance based on good reasons that any normal person can accept as rationally binding, the temptation to engage in corruption, especially under conditions approaching those of perfect injustice, as in the case of Gyges, may be too tempting and too strong for some people to resist; perhaps even most people. And rationally speaking, why resist if there are no rationally authoritative reasons to do so, and moreover you can take advantage of self-beneficial corrupt conduct with minimal or no cost to oneself.

This is an important question to ask and apply in the case of the Big Tech companies such as Facebook and Google whose self-seeking business models that favors their financial interests over the common good of society, together with their significant power and the complexity and opacity of their algorithms, allows them to remain non-transparent and therefore unaccountable. Instrumental rationality in that case, favors their self-interest over the public good of society. In Chap. 7 we shall examine why external proactive compliance through government regulation becomes essential in making tech companies normatively responsible and compliant with the inculcation of public ethical principles and values within the corporate structures of those companies for the public good of society.

Ethical education of the right kind, both theoretical but most importantly practical, is important in order to overcome the natural tendency in people to behave according to the counsel of instrumental rationality that under conditions of perfect injustice may favor, from an instrumentally rational perspective alone, corrupt conduct. Ethical education is also necessary in overcoming ethical ignorance. For the condition of invisibility that makes corruption instrumentally attractive can also operate in the form of self-deception. Namely, that as long as we can evade detection, it is in our interest to engage in corrupt deeds, especially under conditions

[13] See also Alan Gewirth (1991) Can Any Final Ends be Rational. *Ethics* 102 (October 1991): 66–95.

approaching perfect injustice. Worse still, we might even delude ourselves through specious rationalizations that our actions or motives are not corrupt because they serve some higher purpose or ends – like getting rich quickly. Furthermore, ethical education must be based on clearly defined and justified *universal* principles of morality that are at least in principle *capable* of motivating ethical action and proscribing unethical conduct such as corruption. Compelling universal principles in ethics are particularly crucial for combating corruption that is driven by personal, familial, corporate, or cultural amoralism.

To the extent that we are all instrumentally rational and hence potentially prone to some form or degree of corruption some of the time, especially under conditions approaching perfect injustice, ethical self-reflection becomes essential. The unexamined life is not worth living precisely because of the risk we run of falling into corruption and if Plato is right, corrupting the most valuable asset we possess, namely, our characters. I speculate that it is strategically perhaps for this reason that Plato and Aristotle attempted to offer arguments that were designed to show that acting ethically is always and ultimately in one's own best interest. They were both trying to beat instrumental rationality at its own game. That is, they were trying to show that short-term selfish interest, that may seem to be favored by instrumental rationality narrowly conceived, is not the same as long term self-interest that on closed reflection may be equally favored by both morality and instrumental rationality broadly conceived. Their respective arguments are essentially arguments from a *eudaimonic* perspective. It is no coincidence that although the Greek and Hellenistic philosophers of antiquity, Plato, Aristotle, the Stoics, the Epicurean, the Cynics, and the Sceptics differ in the details and approach of their ethical theories, all of them made *eudaimonia* or happiness through virtuous conduct, based on the moral virtues of *courage*, *prudence*, *moderation* and *justice* (the four cardinal virtues), both the primary objective for a good life as well as the necessary condition for its attainment. Going one step further, the Stoics made it also a sufficient condition. At present, Stoic philosophy, through mainly its online presence on the Internet and through a global social media network, has undergone a new renaissance unprecedented since the time of its significant influence during the Hellenistic period and the Roman Empire that boasts several prominent Stoic philosophers such as its founder Zeno of Citium, Chryssipus of Cilicia, Emperor Marcus Aurelius, Seneca, and Epictetus. Just as then so as now, Stoic philosophy appeals as an antianxiety remedy or *pharmakon* for troubled times. The pandemic of the coronavirus is no exception and offers both theoretical and practical attraction for Stoic philosophy, whose main core principle is that the attainment of *eudaimonia* or happiness is entirely within our personal control, since our moral character is, regardless of the 'slings and arrows of outrageous fortune' (Shakespeare, *Hamlet*).

External compliance measures alone against corruption are not enough. This merely leads to an ever- escalating white-collar war between on the one hand compliance enforcement and compliance deviance on the other. What is required in addition to government external compliance is effective ethical self-regulation. This in turn requires the kind of ethical training of a virtuous character recommended by Plato, Aristotle and later the Stoics and other Hellenistic philosophers. Moreover, this in turn requires not merely individual, but also collective social ethical education. This is important for establishing and re-enforcing social capital in terms of trust and trustworthiness. In the general ethical scheme, I have been advocating in this chapter, trust plays a crucial and necessary role. Especially, if I am right in maintaining that a fiduciary relationship of trust and trustworthiness is an essential feature of anti-corruption; for if the state is sometimes rotten it is because there is not enough social capital in the form of mutual trust based on mutual respect. Namely, a mutual ethical respect that is universal and not merely particular. This may sound utopian, but it is equally utopian to think that we can combat corruption effectively through merely ever- escalating costly external compliance enforcement and privacy-intruding surveillance measures.

What is ultimately required is not ethical information about ethical rules and arguments important as these of course are, but also and more importantly what is required is ethical transformation through promoting a culture of public ethical values and virtues. Namely, a culture that is publicly supported and promoted both socially and institutionally through appropriate ethical educational programs that view self-regulation in the public and professional spheres as primarily the ethical self-regulation of each individual agent as well as the professional and political institutions that support the democratic system. *Surveillance capitalism* that is practiced and perpetrated widely at present by the Big Tech companies such as Facebook, Google, Apple and Amazon undermine, through their self-rewarding financial business models, infringes and violates our collective human rights as citizens, rights of privacy, autonomy, security, truth and the integrity of our information and communication systems, thus, undermining the common good of society.[14]

For this to work adequately and effectively, however, what is needed is civil and institutional education of ethical principles and values that can provide at least adequate justification and motivation in support that can guide not merely individual ethical means but also and more importantly individual and collective ethical ends for the common good of society. It is precisely for this reason that the authoritative question of ethics "why be moral?" and its related but equally important motivation question "why care about being moral?" is a central and important question not only in theoretical ethics but also and crucially in applied practical ethics. Unless this question is properly and publicly addressed and adequately answered, instrumental rationality favoring self-interest over the common good, especially under conditions approaching perfect injustice, will continue to encourage corruption. The *alignment* of public ethical principles and values and compliance through government regulation will be examined as a measure of anti- corruption, in Chap. 7.

[14]For more detail about Surveillance Capitalism see Shoshana Zuboff (2019), *The Age of Surveillance Capitalism*. London: Profile Books Ltd.

3.10 Conclusion

This chapter has presented a general philosophical account of corruption that applies to all forms of corruption be it political, financial, corruption in the clergy, police corruption, sports corruption, and media corruption, which demonstrates why such practices are not only unethical but also corrupt. Such practices are of great normative concern as they have the tendency not only to cause harm to individual persons or groups of persons (for example, by invading their privacy or undermining their autonomy) but also cause harm to the institutional structure of the democratic system itself. Insofar as this is the case, the harm that is caused by corruption and specifically media corruption, affects every citizen. However, like the proverbial fifth-phalanx, media corruption is not always apparent and when apparent is not understood as media corruption as other forms of corruption are. As in Plato's Myth of Gyges that was examined in this chapter, the media, merely "appears just, when it is not". Having determined the essential characterizing features of corruption as well as its necessary and sufficient conditions, the chapter provided a taxonomy of corruption of its various types and manifestations.

Plato, whose Myth of Gyges first alerted me to the essential key characterizing features for identifying corruption in all its different forms, including media corruption (Spence 2008) would probably have called contemporary corruption "a perfect injustice – appearing just when one is not". A possible moral response to Plato's resonant and relevant for us question today, as to why one should be moral or just when one can act immorally or corrupt with total impunity under conditions of perfect injustice, is to say that it may not be possible to do so with total moral immunity to moral jeopardy resulting in bad conscience, loss of integrity with resultant psychological dissonance when one's actions do not match one's character, and a potential loss of one's peace of mind and possibly loss of eudaimonia or happiness.

> Overall, the balance sheet does not seem to favor corruption in the long term, even if it appears to do so in the short-term. Ethical behavior might pay in the long term just because it can not only keep us honest but might also be able to protect us from making ourselves unhappy. (Spence 2006)

If happiness is ultimately what matters most in people's lives, then honesty and integrity might be the best policy in the long run.

References

Applbaum, Arthur Isak. 1999. *Ethics for Adversaries: The Morality of Roles in Public and Professional Life*, 85–99. Princeton: Princeton University Press.

Fukuyama, Francis. 1996. *Trust: The Social Virtues and the Creation of Prosperity*. London: Penguins Books.

Gewirth, Alan. 1978. *Reason and Morality*. Chicago: The University of Chicago Press.

———. 1991. Can Any Final Ends be Rational. *Ethics* 102 (October 1991): 66–95.

Hobbes, Thomas. 1651. *Leviathan*. http://www.gutenberg.org/ebooks/3207. Accessed 3 July 2020.

Lipset, Seymour Martin, and Gabriel Salman Lenz. 2000. Corruption, Culture and Markets. In *Culture Matters: How Values Shape Human Progress*, ed. Lawrence E. Harrison and Samuel P. Huntington. New York: Basic Books.

Miller, Seumas. 2018. *Corruption. Stanford Encyclopedia of Philosophy*, ed. Edward N. Zalta. (Winter 2018 Edition).

Miller, Seumas, Peter Roberts, and Edward Spence. 2005. *Corruption and Anti-Corruption: An Applied Philosophical Approach*. Upper Saddle River: Pearson/Prentice Hall.

Pasquale, Frank. 2015. *The Black Box Society: The Secret Algorithms That Control Money and Information*. Cambridge, MA: Harvard University Press.

Plato. 1952a. *The Republic, The Dialogues of Plato*. Trans. Benjamin Jowett, Book II: 359–361. Chicago: Encyclopedia Britannica Inc.

———. 1952b. *The Republic, The Dialogues of Plato*. Trans. Benjamin Jowett, Book X: 10.614–10.621. Chicago: Encyclopedia Britannica Inc.

Searle, John. 1969. *Speech Acts: An Essay in the Philosophy of Language*, 33–42, 50–53. Cambridge: Cambridge University Press.

Simmons, Peter, and Edward Spence. 2006. The Practice and Ethics of Media Release Journalism. *Australian Journalism Review* 28 (1): 167–181.

Spence, Edward. 2006. Corruption doomed to fail in long term. *Financial Review*, January 14, 2006.

———. 2008. Corruption in the Media. *International Journal of Applied Philosophy* 22 (2 – Fall): 231–241.

———. 2014. The Advertising of Happiness and the Branding of Values. In *Business Ethics*, ed. Michael Boylan, 2nd ed. Upper Saddle River: Pearson/Prentice Hall.

———. 2017. Corruption in the Media. In *The Handbook of Business and Corruption: Cross-Sectoral Experiences*, ed. Michael S. Aßländer and Sarah Hudson, 453–480. Bingley: Emerald Group Publishing.

———. 2018. Harm in Media Marketing: The Branding of Values. In *The Handbook of Media Ethics*, ed. Patrick Plaisance, 237–225. Berlin: Walter de Gruyter GmbH.

Spence, Edward, Andrew Alexandra, Aaron Quinn, and Anne Dunn. 2011. *Media, Markets and Morals*. Oxford: Wiley- Blackwell.

Zuboff, Shoshana. 2019. *The Age of Surveillance Capitalism*. London: Profile Books Ltd.

Chapter 4
Media Corruption – Types, Causes and Contexts

So let the unjust make his unjust attempts in the right way, and lie hidden if he means to be great in his injustice: (he who is found out is nobody:) for the highest reach of injustice is, to be deemed just when you are not.

From the Myth of Gyges, Plato, The Republic, Book II.

4.1 Introduction

This chapter will identify and examine the presence of corruption as it is manifested in the media. As in the case of the general account of corruption that was examined in Chap. 3, this chapter will also examine media corruption by reference to Plato's Myth of Gyges (*The Republic*, Plato 1952) as this has contemporary significance and relevance in explaining corruption generally and specifically as it applies to the media. To that end, this chapter will use a *model of media corruption* that shares the same characteristics and features of the general account of corruption that was examined in Chap. 3 but specifically designed and developed for application to the phenomenon and practice of corruption in the media (Spence 2008, 2017).

The primary objective of this chapter is to identify and categorize the different types of media corruption, the ways in which these are caused, and the contexts in which they are manifest in current physical and virtual media environments and practices. Whereas much has been written on other forms of corruption, including corporate, political, financial, sports corruption, and police corruption, media corruption has been largely overlooked. Although identified as unethical within the general corpus of media ethics, practices such as *cash-for-comment* and *media release journalism*, including *video news releases* (VNRs), fake news, *staged news*, *advertorials*, and *informercials*, among others, have not been commonly defined as corrupt practices. In addition, there has been no systematic theoretical study of why and how such practices constitute media corruption.

E. H. Spence, *Media Corruption in the Age of Information*, Library of Public Policy and Public Administration 15, https://doi.org/10.1007/978-3-030-61612-0_4

The chapter will apply the aforementioned philosophical model of media corruption to identify and categorize major types of corruption that arise in the media. Diachronic historical key case studies will provide a practical illustration and contextualization of those major types of media corruption, as well as demonstrate that the phenomenon and practice of media corruption continues in various forms across a span of several years to manifest itself in some of the current practices of the social media and the Tech Media, such as Facebook and Google, a topic we will examine in more detail in Chap. 5.

Before proceeding to examine what are the various types of media corruption, it would be useful to recall what are the six features of corruption that emerge from an examination of the Myth of Gyges in Plato's *Republic*, as well as what are the necessary and sufficient conditions of corruption that apply generally to all forms of corruption including media corruption.

4.2 The Characterizing Features of Corruption

The six features that characterize corruption as examined in Chap. 3, are: the *possession of power*, *disposition* to exercise that power, *opportunity* to exercise that power, *invisibility* or concealment, *self-regarding gain*, and a pre-existing *fiduciary duty of trust*.

As explained in Chap. 3, *possession of power* is the ability or capacity to act in a manner capable of bringing about a certain intended desired outcome; a *disposition to exercise that power* is the possession of a predisposition, pro-attitude or willingness to purposefully exercise that power; *opportunity* is having the opportunity, either presented to oneself or engineered by oneself, to engage in some activity for which one has the power and the predisposition in which to engage; *invisibility* or *concealment* is the ability or quality an agent has for keeping the motives and the identity of the agency of his actions invisible, concealed, or hidden from the gaze of others; *Self-regarding gain* is any gain, not necessarily financial, that accrues to the agent personally or to a group of which he is a member, as a result of his or the group's actions; *fiduciary duty of trust* is a socially pre-established and widely acknowledged fiduciary relationship of trust that exists between the corrupt person or corrupt group and the person or group of persons who are wronged or harmed in some way by the corrupt person's or the corrupt group's actions. With regard to the condition of invisibility, while the actions themselves would be visible at least with regard to their effects and consequences, the identity of their agency is invisible. Or at least the corrupt agent's intention is to keep his agency invisible or concealed.

Many of the characterizing features of corruption are present and accompany nearly all acts of corruption. For without power, one cannot commit a corrupt act. Possessing power is not enough; one must have the disposition to exercise that power willingly. Similarly, through lack of opportunity, one cannot engage in corrupt activity, even when one has both the power and the disposition to act corruptly. Invisibility seems to also be a characterizing feature of corruption that is usually, if not always, present in instances of corrupt activity.

Invisibility seems to be at least instrumentally desirable-, for without invisibility, one might not be able to evade detection, which is essential to escape possible social disapproval and punitive retribution from others or the state. Even for a Gyges-like person, keeping the identity of his agency in committing the immoral acts hidden would be prudent, lest he invokes social disapproval, which may eventually undermine his power to rule and invite retribution from those he harms through his unethical conduct. Like Glaucon's perfectly unjust person, perfectly corrupt persons maintain an outward appearance of probity, justice, and morality, while carrying out their corrupt deeds in secret. In this way they maximize their self-regarding gain, which can accrue to them personally or to a group to which they belong or cause to which they are committed, with little or no instrumental cost to themselves, their group, or their cause.

A socially pre-established and widely acknowledged fiduciary relationship of trust is also a necessary characterizing feature of corruption that must be present in all types of corruption, especially institutional corruption. For though the actions of a house burglar or bank robber, for example, may share the other five features of corruption cited above, namely, possession of power, disposition to exercise that power, opportunity to exercise that power, invisibility or concealment, and self-regarding gain, the missing sufficient condition for characterizing their actions as also corrupt, is the absence of a pre-existing fiduciary duty of trust that exits between the house burglar and the bank robber and the house owners and the banks and customers that have been harmed by their actions. Violation of a fiduciary duty of trust is therefore a necessary characterizing feature of corruption. The fiduciary relationship can be articulated in political, professional, educational, social, or the duties relating to the institutional role of the clergy. Thus, for example, a priest or minister of religion, or teacher who sexually abuses children in his or her care is acting corruptly, even though there might not be any financial gain, as the self-regarding gain as a feature of corruption need not be financial but any gain that accrues to a person of group engaging in corruption.

4.3 The Necessary and Sufficient Conditions of Corruption

As in the case of the characterizing features of corruption referred to above, it would also be useful to recall the necessary and sufficient conditions of corruption, with regard to corruption generally and as they specifically apply to media corruption (Miller 2018; Spence et al. 2011).

1. An instance of institutional corruption is an instance in which an action or joint action or set of actions performed by an agent or set of agents undermines or has a tendency to undermine or contribute to the undermining of a legitimate institutional role, process, goal(s) or purpose(s) (understood as a collective good) of that institution and/or an effect of the despoiling of the moral character of an

institutional role occupant (s), qua role occupant of that institution. This is the *Institutional Actor Condition.*
2. An action or set of actions is corrupt only if it corrupts something or someone. This constitutes the *Cause and Effect Condition.*
3. An action or set of actions is corrupt only if the role occupant(s) who performs that action(s) intended it or foresaw the corrupting effects of that action(s) – or at the very least, could and should have foreseen the corrupting effects – or could have reasonably avoided the action(s). This is the *Moral Responsibility Condition.*

A common trait of institutional corruption that is not, however, a *necessary condition,* is its predominantly *systemic* nature. It is not a necessary condition for even if the corruption as illustrated by the Cambridge Analytica case that will be examined in Chap. 5 was a one-off case, it would still count as corruption because of its high societal impact and wide unethical repercussions and damage to public trust.

Another general feature of corruption is that all forms of corruption are immoral, though not all forms of immorality constitute corruption. So, although a burglar who breaks into your house to steal has committed an illegal act, he has not acted corruptly. Corruption requires a pre-exiting fiduciary duty of trust that renders the act corrupt though the act may not be illegal. Many forms of corruption, such as political bribery, are illegal, though some, like fabricating stories in journalism and advertorials, are not (Spence 2008; Spence et al. 2011). Corruption as understood and explained in this chapter is therefore fundamentally a moral problem (Spence et al. 2011; Miller 2018). This is further demonstrated by the close conceptual connection between corruption and unethical conduct and the Dual Obligation Information Theory (DOIT) as illustrated by the types of media corruption in this chapter.

4.4 Types of Media Corruption

The following sections present key illustrative examples of major types of media communication messages, which, insofar as they possess the aforementioned six characterizing features of corruption and meet the necessary and sufficient conditions of corruption, constitute media corruption. These illustrative cases spanning a period of several years although some of them now dated have been purposely chosen to emphasize the *diachronic nature* and *historical continuity* of media corruption (Spence 2008; Elliott and Spence 2018). As well, the timeless significance of those case studies highlight how such cases constitute *typical cases* of media corruption over a period of time marked by many far-reaching changes in the media, from the fourth Estate to the fifth Estate, and currently the sixth Estate of the Tech Media companies, a topic to be examined in Chap. 5.

4.4.1 The Inside Job: Fictional News, Biased News, and News for Sale

Fictional News: Three central cases, those of Jayson Blair of the *New York Times* in 2003, Stephen Glass of the *New Republic* in 1998, and the *Der Spiegel* journalist Class Relotious in 2018, are illustrative examples of this type of internal corruption.

All three journalists wrote fabricated stories, mixing fact with fiction, and presented them as news. For example, among the fabricated stories written by the *New York Times* reporter Jayson Blair was an interview with the parents of Jessica Lynch, the Iraqi prisoner of war freed by U.S. troops. The story later proved to be entirely a product of Blair's fertile imagination. Ironically, the veracity of the reporting of the rescue of Private Jessica Lynch itself came under doubt and media scrutiny with regard to whether the incident happened as reported or whether it was staged by the US military spin machine as political propaganda.

Almost 20 years ago since the Stephen Glass scandal, another recent case in 2018 is that of the *Der Spiegel* journalist Class Relotious who like Stephen Glass and Jayson Blair before him, had a literary talent for writing fabricated 'investigative' stories that mixed fact with fiction. Relotius' fictional reporting proved so successful that before he was exposed, he had won the *Reporterpreis,* the highest prize for German journalists, four times over 6 years. Ironically, his exposure and resignation came from another De Spiegel colleague, Juan Moreno, in a book he published in 2019 titled *Thousand Lines of Lies* (Oltermann 2019). It highlights once again the importance of good investigative journalism as an effective measure of exposing and reporting corruption, including media corruption as in this case, a theme that runs throughout this book and is a topic examined in more detail in Chap. 6.

Biased News: Robert Greenwald's documentary film *Outfoxed: Rupert Murdoch's War on Journalism* (2004) raises searching questions about corporate influence in the media and in particular the right-wing political agenda of News Corporation's *Fox News,* and, as such, provides an illustrative case study for bias in the media and its conduciveness to corruption. Another illustrative case study involves CBS anchor Dan Rather, who admitted that the authenticity of the documents he used to question President Bush's National Guard record in his *60 Minutes* program in 2005 was unauthenticated and thus questionable regarding their veracity. Was this a case of a genuine mistake, sloppy journalism, or a deliberate attempt to skew the news? This case might provide an illuminating analysis of how bias, even when not intentionally used to slant the news might lead to biased news though negligence. Insofar as negligence in reporting meets the characterizing features of corruption, it can be argued that it is a form of corruption. Negligence meets the characterizing features of corruption because is a dereliction of duty. The journalist's duty is to inform the public on matters of public interest truthfully and reliably, as a doctor's duty is to heal her patients or at least not cause them harm through negligence.

Yet another form of media corruption by biased reporting is that involving the use of *unidentified sources*. Are there cases where the undisclosed sources are the product of "creative journalism," made up to tell a particular story that serves the media organization's political or social agenda? One case concerning the creation and use of an "unidentified source" to tell a biased story, one that turned out to be entirely false, involved the *Daily Express*. The gist of the story was that "a suspected Al Qaeda plot to target Tony Blair's home has been foiled …" (*Daily Express*, August 16, 2004). The source of the story was unidentified "security sources." However, just hours after the story was published, the Durham police categorically denied the authenticity of the story. According to them, the whole incident involved a couple of Lithuanians in a stolen Vauxhall, who had been picked up by police a few miles from Blair's house, not at the time reported in the *Daily Express* article but a year earlier. Not dissuaded by the British police's denial concerning the authenticity of the story, News Corp newspapers throughout Australia published similar stories: "Plot to kill Blair foiled—Al Qaeda linked to assassination plan." (*Daily Telegraph*, August 17, 2004), and others like it.

News for Sale**:** *Advertorials* or *infomercials* exemplify another type of corruption that is generated from within journalism itself. It usually involves the selling of pseudo "editorials" or "news" as part of an overall advertising package by media organizations in the forms of both print and broadcast journalism. At least one case study that indicates this type of media corruption involved a Sydney suburban newspaper, the *Sydney Weekly Courier*, that offered professionals, business people, and even candidates in local council elections advertising packages that included the sale of four ads with three complimentary "editorials" written by the clients themselves. In all cases, there was no disclosure by the *Courier* that those texts, presented as editorials, were a form of advertising or advertorials. In its defense when exposed by *Media Watch*, a weekly program of the Australian Broadcasting Corporation (ABC) that monitors and reports on the ethical blunders and lapses of the Australian media, the *Courier* replied that the complimentary advertising pieces were separated from other news and editorial content by their labelling as a "Special Feature."

Although smaller in scale and perhaps significance than other forms of media corruption, this type of corruption is not uncommon and typically indicative of the ill effects of the commercialization of media on the proper role of journalism: informing the public as citizens, truthfully and fairly, on matters of public interest. Simply put, advertorials and infomercials are a perversion and a corruption of that important civic role.

A more substantial and well-known example of this type of corruption is the case involving the *Los Angeles Times* and the Staples Center. Back in 1999, the journalists assigned to write a story on the new Staples Center sports arena for a special issue of the Sunday magazine, were unaware that the publisher of the *Times* had agreed to split the advertising revenue from the issue with the Staples Center. The article was published without disclosing the *Times*'s financial interest in the reported story.

Advertorials, ads for media paid- for- comment or paid embedded segments in News programs, have been presented as editorial content on programs of TV Commercial stations for some time now, with no sign that they will be regulated any time soon. At least three recent cases in 2018 and 2019 were reported on *Media Watch*, the weekly program of the Australian Broadcasting Corporation (ABC).

The first, involved a paid- for-segment on a program on heart disease on a news program of Channel 10, a commercial TV station in Australia, after the sudden death of a famous rugby player from heart failure. During the program, a garlic extract product was promoted by the panel of journalists and a single cardiologist invited on the program, as an effective antidote for heart disease. However, the information about the effectiveness of the product was not confirmed on the basis of any independent credible scientific evidence, other than evidence provided by a study conducted by the manufacturer of the advertised product that was a also the sponsor of the news program that advertised its aged garlic product on Channel 10 (Media Watch, 5 March, 2018). Although the paid- for sponsorship of the news program was disclosed by Channel 10, it is still epistemically and ethically questionable that a commercial product was presented in the context of an important topic of public interest, as a news item. Moreover, it was presented as a news item without any independent credible scientific evidence other than the evidence provided by a study sponsored by the manufacturer of the advertised product, and the personal testimony of a single cardiologist.

The second case of an advertorial reported by *Media Watch* (24 June 2019) concerned a news story on *Ikea* presented on the Australian TV Channel 9 but without disclosure that the 'news story' was in reality a paid-for-ad by *Ikea*.

And finally, a third recent case of an advertorial disguised as editorial comment, again reported by *Media Watch* (30 September 2019), concerned a news segment on the TV Channel 10. It involved a commentary in the form of editorial comment offered by their in-house car expert reporting from the Frankfurt Motor Shaw. During that segment he is shown promoting a new Volkswagen model without any disclosure that the in-house car expert of Channel 10 was also unbeknown to the audience the "PR and Brand Experience Manager" of Volkswagen.

The general problem of advertorials, as illustrated by the cases above, is that they present paid-for-ads in the context of news and editorial comment without making a clear distinction between the two. Later in this chapter, we will examine the underlying conceptual and normative incompatibility between the two.

4.4.2 Deception by Collusion: Fake News, Staged News, and Cash-for-Comment

This type of media corruption is the result of collusion, intentional at worst and negligent at best, between journalists and public relations and advertising organizations or government agencies. This is perhaps one of the most insidious and pervasive forms of media corruption. It not only corrupts the communication of information processes and products, but more nefariously, it corrupts the institutional processes of the democratic system itself. It harms every citizen both individually and collectively, as it violates their fundamental right to make informed choices on the basis of accurate information that is free of deception and manipulation.

> <u>Fake News:</u> *Over a ten-month period, the Center for Media and Democracy (CMD) documented television newsrooms' use of 36 video news releases (VNRs)—a small sample of the thousands produced each year. CMD identified 77 television stations, from those in the largest to the smallest markets, that aired these VNRs or related satellite media tours (SMTs) in 98 separate instances, without disclosure to viewers* [that the information was produced by those with private interests rather than by journalists]. *Collectively, these 77 stations reach more than half of the U.S. population. The VNRs and SMTs whose broadcast CMD documented were produced by three broadcast PR firms for 49 different clients, including General Motors, Intel, Pfizer and Capital One. In each case, these 77 television stations actively disguised the sponsored content to make it appear to be their own reporting. In almost all cases, stations failed to balance the clients' messages with independently-gathered footage or basic journalistic research. More than one-third of the time, stations aired the pre-packaged VNR in its entirety.*

The above passage, published on the website of the *Centre for Media and Democracy* and written by Diane Farsetta and Daniel Price (2006), highlights an ever-increasing trend of using media releases, including video news releases (VNRs) by public relations organizations to promote and publicize their clients' products, services, or interests in the form of pseudo-"objective and independent news stories" without no or insufficient disclosure that these are paid-for media releases. Designed to look like editorial and journalistic comment in print or broadcast media forms, these hybrids of information and persuasion, what is referred to as *media release journalism* (Simmons and Spence 2006), are designed to deceive by stealth. Starting in college, students in public relations studies are taught how to design sample media releases for clients that look, smell, and feel like the real thing: editorial journalistic columns or segments of broadcast news.

In design as well as execution, the practice of media release journalism has the hallmark of media corruption, as illustrated by the Myth of Gyges in Plato's *Republic*: they appear just, in that they are misleadingly presented as journalistic accounts; yet they are not as they are designed to advance client interests over public interest.

An example of media release journalism is the case involving a campaign to deceive the Australian public orchestrated by an Australian PR consultancy firm on behalf of a client, *Abbott Australasia*, a pharmaceutical company. The unidentified PR firm, for ease of reference let's refer to it as XYZ, targeted several regional newspapers around Australia with the strategic intention that these newspapers, given their known limited staff resources, would in all probability publish its media releases as journalistic opinion pieces. They did. This is a well-known and pervasive PR strategy that targets and uses journalists as "credible third-party endorsers" – of their client's paid for information – (Johnston and Zawawi 2004, 263). Of course the public that receives such information remains, through the absence of a qualifying statement that these are media releases, unaware that the information presented to them as journalistic comment or opinion is, quite often, a word-for-word media release, in some cases with the journalist's byline attached to it for extra credibility.

Staged News: One of the most infamous examples of this type of media corruption is a case that involved the international public relations firm Hill and Knowlton. Just before the first Gulf War of 1991, it staged a fabricated story using the daughter of Kuwait's ambassador in the United States. She posed as a nurse who claimed that she had witnessed Iraqi soldiers in a Kuwait hospital throwing babies out of their incubators, onto the floor, and leaving them to die. That story went a long way in swaying American public opinion and won Congress approval for waging war against Iraq in the first Gulf War (Stauber and Rampton 1995, Chapter 10).

A related case was the staging of the fall of Saddam Hussein's statue after the capture of the Iraqi capital by U.S. troops in 2003. According to a Marine colonel, the toppling of the statue was not the spontaneous and joyous action of Iraqi civilians, as indicated by the striking TV images that were beamed around the world. Contrary to those images, it was rather a carefully staged event by the U.S. Army's psychological operations team that selected the statue as a "target of opportunity," one that resulted in a brilliant piece of modern-day war propaganda (Zucchino 2003).

Cash-for-Comment: Journalism manifests corruption by sometimes operating under conditions of more or less perfect injustice, both at the level of individual journalists and the level of news corporations and in both print and broadcast journalism. At the individual as well as the corporate levels, journalism will, at times, publicly advocate and endorse its role of serving the public interest by informing the public truthfully and accurately, with balance and fairness—while at the same time undermine the public interest by presenting information to the public that is knowingly untrue, either because it is inaccurate or incomplete and it is biased, unfair, and motivated primarily by money and self-interest rather than morality. Similar to media releases, *cash-for-comment* is a type of media corruption that involves presenting paid advertisements as editorial comment or opinion. Not unlike advertorials which they resemble in presenting paid for information as editorial comment or news, cash-for-comment cases exemplify the double standards of corrupt journalism that engages in such practices.

Armstrong Williams, a prominent black commentator, was paid $240,000 by the Bush administration to promote the government's "No Child Left Behind" (NCLB) education law reform policy, in the hope of winning support among black families. The deal required Williams to "regularly comment on NCLB during the course of his broadcasts" and to interview Education Secretary Rod Paige for TV and radio spots that aired during the show in 2004 (Toppo 2005). The deal with Williams was only part of a $1 million package with the public relations firm Ketchum that included the use of VNRs to promote the government's NCLB nationwide. The Bush administration had also used VNRs designed to look like news reports to promote its Medicare prescription drug plan the previous year.

4.4.3 Seeing Is Not Believing – How Pictures Lie

This section will examine and evaluate the practice of photo-manipulation as a form of media corruption of the visual kind. The digitalization of photography has made the manipulation of photographic images much easier and less detectable. Pictures, for example, can be cropped to remove certain details and altered to add other details extraneous to the original photograph. This ease of undetectable alteration lends itself to the potential misuse of photographic images to deceive and misinform. Arguably, insofar as photographic images used by the media are being manipulated to deceive and misinform the public, they constitute media corruption. If a picture is worth a thousand words, it can worth its weight in gold as a means of media propaganda. One infamous example of photographic manipulation that succeeded in deceiving the public and to some extent an uncritical media, is the Australian case known as "Children Overboard". The following is a short description of the case as reported in the UK *Guardian* (Hamilton 2002):

> *On October 7 last year* [2001] *the Immigration Minister, Philip Ruddock, told the media that people on board the vessel, known as SIEV 4, had thrown their children into the sea—claims to which Mr. Howard referred repeatedly in the days following. Three days later, Mr. Reith* [minister of defense] *released photographs purporting to support the claims, but the inquiry discovered the pictures of children in the water were taken when the vessel sank on October 8.*
>
> *Senator John Faulkner, Labor, said the senate inquiry committee had exposed "an extraordinary story of deceit" and said the Government owed Australians an apology. The Committee has established on no less than 13 occasions that the Prime Minister, his department, or his office [and] that on no less than 14 occasions the Minister for Defense at the time, Mr. Peter Reith, or his office had been informed that children had not been thrown overboard from SIEV 4 or that the photographs of people in the water represented that event."*
>
> *Key findings of the report were:*
>
> ** No children were thrown overboard from SIEV 4;*
>
> ** Minister Reith made a number of misleading statements, implying that the published photographs and a video supported the original report that children had been thrown overboard well after he had received definitive advice to the contrary;*
>
> ** Despite direct media questioning on the issue, no correction or retraction was made prior to the general election on November 10, 2001.*

The general election referred to in the *Guardian* report resulted in the re-election of John Howard's government. It would be no exaggeration to say that the "children overboard" affair helped the Howard government back into office. It did so by instilling fear in the electorate of an imminent invasion by hordes of asylum seekers in boats, mostly from poor Muslim and Asian countries to the north of Australia. The electorate with the help of an insufficiently critical Australian media, had responded favourably to Howard's tough anti-immigration policies, boosted no doubt by the "children overboard" fiasco, as well as by the 9/11 events in America that had proceeded it, and voted his government back into office. All it took was a cropped picture cleverly manipulated by the government's public affairs department that falsely depicted, by implication mostly, parents throwing their children into the sea. The truth of the matter was that the children had ended up in the water together with everyone else in the boat, known as SIEV 4, after it had sunk.

This case is important in highlighting at least three crucial elements: one, the ease by which photographs can be manipulated to misinform and deceive the public; two, the need for a vigilant, critical and independent media in keeping governments in check in their role as the fourth Estate; and three, how, on the contrary, a complacent and less than critical media can be manipulated by morally unscrupulous governments and either willingly or unwittingly become complicit in a government's deception of its citizens as attested by the Children Overboard case in Australia and the Weapons of Mass Destruction (WMD)s case in the USA.

Of serious concern of not always believing what you see is what has come to be known as ***deep fakes***. Created by Artificial Intelligence (AI) programs deep fakes are false visual images that not only distort and misrepresent reality but, in some cases, change it entirely. Technology using big data and AI algorithms can create misinformation through misrepresentation and fabrication of oral and visual communication. In May 2018 a video on the internet showed Donald Trump offering advice to the people of Belgium on climate change: "As you know" he says, looking directly into the camera, "I had the balls to withdraw from the Paris climate agreement, and so should you". The video was created by a Belgian political party, Socialistiche Partij Anders, or sp.a, and posted on sp.a's Twitter and Facebook platforms. The provoked outrage and anger against Trump that followed through a deluge of comments turned out to be unwarranted and misdirected as the video was subsequently revealed to be a hi-tech forgery (Schwartz 2018). Sp.a admitted it had created the deep fake video using a machine learning computer program to raise awareness of climate change and direct people after viewing the video to an online petition calling on the Belgian government to take climate action.

According to Sp.a this was intended as a practical joke to catch people's attention, but a practical joke that had gone bad. A 'joke' that had demonstrated how deep fake videos together with fake news can manipulate public opinion in a political context that can have far wide harmful implications for democracy. As we shall see in Chap. 6 in more detail, this example of media manipulation illustrates the crucial importance of investigative journalism in uncovering and exposing media corruption.

The case of the Trump fake video is conceptually of a kind with the *Jonathan Moylan hoax*. Moylan, an Australian climate change advocate, successfully perpetrated a hoax by issuing a fake media release claiming that the ANZ Bank of Australia had withdrawn its $1.2 billion loan from Whitehaven Coal mines, plunging the share value of that public company and disrupting the financial markets in Australia. In both cases, that of Moylan and Socialistiche Partij Anders, one could reasonably claim that the intention was to draw attention to a good cause, saving the environment from mining degradation and climate change. However, the good-intended actions in both cases had the unjustified effect of creating disinformation. Insofar as these cases have the characterizing features of corruption as they seem to do, including a fiduciary duty of trust as communicators of information of the fifth Estate in their role of citizen journalists concerning a matter of public interest, that of climate change; and insofar as they meet the necessary and sufficient conditions of corruption, which those two cases also appear to do, their actions constituted media corruption; institutional in the case of Socialistiche Partij Anders as a political party, and at least personal corruption, in the case of Moylan. That cannot be good, certainly for the common good of society, as it undermines trust in the integrity of the Internet, which we all rely on for the dissemination of truthful and reliable information and its communication as required by the Dual Obligation Information Theory (DOIT). At the very least, corruption of the cybersphere is nearly as bad as corruption of the biosphere and both self-defeating as we are of necessity reliant on both for our survival.

Media corruption is ultimately bad for everyone as it leads to truth decay and reality apathy, when people stop trusting what they see and hear, and everything is regarded as deception. As Danielle Citron, a professor of law at the University of Maryland, is quoted as saying, "ultimately, deep fakes are simply amplifying what I call the liar's dividend. When nothing is true then the dishonest person will thrive by saying what's true is fake." (Schwartz 2018). As we have seen this past decade, especially since 2016, the "liar's dividend" has been weaponised and put to effective use in several political contexts, posing a real threat to democracy itself. For this reason alone, a robust, independent, and trustworthy journalism, as represented by both the fourth Estate as well as the fifth Estate, is needed now more than ever before. Just as democracy has proved an effective measure against dictatorship, investigative journalism, as we shall examine in Chap. 6, has proved, at least until now, an effective measure against corruption including media corruption.

4.4.4 Media Corruption in the New Digital Media

How does corruption manifest itself in the new digital media? Are the sources, content, and the technologies of the new digital media themselves less or more liable to corruption than those in the traditional corporate media? It could turn out that the situation is more complex still, namely, that the new digital media are less liable to certain forms of corruption and more liable to other forms of corruption. For example, web blogs can be used covertly by advertisers and public relations practitioners to generate cash-for-comment, media release journalism, and advertorials, as well as *product placements*, by misrepresenting paid-for information or advertising as independent editorial comment or opinion. Insofar as advertorials, infomercials, media release journalism, and cash-for-comment practices are types of media corruption, then similar practices that occur in the new digital media also constitute corruption and are thus ethically objectionable.

At least one example concerning a cash-for-comment case involved the digital media was that of Marqui, a company in Vancouver, that paid bloggers, who claimed to be independent, to mention the company (Businesswire 2004). A prediction in the UK *Guardian* in 2006 that the Internet would overtake national newspapers in the competition for advertising spending (Milmo 2006) proved correct. A report by the *Poynter Institute* (James Rose 2018) claimed that as at 2018 Facebook and Google dominated online advertising with 85% of total digital advertising revenue worldwide. The implication is that newspapers have less advertising revenues and therefore less resources to spend in covering the costs of quality reporting and especially of investigative journalism. It is to their credit that newspapers such as *The Guardian*, the UK *Times*, the *New York Times,* the *Financial Times,* the *Washington Post,* the *Wall Street Journal* and *The Sydney Morning Herald* and the *Age*, among many others across the world, continue to produce and deliver high quality journalistic reporting. It also implies that the use of blogs and other digital media will increasingly become an attractive and lucrative target for advertising spam and public relations spin. Although we can expect more and different types of media corruption in the ever-expanding cyberspace, the basic characterizing features of media corruption, as the ones examined in this chapter, would remain largely the same even if their contexts and modes of expression change.

A case of a blogger misleading her audience is that of the Australian blogger Belle Gibson (Davey 2015). Gibson started a digital community and sold recipe books based on her claims that she cured herself of terminal brain cancer through diet and lifestyle. Upon further media investigation she was, however, obliged to admit that she lied about having cancer and her claims that her diet cured her of cancer were in fact, untrue. We can think of this case as another example of a cash-for-comment case, as Gibson sold her diet book to her online community on false claims and misinformation.

Worth mentioning here is that given our understating of *media convergence*, which was examined in Chap. 2, the dissemination of information on the Internet, which involves no sharp distinction in principle between information communicated by journalists of the fourth Estate and that of the fifth Estate, and by everyone in fact who communicates *information* to an intended audience, such as citizen journalists, bloggers etc., the Belle Gibson's cash-for-comment case highlights the important point of how media corruption can arise also and prominently in media convergent communication practices. The Dual Obligation Information Theory (DOIT) that was examined in Chap. 2, which was conceived and designed specifically for the normative evaluation of the global dissemination of information on the Internet (Spence 2009a) demonstrates that everyone who communicates information to an intended audience in the infosphere with journalistic intent, is committed, at least personally if not institutionally, to ethical and epistemic principles, such as reliability, trustworthiness and truthfulness as well as respect for the information rights of their recipients.

Cash-for-Posts (Francis 2015) and *Cash-for-Tweets* (Barber 2012) where celebrity social media personalities or *influencers* get paid-for endorsement of products and services on social media sites such as Instagram and Tweeter without disclosure to their thousands of followers that their endorsements are paid-for by marketing and advertising promoters, is becoming common practice. Nondisclosure of paid comment is misleading and a form of deception. Clearly, then, it is ethically objectionable on the basis of DOIT. The information communicated is neither reliable nor trustworthy, since its source, namely, the paid endorser, is not unencumbered and independent but undisclosed paid-for-comment. However, even if unethical, does it constitute media corruption?

One way of thinking about this issue is that it all depends on whether the social media endorser (who is not a journalist but a social media commentator) has a *fiduciary duty of trust*, as in the case of a journalist, to inform their followers and readers with truthful, reliable, and trustworthy information or comment. Given the fluidity between journalists, bloggers, tweeters, and other social media commentators in the convergent digital media of today, perhaps one could make the case that this is a form of personal *information corruption*. Although it could be argued that it is not of the same degree as serious *institutional media corruption* that impacts on matters of public interest such as information concerning government, education, health, and matters of state.

The *Gay Girl of Damascus*, a case of media convergence that was examined in Chap. 3, is also an illustrative example of digital media corruption. For it violated the normative requirements of Dual Obligation Information Theory (DOIT), as well as displaying the characterizing features of media corruption and satisfying its necessary and sufficient conditions. And as in the Bell Gibson case, the question is raised whether the condition of a fiduciary duty of trust is present in this particular case. As in the Bell Gibson case given the fluid role of what a journalist is in the ever-expanding cyberspace of the social media and the fifth Estate it is reasonable to argue that in their role of disseminating information to the public, they are indeed bound, at least personally if not institutionally, by the normative requirements of DOIT. And insofar as they undermine those requirements through willful and intended misinformation and deception for their personal interest and gain at the moral expense of the users of that information and society generally, then their actions constitute, if not institutional corruption, at least personal media corruption.

The *deep fake* case we also examined in the previous section also illustrates how, as in the *children overboard* case, digital media with the aid of AI algorithms that for the most part remain incomprehensible, non-transparent and unaccountable, provide fertile ground for media corruption to a much greater and alarming extent, in the age of information.

4.5 The Faustus Pact[1]: Media Corruption by Collusion

This section of the chapter examines the different and potentially conflicting roles of the media as journalism, public relations, and advertising. The notions of information and persuasion that underlie these separate roles will be subjected to a

[1] This title is a metaphorical reference to the story of Dr. Faustus, an erudite scholar who made a pact with the Devil, selling his soul in exchange for unlimited knowledge and worldly pleasure. The story was immortalised in two literary works by Christopher Marlowe in the sixteenth century, and 200 years later in the eighteenth century, by the celebrated German writer, Johann Wolfgang von Goethe.

conceptual comparative analysis to determine in what ways they are compatible or incompatible. In a commercial environment that promotes and supports increasing media conversion, are the traditional distinctions between journalism, public relations, and advertising tenable? However, if they are no longer tenable, where does that leave the communication of accurate, balanced, and fair information, which was traditionally the role of the fourth estate? It will be argued that the convergence of the three primary modes of media communication, journalism, advertising and public relations, renders journalism and specifically, investigative journalism, more important and necessary in our information age than ever before, especially, in the face of increasing corruption within the media, partly through the convergence of those conflicting roles. This as we shall examine in depth in Chap. 5 is of particular concern in the case of the big Tech Media Companies such as Facebook and Google, for example, whose business models, based predominantly on advertising revenue, appears to be in direct conflict with their media role of collecting and curating users' information that then sells to advertising companies for profit; often without the users' informed consent as illustrated in the *Cambridge Analytica* case. As Rana Foroohar correctly observes in her recent book, *Don't Be Evil: The Case Against Big Tech* (2019, 55), the "deeper problem" of Big Tech such as Facebook, and Google,

> Is...their core business [that] fundamentally depends on data mining by manipulating behavior, using an odd mix of Las Vegas-style techniques and opaque and opaque algorithms to keep users hooked.

We shall examine in more detail the "deeper problem" at the heart of Facebook' and Google's business model in Chap. 5, which as demonstrated in that chapter, is conducive to media corruption. Suffice to say here that as Foroohar suggests, the 'odd mix of techniques' of mixing information with advertising is not new and has being in practice in the legacy traditional media for a long time, well before Big Tech arrived on the scene. As we shall examine later in this chapter, it involves an 'unholy alliance' between journalism, adverting, and public relations, with the sole aim of manipulating consumer behaviour for profit. What is of more concern and harmful in the case of Big Tech, is that it is done on a much larger global scale.

Moreover, insofar as the commercialized media treats information itself as just another valuable *commodity*, and the public predominantly as *consumers*, journalism whose primary role is to ensure an informed citizenry on matters of public interest, becomes crucial to the democratic process itself in an age in which information has been monetized and commercialized to an unprecedented extent, making the *Big Tech companies*, such as Facebook, Google, Amazon, Apple and Microsoft, five of the wealthiest companies in the world with a collective capital value of trillions of dollars and rising. Whereas oil once used to be the dominant currency of wealth, now, and in the foreseeable future, it is information; predominantly our information that is under constant surveillance[2] and harvested by tech

[2] See Shoshana Zuboff's informative and detailed book on surveillance for profit by the big tech companies, *The Age of Surveillance Capitalism*, 2019.

companies such as Google and Facebook for profit. As Rana Foroohar perceptively argues (2019: 11),

> Big Tech is taking on the role of Big Brother right here in the United States, working with local, state, and national authorities to create what is starting to look a lot like a surveillance nation (p. 11).

In the current political and free market environment in which information has been *monetized* and *weaponised* (two neologisms used increasingly in the media) and viewed as the primary valuable commodity, an independent, reliable, accurate, and trustworthy media in the form of journalism is much needed, as highlighted recently in the *Panama Papers* scandal that led to the exposure by the International Consortium of Investigative Journalists (ICIIJ) of widespread corruption of global dimensions. As examined in Chap. 2, the symbiotic relationship between the fourth Estate and the fifth Estate has also proved an effective measure in bringing to light various forms of institutional corruption. The continuous diachronic exposure and reporting of corruption, including media corruption by investigative journalists and whistleblowers, will be examined in more detail in Chap. 6.

To the extent that this is indeed the age of information and insofar as the media, and in particular the digital media that under the direct influence of powerful and unaccountable tech companies are increasingly turning information into just another marketable commodity, the potential consequence of turning citizens into consumers might have detrimental and harmful effects on the social and moral fabric of society.

In this section, we first examine if and how the relationship between different types of media communication modes such as journalism, advertising, and public relations is not only unethical but also conducive to media corruption. Is this a case of an unholy alliance? How can these different modes of transmitting information with different and potentially conflicting objectives and roles be so closely aligned? Where the alignment is purposeful and planned, does it constitute a collusion of unethical complicity resulting in media corruption?.

Advertorials (advertisements masquerading as editorial comment) as we saw above, may be viewed as an example of such unethical complicity that is directly conducive to media corruption. The use of advertising or of public relations media releases as a form of propaganda by governments or political contestants during election campaigns to manipulate or influence public opinion, seems equally ethically problematic and conducive to media corruption, which the Cambridge Analytica case illustrates in Chap. 5.

For if the communication of accurate, true and fair information can potentially come into conflict with the demands of successful persuasion, then the two principles operating within both advertising and public relations, those of information and persuasion, are locked in an *inherent conflict of interests*; at least a potential conflict. Moreover, the conflict of media roles between journalism on the one hand, and advertising and public relations on the other, as examined above, is conducive to media corruption. Specifically, the corruption of the dissemination of information to the public.

The section concludes by showing that journalists cannot allow themselves to treat the public as simply advertising or public relations consumers since the role of journalism and the roles of advertising and public relations are seemingly epistemically incompatible and potentially ethically incompatible and moreover, conducive to media corruption as we saw in the case of advertorials and cash-for-comment examples in this chapter. Thus, journalists cannot compromise their professional role by being in any way involved in the production or dissemination of misleading or deceptive advertorials or infomercials.

To answer the question if the close association between journalism, advertising and public relations in the process of media communication constitutes an "unholy alliance" that raises epistemic and ethical concerns, not least because in certain cases as those examined in this chapter above may constitute media corruption, we must first determine what the generic professional and institutional role of each of the three communication mediums is.

This will assist us in ascertaining the *role morality* (Spence et al. 2011) of each medium in order to determine if those roles are professionally and ethically compatible or not. For any ethical concerns that may arise from the association of these different communication mediums may be the result of the association of professionally and ethically incompatible roles. More specifically, ethical concerns may arise as a result of the ambiguity or the blurring of these roles so that consumers and citizens are either unaware or uncertain if the source of the information communicated to them is independent editorial fact, comment or opinion, or paid-for advertisements or public relations media releases, masquerading as editorial reporting.

4.6 The Primary Professional Roles of Journalism, Advertising and Public Relations

What are the primary generic roles of Journalism, Advertising and Public Relations[3]? To answer that question this section will first examine the traditional and historical perceived roles that each of those professions has and then conduct a conceptual comparative analysis to determine what the relationship between those three

[3]The primary generic roles described here are the manifest common roles that emanate from a general social conception and understanding of the respective professional or institutional practices of journalism, advertising, and public relations. Of course, it is possible that some of the specific roles and practices of journalism, advertising, and public relations deviate in various ways from the primary generic roles described here. However, insofar as the primary generic roles of these professions or institutions describe in general terms what the basic and ultimate roles of these professions or institutions are, then these general descriptions are adequate to our purpose of ascertaining the degree of compatibility between those roles.

professions is and how those professions are similar or different from each other. This would help us determine the epistemic and ethical responsibilities of each of those profession.

4.6.1 Journalism

The primary generic role of journalism is to convey information, ideas and opinions to the public that are either of interest to the public or of public interest.[4] Journalism should inform citizens and animate democracy. It should do so with honesty, fairness, independence, and respect for the rights of others. Its agents should strive for objectivity, without allowing personal or commercial interests to undermine accuracy, justice, or impartiality. Two of the primary fundamental principles of journalism are truth and the right of the public to be informed on matters of public interest.[5]

4.6.2 Advertising

The primary generic role of advertising is to present products or services in ways that enhance their marketability and renders consumers favorably pre-disposed towards those products or services for the ultimate objective of promoting their sale.

4.6.3 Public Relations (PR)

The primary generic role of public relations is to mediate or facilitate information between PR clients and the clients' targeted audiences and/or the general public through various media outlets. The ultimate objective of this role is to present the PR clients in a favorable light or at least present them in a less unfavorable light to their targeted audiences and/or the general public.

[4] "Public interest" is any interest which impacts directly or indirectly on the collective rights of freedom and wellbeing of the public which comprises of all the citizens of a state or a nation locally, and all the citizens of the world globally.

[5] The journalistic principles referred to here are those described in the current Australian journalistic code of ethics, the *Media and Entertainment Arts Alliance (MEAA) Code of Ethics*, but those principles are common to most international journalistic codes of ethics, especially those of democratic states around the world.

4.7 What Are the Minimal Primary Professional and Instrumental Requirements for Achieving Those Roles?

4.7.1 Journalism

The information conveyed to the public must be independent, balanced, fair, unbiased, accurate, true, or at least truthful (intended to be true) and as far as possible, objective. Opinions must be clearly and unambiguously demarcated from facts and other advertising and public relations material.

4.7.2 Advertising

The advertisements promoting the products or services to the consumers must be effectively persuasive and marketable to render the products and services advertised attractive to consumers.

4.7.3 Public Relations

The PR campaigns and strategies addressed to the public on behalf of clients must be persuasive and influential in creating a positive impression of the clients or at least minimizing any negative impressions about the clients in the minds of the targeted audiences and/or the public.

4.8 Are Those Roles and Their Realization Compatible with Each Other?

4.8.1 Journalism and Advertising

By the avowed principles of journalism as supported by its code of ethics, *journalistic information* must meet the standards of balance, fairness, honesty, independence, truth, accuracy, objectivity, disclosure of all essential facts, avoidance of distorting emphasis, and avoidance of unnecessary emphasis on personal characteristics (race, gender, ethnicity, etc.,). Personal interest or advertising and commercial considerations must not undermine accuracy, fairness, or independence. Pictures and sounds presented in publications must be true and accurate.[6]

To the extent that most if not all of the above journalistic standards and principles are *not* applicable because not relevant to advertising, then the roles of journalism and advertising are significantly different and potentially incompatible. As argued by Edward Spence and Brett van Heekeren (2005, Chapters 6 and 8) truth, independence, objectivity, the absence of distorting emphasis are often not relevant to advertising, which often relies on metaphor, fiction, and fantasy, rather than facts in its communication strategies. If the primary objective of advertising is effective *persuasion* and that of journalism, accurate *information*, which must be true or at least truthful, we can see how those two primary objectives can potentially come into opposition and result in a conflict of interests or conflict of roles.[7] For insofar as the primary ultimate objective of advertising is the successful promotion or placement of consumer products or services for persuading consumers to purchase them, effective persuasion need not have any of the traditional epistemological characteristics of journalistic information.

Persuasion strategies, as the dominant communication strategies used in advertising, can succeed just as effectively and sometimes even more so in persuading consumers to feel pre-disposed towards the products or services advertised. A mere appeal to consumers' desires, fears, aspirations, fantasies, and other emotions renders an appeal to factual, truthful, unbiased and objective information persuasively irrelevant or redundant.

4.8.2 Journalism, Public Relations and Advertising

The primary role of public relations is to manage the communication of information on behalf of its clients for the ultimate objective of influencing public opinion in favor of its clients' reputation. Like advertising, its primary operative principle is persuasion. Information is mainly used as a tool or strategy of persuasion. Like advertising, public relations seeks to primarily render its targeted audiences favorably pre-disposed or at least less unfavorably disposed towards its clients' products or services. Similarly, as with advertising, public relations operates with two potentially incompatible and conflicting principles, namely, the principle of information and the principle of persuasion. Unlike journalism, which, in principle, is committed to inform the public truthfully and objectively on matters of public interest, independently of any other commercial interests, public relations, as advocate for its clients, is primarily committed to inform the public only on matters pertinent to its

[6]As per the current Australian Journalism Code of Ethics, the *Media and Entertainment Arts Alliance (MEAA) Code of Ethics,* and most other International Journalism Code of Ethics.

[7]For conflict of interest and conflict of roles conducive to media corruption see Spence (2003) *Conflict of Interest and Corruption*. Melbourne: Australian Journal of Professional and Applied Ethics Vol. 5, No. 2, pp. 25–36.

clients' interests. Moreover, it does so in a manner that is partial and favorable to its clients, even if it means "spinning" the truth a little to adjust reality to fit the favorable image or reputation they are required to convey to the public on their clients' behalf.

Journalism is committed by its professional role to disseminate information to members of the public, qua citizens, that is concomitant of the *public's interest*. Advertising and public relations by contrast are only committed by their role as commercial advocates of their clients to convey information to members of the public, qua consumers, that is concomitant to their *clients' interest*. Such information is only at best derivatively of interest to the public. For the primary interest that advertising and public relations clients have is creating a good impression of themselves and their products and services in the minds of their consumers. This is so whether the consumption relates to products or information.

The following analysis of advertorials is a key example of how the two potentially conflicting principles of persuasion and information, present in both advertising and public relations, can result in a conflict of interest or roles. This is potentially detrimental to the public in their dual capacity as both consumers and citizens. Advertorials are an illustration of an epistemological and ethical inherent incompatibility between journalism on the one hand, and advertising or public relations on the other. They constitute, in effect, a complicity of deception generated by the covert and undisclosed mixing of journalistic informational practices with those of advertising or public relations persuasion practices. The following analysis will focus primarily on how advertorials raise potential and actual ethical problems for both journalism and advertising, which as we saw in earlier can result in media corruption.

4.9 The Systemic Problem of Advertorials

The *inherent problem* with advertorials is the combining of two modes of communication that are epistemically incompatible, that of journalism as communication of information for citizens, for the public interest and that of advertising as persuasion of consumers, for the primary interest of clients.

The *ethical problem* with advertorials is that they are designed to deceive. They rely on the epistemic credence of journalistic information to render the advertising more credible and reliable in the eyes and ears of the consumers.

Part of that deception has to do with the *approach problem* which involves advertorials seeking to communicatively approach consumers qua consumers not as consumers but as citizens who are purportedly being informed on some matter of public interest, as in some of the cases we examined earlier in this chapter. This problem also highlights the inherent epistemological and ethical incompatibility of journalism and advertising as media of communication, for journalism approaches its audience as *citizens* whereas advertising approaches its audience primarily as *consumers*. Even if we accept that in the age of information, information has become just another commodity, the difference between journalism and advertising remains. For even if information is perceived as just another commodity, journalism communicates that information *as information,* an *end* in itself, whereas advertising communicates information merely as a *means* of promoting the consumption of a product or service; which, can also take the form of a political cause or campaign in the form of propaganda when the aim is to persuade rather than inform.

4.9.1 Advertising Laws: Cash-for-Comment

John Laws, a well-known commercial radio celebrity in Australia, abused his editorial power for the purpose of influencing the opinion of his two million strong audience favorably towards a group of banks for a sum of $1.2 m. The financial transaction of the $1.2 m between Laws and the banks was carried out in secret and concealed from the public, including his audience. John Laws' favorable comments on the banks following the $1.2 m deal can be seen as a typical instance of an advertorial. The public would have been led to think John Laws was expressing a genuinely unbiased and informed honest view about the banks when in fact and unbeknown to his listeners he was advertising the banks' 'merits' for a price, offering editorial comment for cash.

In that "cash-for-comment" case, we observe an important distinction between the dictates of advertising versus journalism: those of *external* versus *internal instrumentalism.* In an *external instrumentalism,* "the means or instrument is external to the end, in that it need not have any of the distinctive characteristics of the end. In *internal instrumentalism*", by contrast, the means or instrument is internal to the end: it is instrumental to the end not merely as causal means but also intrinsically in that its features are also constitutive of the end. It serves as an instrument to the end by bringing about a certain result, while at the same time it has the distinctive characteristics of the result (Alan Gewirth 1986, p. 295). To illustrate the difference between internal and external instrumentalism, Gewirth gives the example of a "lecture on some scientific or philosophical topic":

> If the lecture is delivered simply or mainly in order to earn money, then the lecture, as means or instrument, is external to the end: spreading enlightenment or under- standing on scientific or philosophical topics is conceptually distinct from earning money, since each can be done without the other. If, on the other hand, the lecture is delivered for the purpose of improving its hearers' understanding of the topics with which it deals, then the lecture, as means or instrument, is internal to the end: the very process of presenting the relevant intellectual considerations exhibits and conforms to the same intellectual criteria as constitute the end of improving the understanding of the subject matter (Gewirth 1986, 295–296).

In the case of advertorials what we have is a conflict between internal instrumentalism and external instrumentalism. In the case of journalism, its means or instrument of communicating information to the public truthfully and fairly is *internal* to its end of informing the public on matters of public interest. By contrast, in the case of advertising, whose main purpose is the successful persuasion of consumers to purchase a range of products or services, the means or instrument of communicating information to the public on those products and services is *external* to its end of providing information to the public.

In the case of journalism, both the means and the end of communicating information conform to the same conceptual and professional criteria of providing true and fair information to the public. By contrast, in the case of advertising the strategies of persuasion as a means of informing the public on consumer products or services so they would buy them is external to the provision of information, and even sometimes irrelevant. For the end of communicating information so as to provide knowledge to consumers about products or services is conceptually distinct from the means of informing them for the mere purpose of persuading them to buy products or services. Moreover, unlike information that of necessity must be true or truthful, persuasion need not be.[8]

As we shall see in Chap. 5, the political campaigns launched in the U.S. Presidential elections and the UK Brexit Referendum in 2016, with the aid of Cambridge Analytical and Facebook, misinformation through half-truths, lies and deception can be just as effectively persuasive as the truth, and sometimes in advertising and PR relations campaigns, even more so. The problem of fake news and deep fakes in the form of fake videos, is their ability to persuade through misinformation and deception. In the political context that can be detrimental to the democratic system itself.

The above discussion of advertorials should alert us to how conflict of roles and principles across different professions or institutions, whose professional and institutional instrumentalism can be at odds with each other, can result, as in the John Laws "cash-for-comment" case study, in unethical practices and moreover, in media corruption. Such practices can prove detrimental to the public good. It is because of the importance that professional and institutional roles have in the determination of role morality, that those roles should be clearly defined, demarcated and understood by all stakeholders. For quite often unethical practices are the result of an ambiguity or opaqueness or in the most extreme cases, ignorance, of what is one's professional institutional, or other socially determined role. Moreover, unethical practices can and do arise because of an ambiguity or ignorance of how one's professional role inter-relates and sometimes comes into conflict with other professional roles in the media, which typically operates across increasingly convergent roles in the marketplace of information. When confronted with the "cash-for-comment" charge, John Laws' defensive response was to claim that he was 'an entertainer not a journalist and so journalistic standards didn't have an ethical hook on him'.

It was correctly pointed out to Laws, however, that the crucial factor was not what *he* thought his role was when offering favorable comments about the banks but what his *audience* perceived his role to be. Most if not all the listeners of Laws' radio program would have been led to believe that Laws was expressing his own

[8] For the relevance of truth and knowledge to advertising, see Spence and Van Heekeren 2005, Chapter 6.

informed and honest opinions about the banks and not running a paid advertisement for the banks. So naturally they would have thought Laws' role to be that of someone who offers, like a journalist, objective comment, or opinion on some important issue with journalistic intent. He was therefore ethically committed to that perceived role. This was a perception he encouraged by concealing the payment of $1.2 m he had received from the banks for advertising their cause.

Another example of role ambiguity is the ambiguity relating to the role of public relations practitioners; a role as mediators or facilitators of paid-for communication that can potentially result in unethical practices. Functioning as advertorials or infomercials, public relations *media releases*[9] produced and disseminated on behalf of paying clients, appear as editorial pieces in newspapers or other media publications, sometimes with a journalist's byline at the end of entirely unaltered press releases. Like advertorials, these media releases amount to deception. And as in advertising, so too in public relations, the purpose of communicating information through persuasion strategies on behalf of paying clients is not always congruent with the true role of communicating information, which in accordance of the requirements of the Dual Obligation Information Theory (DOIT) we examined in Chap. 2, the communication of information must be truthful and trustworthy since information of necessity must be true and accurate whether it is persuasive or not.

To see more clearly how the *role moralities* of the different media fit in with the *internal and external instrumentalism* that applies to them, consider the following argument: We have seen that the primary role of information is to provide the public, either as citizens or consumers, with knowledge about something, for example, news, products and services. In the case of journalism whose primary role is to inform the public on matters of public interest, the *instrumental role* of information of providing knowledge and the role morality of journalism of providing information to the public are on the same page. Both roles are instrumentally internal since they are means to the same end – the end of providing factual information or knowledge. Moreover, those instrumental means are internal to that end and have the same characteristics as that end since the means (information) and the end (knowledge) are of the same kind. Both must be true or truthful. By contrast, in the case of advertising and public relations, the instrumental role of information for providing knowledge and the role moralities of advertising and public relations are not on the same page, or at least need not be on the same page as in the case of journalism. This is because the primary but not exclusive role of advertising and public relations is to persuade rather than to inform. Information is merely an instrumentally external means to their ultimate end of persuasion. Moreover, the *means* of informing does not have the same characteristics as the *end* of persuasion. Information of necessity must be true whereas persuasion need not be. Propaganda can be persuasive without being true. Often it is not.

[9] For a detailed analysis and evaluation of the ethics of *media release journalism* see Simmons, P. and Spence, E. (2006).

In sum, as means of informing, editorial comment is congruent to its end of providing information to the public. By contrast, public relations media releases that seek to emulate editorial comment through the disguise of infomercials are merely externally instrumental to the end of providing information and often antithetical to the essence of information understood as a type of knowledge; which of necessity has to be true or truthful. Notice that if the role of information in the process of communication is to impart knowledge both the means and the end of that role must be the same. The means must track the end and the end must be responsive to the means. This at least is what is meant to happen when journalism operates as it ought to: conveying information to the public on matters of public interest and matters that are of interest to the public. By contrast the role of advertising and public relations as a form of advocacy on behalf of paying clients is to convey information for the goal of persuasion. Those are their respective role moralities of advertising and public relations as industries of persuasion. The information conveyed by them can of course be true but need not be and as we saw from the *John Laws* case and messages of persuasion masquerading as 'information' are often conveyed to consumers in misleading and deceptive ways, by commission as well as by omission. For if the primary role of those industries is to persuade rather than to inform, then the means of persuading need not be congruent with the misleadingly presumed and avowed end of providing 'information' on products, services or clients for the benefit of the public.

Both advertorials and infomercials, in the form of advertising or media releases presented by journalists as "news" without any acknowledgement that these are advertising or media releases, involve two opposing principles. In their intent to appear as editorial comment, they embody the *principle of information*, which requires information to be true, truthful, and justified through independent corroboration and verification. On the other hand, as a form of paid-for advertisements or public relations media releases, they embody the *principle of persuasion*. This principle does not necessarily require the information communicated to be true, truthful, or even justified. Of course, information that is true and justified can and often is persuasive. However, persuasion need not necessarily be achieved through information that meets the condition of truth since misinformation, half-truths, and lies can just as easily be persuasive if presented in the right format. Successful propaganda is a case in point. Another way of making the same point is as follows: If the primary purpose of communication is to persuade, then the "information" communicated need not be true. It can of course be true, but it need not be. By contrast, if the primary purpose of communication is to inform by imparting knowledge then the information communicated must of necessity be true or at least intended to be true. So, whereas truth and truthfulness are *intrinsic and necessary* to the communication of information it is only *extrinsic and contingent* to communication by way of persuasion. In the case of communicating information for imparting knowledge, truth is *internal* to the process of communication whereas truth is at best *external* in the case of communicating information for the purpose of persuasion. Clearly then the notion of *internal instrumentalism* applies to and fits in with communication by way of information whereas by contrast, external instrumentalism applies to and fits in with communication by way of persuasion.

Interestingly, the ambiguity of the professional role of public relations makes it difficult to determine what the public relations industry's fiduciary duties of trust are and to whom they are owed. For example, does the public relations industry as communicators of information have a fiduciary duty of trust to the public for ensuring that the information mediated by them to the public through the media is accurate, true and fair? If the answer to that question is yes, then the public relations industry faces a conflict of interests or roles that is inherent to its own practice. For if the communication of accurate, true and fair information can potentially come into conflict with the demands of successful persuasion, then the two principles operating within public relations, those of information and persuasion, are locked in an *inherent conflict of interests*; at least a potential conflict. To the extent that this is the case, then the practice of public relations is by virtue of the nature of this inherent conflict prone to unethical conduct in violation of the normative requirements of the Dual Obligation Information Theory (DOIT) and moreover, that inherent conflict also renders PR practices of misinformation and manipulation, as illustrated in the aforementioned case study of the "Media Drug Dupes" involving the XYZ PR firm, conducive to media corruption. In Chap. 5 we shall examine how in the case of Facebook the inherent conflict of interest between their role as a media company and their business model, makes that conflict conducive to media corruption, as illustrated by Facebook's part in the Cambridge Analytica controversy.

4.10 Citizens and Consumers

Citizens require information to enable them to make informed decisions about important issues of public interest, which effect or could potentially affect their rights to freedom and wellbeing. To that end, citizens, collectively the public, have a right to such information and that right is rationally supported and justified by the Dual Obligation Information Theory, as we saw in Chap. 2. That information must be true, balanced, fair, accurate, and objective. To that end, the source of that information must be independent, credible and reliable. In their role as providers of information to the public on matters of public interest, journalists are thus committed to those epistemic values. Their journalistic or press freedom to inform the public on matters of public interest and also less significantly on matters that are of interest to the public, is conditional on the journalists' professional and ethical obligation to inform the public according to those epistemic and ethical values and standards. By contrast, as consumers, people are provided with information that is primarily designed to persuade them to consume products (advertising), services or comments or other packaged information favorable to particular individuals, corporations, or institutions (public relations).

In their avowed role as providers of information to the public on matters of public interest, journalists cannot allow themselves to treat the public as advertising or public relations consumers since the roles of journalism on the one hand and the roles of advertising and public relations on the other are inherently epistemically and ethically incompatible. Thus, journalists cannot compromise their professional role by being in any way involved in the production or dissemination of advertorials or infomercials.

Advertorials that seek to influence public policy or exert influence on matters of public interest undermine the independent and fair flow of information that in turn undermines the democratic process that relies for its effectiveness on an informed citizenry. To the extent that they interfere with the free and independent flow of information on matters of public interest as examined earlier, they are a form of media corruption.

The fundamental difference between journalism on the one hand, and advertising and public relations on the other, is that the former, according to its own avowed role, seeks to approach the public primarily as citizens whereas the latter, seek to approach the public primarily as consumers of products, services and even information. Advertising and public relations' respective presentations of "information" often fail the conditions of knowledge that characterize or should characterize information due to the absence of truth and epistemological independence and objectivity. By contrast, to the extent that journalistic information meets the requirements of truth or at least truthfulness and epistemic independence, reliability, and objectivity, it can qualify as a type of knowledge.

4.11 Conclusion

This chapter has identified and examined the presence of corruption as it is manifested, specifically in the media. As in the case of the general account of corruption that was examined in Chap. 3, this chapter examined media corruption by reference to Plato's Myth of Gyges (*The Republic*, Plato 1952) as this has contemporary significance and relevance in explaining corruption generally and specifically as it applies to the media. To that end, the chapter applied a *model of media corruption* that shares the same characterizing features of the general account of corruption that was examined in Chap. 4 but that was designed specifically and developed for application to the phenomenon and practice of corruption in the media (Spence, E. 2008, 2017). Finally, the chapter provided a taxonomy of media corruption by identifying and categorizing the different types of media corruption, the ways in which these are caused, and the contexts in which they are manifested in current physical and virtual media environments and practices.

The chapter then explored the question how corruption in the media manifests itself in the new digital media of today. Are the sources, content, and the technologies of the new digital media themselves less or more liable to corruption than those in the traditional corporate media? Is the new digital media less liable to certain forms of corruption and more liable to other forms of corruption?

In answering those questions, the chapter examined how web blogs, cash-for-posts (Francis 2015) and cash-for-tweets (Barber 2012) used by celebrity social media personalities or *influencers* get paid-for endorsement of products and services on social media sites such as Instagram and Tweeter without disclosure to their thousands of followers that their endorsements are paid-for by marketing and advertising promoters, may constitute media corruption. As examined in this chapter, nondisclosure of paid-for comment is misleading and a form of deception. Arguably then, it is ethically wrong and objectionable on the basis of DOIT. However, even if unethical, do such practices constitute media corruption?

The issue depends on whether the social media endorser (who is not a journalist but a social media commentator) has a *fiduciary duty of trust*, as in the case of a journalist, to inform their followers and readers with truthful, reliable, and trustworthy information or comment. Given the fluidity between journalists, bloggers, tweeters, and other social media commentators in the convergent digital media of today, one could argue reasonably that this is a form of personal *information corruption,* even though it is not of the same degree as serious *institutional media corruption* that impacts more widely on matters of public interest such as information concerning government, education, health, and matters of state.

Finally, the chapter investigated how the conflict of roles between journalism, adverting and public relations that lead in some cases, as those examined in this chapter, to media corruption. They do so by collusion through deceptive and misleading practices in the form of advertorials or infomercials, including advertising strategies that disseminate inaccurate information in the form of propaganda or misleading public relations practices in the form of media release journalism, which, based on the Dual Obligation Information Theory, are epistemically and ethically wrong and violate the internal codes of ethics of those professions that proscribe such practices of misinformation.

References

Barber, Dylan. 2012. Tweet for your supper: The new wave of cash-for-comment. *Crikey.Inq (Independent Inquiry Journalism)*, April 24, 2015. https://www.crikey.com.au/2012/04/24/tweet-for-your-supper-the-new-wave-of-cash-for-comment/. Accessed 26 Mar 2020.

Businesswire. 2004. Marqui Pays Bloggers In Revolutionary Marketing Move; Generates 244,000 Google Hits in One Week, December 02, 2004. https://www.businesswire.com/news/home/20041202005541/en/Marqui-Pays-Bloggers-Revolutionary-Marketing-Move-Generates. Accessed 26 Mar 2020.

Daily Express. 2004. Al Qaeda scouts found ½ mile from PM's home, August 16, 2004.

Daily Telegraph. 2004. Plot to kill Blair foiled—Al Qaeda linked to assassination plan, August 17, 2004.

Davey, Melissa. 2015. 'None of it's true': Wellness blogger Belle Gibson admits she never had cancer. *The Guardian*, April 22, 2015.

Elliott, Deni, and Edward Spence. 2018. *Ethics for a digital era.* Oxford: Wiley-Blackwell.

Farsetta, Diane, and Daniel Price. 2006. *Fake TV news: Widespread and undisclosed.* Centre for Media and Democracy. http://www.prwatch.org/fakenews/execsummary. 6, April.

Foroohar, Rana. 2019. *Don't Be Evil: The Case Against Big Tech*. London: Allen Lane, Random House.

Francis, Hannah. 2015. Cash-for-posts: The murky ethics of social media stardom. *The Sydney Morning Herald*, November 7, 2015. https://www.smh.com.au/technology/cash-for-posts-the-murky-ethics-of-social-media-stardom-20151105-gkrs29.html. Accessed 26 Mar 2020.

———. 1986. Professional Ethics: The Separatist Thesis. *Ethics* 96: 282–300.

Greenwald, Robert. 2004. *Outfoxed: Rupert Murdoch's War on Journalism*, documentary film. https://en.wikipedia.org/wiki/Outfoxed. Accessed 25 Mar 2020.

Hamilton, Janice. 2002. Inquiry highlights cover-up by the major parties. *The Guardian*, November 6, 2002.

Johnston, Jane and Zawawi, Clara (eds) 2004. Media Relations. In *Public Relations Theory and Practice*, 2nd. Sydney: Allen and Unwin.

Miller, S, (2018). Corruption. Stanford Encyclopedia of Philosophy. (Winter 2018 Edition), Edward N. Zalta (ed.).

Milmo, Dan. 2006. Net advertising 'to overtake national newspapers'. *The Guardian*, May 31, 2006.

Oltermann, Philip. 2019. The inside story of Germany's biggest scandal since the Hitler diaries. *The Guardian*, December 9, 2019.

Plato. 1952. *The Dialogues of Plato*. Translated by Benjamin Jowett, 359–361. Chicago: Encyclopedia Britannica Inc., Book II.

Rose, James. 2018. Facebook and Google dominate online ads. Can alliances between news publishers compete? May 24, 2018. https://www.poynter.org/business-work/2018/facebook-and-google-dominate-online-ads-can-alliances-between-news-publishers-compete/. Accessed 26 Mar 2020.

Schwartz, Oscar. 2018. You thought fake news was bad? Deep fakes are where truth goes to die. The *Guardian*, November 12, 2018.

Simmons, Peter, and Edward Spence. 2006. The practice and ethics of media release journalism. *Australian Journalism Review* 28 (1): 167–181.

Spence, Edward. 2003. Conflict of Interest and Corruption. *Melbourne: Australian Journal of Professional and Applied Ethics* 5 (2): 25–36.

———. 2008. Corruption in the Media. *International Journal of Applied Philosophy* 22:2 – Fall 2008: 231–241.

———. 2009a. A Universal Model for the Normative Evaluation of Internet Information. *Ethics and Information Technology* 11 (4): 243–253.

———. 2017. Corruption in the Media. In *The Handbook of Business and Corruption: Cross-Sectoral Experiences*, ed. Michael S. Aßländer and Sarah Hudson, 453–480. Bingley: Emerald Group Publishing.

Spence, Edward, and Brett Van Heekeren. 2005. *Advertising Ethics*. Upper Saddle River: Pearson/Prentice Hall.

Spence, Edward, Andrew Alexandra, Aaron Quinn, and Anne Dunn. 2011. *Media, Markets and Morals*. Oxford: Wiley-Blackwell.

Stauber, John, and Sheldon Rampton. 1995. *Toxic Sludge Is Good For You: Lies, Damn Lies and the Public Relations Industry*. Monroe: Common Courage Press.

Toppo, Greg. 2005. Education Dept. paid commentator to promote law. *USA Today*, July 1.

Zuboff, Shoshana. 2019. *The Age of Surveillance Capitalism*. London: Profile Books Ltd.

Zucchino, David. 2003. Army Stage-Managed Fall of Hussein Statue. *Los Angeles Times*, July 3.

Chapter 5
Tech Media Corruption in the Age of Information

The fault dear Brutus is not in our stars but in ourselves
(Shakespeare, Julius Caesar, Act I, Scene III, L. 140–141).

5.1 Introduction

This chapter will examine some of the invasive practices of the Big Technology Companies (Big Tech companies) such as Facebook and analogously Google, to determine if such practices are not only illegal and unethical but moreover constitute corruption, as defined in Chap. 3 generally, and in Chap. 4 as it applies specifically to the media (Spence 2020).[1] Recent publications by scholars such as Shoshana Zuboff (2019), Rana Foroohar (2019) and Frank Pasquale (2015) among others, as well as several articles by investigative journalists of legacy newspapers such as the *New York Times*, the *UK Times*, *The Guardian*, the *Washington Post*, *The Wall Street Journal*, the *Financial Times*, the *Sydney Morning Herald*, *The Age* and the *Australian*, as well as the *Conversation* provide persuasive evidence that such practices are at least illegal and unethical. Do such practices, however, also constitute corruption and specifically, media corruption?

Digital Media and by extension social media, mediated via Facebook and other tech companies such as Google challenge the traditional role and legitimacy of the traditional legacy media in the form of the fourth Estate, and by extension the digital media in the form of the fifth Estate, which includes user-generated information via the social media (Elliott and Spence 2018, Chap. 6). As we examined in Chap. 2, the fourth Estate together with the fifth Estate constitute the *Convergent Media* as the

[1] This is an extended and revised chapter, based on an earlier abridged version of a published paper by Spence (2020) The sixth estate: media corruption in the age of information. *Journal of Information, Communication and Ethics in Society*, Emerald Publishing Limited, 1477996X.

E. H. Spence, *Media Corruption in the Age of Information*, Library of Public Policy and Public Administration 15, https://doi.org/10.1007/978-3-030-61612-0_5

primary sources of information communicated to the public.[2] Digital media now available through the internet, Twitter, smart phones, and social networks, such as Facebook and YouTube, are having a profound impact on the social life and democratic processes and practices of societies. As we saw in Chap. 2, and throughout this book, the fifth Estate is defined generally as the estate comprising all the world-denizens operating in cyberspace that, as individuals or groups, disseminate information on matters of public interest to the world at large and some who are doing so with journalistic intent in their capacity as citizens–journalists of the fifth Estate. As previously examined in Chap. 3, the *Convergent Media* referred to in this chapter comprises the symbiotic relationship that has developed between the journalists of the legacy media (the fourth estate) and the digital media including the social media (the fifth estate). Many journalists now operate in both those estates. When the symbiotic relationship between the two media estates operates appropriately and in accordance with the normative requirements of the *Dual Obligation Information Theory (DOIT)* it augments the quality and quantity of information disseminated to the public and enhances the substance and scope of deliberative democracy (Elliott and Spence 2018, Chapter 6).

As we saw throughout this book, truth, trust, and the public's right to information are fundamental principles of the Media professions and particularly journalism in their role as the fourth estate and by extension the fifth estate. Those principles are mandatory and required by (DOIT) which was specifically designed to identify, analyse and evaluate normative issues that arise in the media generally on the basis of what information is intrinsically and the normative implications of its different modes of communication in both the fourth and fifth Estates (Spence 2009, 2011). This chapter comprises three main primary objectives:

Choosing *Facebook* as the specific example of what is referred to in this chapter as the *sixth Estate* in order to distinguish it conceptually from the fourth and fifth Estates, the primary objective of the first part of the chapter is to examine if digital information created, disseminated, and mediated increasingly via Facebook is also subject to those same normative principles as the fourth and fifth Estates. If it is,

[2]Traditionally the Four Estates were understood to include, the government, the clergy, the public and the press in the form of the legacy media whose role was to hold the other three estates to account for the public good. In the advent of the Internet and the World Wide Web where anyone with access to the Internet can disseminate and communicate information to the public, nationally and internationally, the fifth Estate is a more recent addition that includes the social media, mediated digitally via Tweeter, Facebook, Google, and other information technologies. The relevance and significance of the fourth and fifth Estates especially through their symbiotic convergence i.e., the *Convergent Media*, is that they act as a monitoring and accountability measure to hold the other two governing estates, that of government and clergy to account. For example, it has been the Convergent Media, including WikiLeaks, that has exposed the misdemeanors and corruption of governments and clergy (police corruption and corruption of the clergy in the form of sexual abuse are two out of many examples).

should we not be consistent and extend the role of the media, as creators, curators, mediators, and communicators of information to include Facebook?[3]

Having established in the first part of the chapter that Facebook is in essence a *media company*, the second part of the chapter will demonstrate, on the basis of the Dual Obligation Information Theory, that Facebook is also subject to the same normative principles and requirements that other media companies of the fourth and fifth Estates, are. This will be illustrated through an examination of Facebook's media role in the Cambridge Analytica case.

The third part of the chapter will examine if Facebook's role in the Cambridge Analytica case not only violated the fundamental normative principles and requirements to which all media companies are subject, but moreover, its actions constituted media corruption. More generally, Facebook's media corruption as illustrated in the Cambridge Analytica case, relates to a conflict of interest emanating from its business model that in its design and practice is conducive to systemic media corruption.

Finally, the chapter will analyse the *corrupting effects* of Facebook's actions in the Cambridge Analytica case on digital information and its communication, which undermine democracy and its underlying political institutions as well as the rights of citizens.

In summary, the overall objective of the argument in this chapter is to demonstrate how some of the information and communication practices of the Tech Media and specifically of Facebook, constitute media corruption (Spence 2008, 2017). To that end, the chapter will first examine what the professional and business role of Facebook is regarding its information/communication practices; It will then demonstrate that its role shows that Facebook is essentially a *media company* and not merely a "platform" and therefore liable to the same normative responsibilities of other media companies on the basis of the Dual Obligation Information Theory (DOIT). DOIT applies generally to all media companies and by parity of argument to all communicative agents that disseminate and share information on the digital media. This is particularly relevant to Facebook in its role of mediating and curating the information of its users, which places upon it a *normative editing responsibility*, qua media company, to ensure both the preventive detection and corrective editing of fake news, as well as other forms of misinformation and disinformation disseminated on its platform.

Finally, applying the philosophical model of media corruption we examined in Chap. 4 the chapter will examine and demonstrate that Facebook's role in the

[3] Insofar as Google, like Facebook, operates functionally as a media company in its information practices through its *search* function and its other communication and curation practices that involve the collection, profiling and harvesting of users information, which like Facebook, sells to advertisers for profit, then Google should also be viewed as being essentially a media company. According to Rana Foroohar (2019: 107) Google's prospectus, when it went public in 2004, shows that "Google wasn't just a tech company. Page 80 of the prospectus laid it out: "We began as a technology company and have evolved into a software, technology, Internet, advertising, and media company, all rolled into one."

Cambridge Analytica case was not only unethical in violation of fundamental media principles such as truthfulness, and trustworthiness, as demonstrated on the basis of the Dual Obligation Information Theory, but moreover, constituted media corruption. The chapter will conclude that argument by claiming that Facebook's media corruption as illustrated in the Cambridge Analytical case is not a one-off case. Rather, it is the result of a systemic and inherent conflict of interest between its business model of selling users' information to advertisers and other information operators for profit, and its role as a Media Company, which renders the conflict of interest between those two roles, conducive to media corruption. Analogously, insofar as Google is also a media company, the chapter will suggest that Google is also subject to the normative epistemic and ethical principles of DOIT, and insofar as its business model, as in the case of Facebook, is in an inherent conflict of interest with its media role, and therefore, it can be argued that Google's practices of harvesting and selling users' information for profit, without its users' explicit informed consent, those practices, as in the case of Facebook, are also conductive to systemic media corruption.

5.2 What Is Facebooks Professional and Institutional Role?

Before we proceed to enquire if and how Facebook is also committed to the same fundamental normative principles of truth and trust, we must first establish what the professional role of Facebook, in its capacity as an Information Technology Company, is. Is the professional role of Facebook that of a Mediator of its user's information? Custodian of its users' information? Curator of its users' information? Trustee of its users' information? Trader of its users' information? Is Facebook essentially, all things considred, a Media information/communication company, or something else entirely, and if so, what is its overarching professional and institutional role? After all, a lot of information and commuinication of information is channeled through Facebook by its billions of information users daily. Prima facie at least, it seems that Facebook is by its function and design if not by name, operating as a media company. If so, Facebook is normatively responsible for the information and communication it handles and should be held both epistemically and ethically responsible and accountable as other media companies are. Why is it not?

Facebook is shy about letting the rest of us know exactly how they themselves perceive its respective professional and institutional role, content to inform us that they are merely a "platform". Which is convenient as the term 'platform' seems topic-neutral and free of any normative commitments with regard to the dissemination and communication of information via Facebook.[4] Which, would appear to suit

[4]Referring to Big Tech generally, which includes Facebook and Google, among others, Rana Foroohar (2019: 50) astutely observes that, "it's a schizophrenia that reflects ambivalence, both, on the part of the companies and society itself, about what they are. Media players? News organisations? Platform technology firms? Retailers? Logisticians?"

Facebook as it alleviates the company of any normative commitments as those that apply to the Convergent Media of the fourth and fifth Estates and generally to anyone that disseminates and communicates information to others on the World Wide Web, on the basis of the Dual Obligation Information Theory (DOIT).

As we examined earlier in Chap. 2, DOIT locates the normativity of the communication of information within the inherent normative strucurte of information that comprise epistemic, ethical and eudaimonic features (Spence 2009, 2011). Those normative features of information commit all communicators of information generally, and especially media complanies, including Facebook qua media company, to principles of truthfulness, accuracy, reliability, trustworthiness and the public good. Furethtmore, as illustrated in Sect. (5.7) through discussion of the Cambrige Analytica case, the violation of those fundamental media principles by Facebook may also constitute media corruption. As we shall see, that systematically occurs when its Bussiness Model of generating advertising revenue on the basis of users' content, comes into direct conflict with its media role, which results in the violation of its normative commitments and responsibilities, as required by DOIT.

On closer examination, and regardless of its self-describing professional role as a "platform" Facebook appears to be a Media Company that handles, curates, mediates, and communicates information generated by its users for profit via advertising and marketing and as such should be viewed in essence as a Media Company. As a media company Facebook is then normatively responsible and accountable to its users and the public generally, as other media companies are, including Radio, Television, Cinema, Video, Newspapers, Magazines, Books and all other types of media broadcasts and publications that generate, disseminate, exchange, mediate and communicate by analog and digital channels information in the public domain. Even if we accept the claim that Facebook is merely operating as a "platform" it is still normatively responsible and accountable for what occurs on its information communication platforms.

Consider the following general argument from analogy. Let's suppose that Mark operates an all-format performance space for use by people that come together to perform and listen to music, share information and have a few social drinks. However, the club is also used for unintended illicit activites by some of its users such as taking illegal drugs that result in non-consensual sex and drug overdoses resulting in death. Upon legal investigation of these illicit activities perpetrated by some of the users of his club, Mark denies any personal responibility for those activities claiming that he is merely the host providing a free space or a platform for people to come together to socialise and express themselves freely and creatively. Would Mark not be expected to at least ensure that such illicit activities did not take place on his premises, especially if they were systemic and not one-off activities, and moreover, activities of which he had or should have had prior knowledge, but chose for convenience and profit to turn a blind eye to those illicit activities? Clearly the answer to that question is that Mark would be ethically and legally held responsible and acountable for those activities.

The genral point of this argument from analogy is that the mere self-labelling of an analog or virtual space as a "platform" does not of itself relieve the proprietor of that platform from responsibility concerning any unethical or illegal practices that occur on the proprietor's self-defined paltform, however that platform is defined or used; no more, than the self-labelled "sports club" relieves the owner of any unethical and illigal systemic activities perpetrated by members of an illegal organization such as the Mafia, let us say, on those premises: "I am sorry your Honour but let's be fair I was merely providing a platform for sports enthusiasts, and as such I bear no responsibility for any illicit or unethical activites of theft and money-laundering carried out by some of the members of the club". I think we can agree that such a defense will not wash in a court of law or if it were presented to an independent ethics committe. Unless of course the court and the ethics committee were bribed. Scott Galloway (2017, 117) presents a similar argument from analogy with regard to Facebook's ethical responsibilities concerning illegal and unethical practices on its platform. According to Galloway,

> Facebook attempts to skirt criticism of its content by claiming it's *not* a media outlet, but a *platform.* This sounds reasonable until you consider that the term *platform* was never meant to absolve companies from taking responsbility for the damage they do. What if McDonald's, after discovering that 80 pecent of their beef was fake and making us sick, proclaimed they couldn't be held responsible, as they arent' a fast-food restaurant but a fast-food platform? Would we tolerate that?

The point Galloway is making here just as the previous argument from analogy is that the mere description of what Facebook does as a "platform" does not absolve that company of responsibility and accountability for any illegal or unethical transgressions that occur on its platform.

To emphasize again the direct relevance of DOIT's normative implications for Facebook's operations we shall examine in more detail in Sect. (5.4), DOIT locates the normativity of the communication of information within the inherent normative strucurte of information that comprises epistemic, ethical and eudaimonic features. These normative features of information commit all communicators of information generally, and especially media companies, including Facebook qua media company, to mandatory principles of truthfulness, accuracy, reliability, trustworthiness and the public good. Furethtmore, as illustrated in Sect. (5.7) through discussion of the Cambrige Analytica case, the violation of those fundamental media principles by Facebook may also constitute media corruption. As we shall see, that occurs systematically, when Facebook's *Bussiness Model* comes into direct conflict with its *Media Role*, which results in the violation of its normative commitments and responsibilities required on the basis DOIT. In Sect. (5.7) we shall see more clearly how DOIT dovetails the Media Corruption model presented in this chapter and one we examined in detail in Chap. 4; both DOIT and the Media Corruption model working in tandem reveal the media corruption that is at the heart of Facebook's bussiness operations.

Let us now explore in more detail what is the actual role of Facebook, as calling it a platform does (a) not clearly define or explain what its overarching role is and (b) calling it a "platform" does not absolve the company of any legal or ethical responsibility in regard to its practices.

5.2.1 Role Morality

This chapter, will use the term *role morality* (Spence et al. 2011) to describe the normative responsibilites to which different professions and insitutions and companies are commited to by virtue of their primary professional or institutional role. Henceforth, the all inclusive term *profession* will be used to encompass all insitutions and companies for convenience.

If what determines the primary role of a professional practice is its ultimate professional objective(s), then that role determines the normative principles to which that professional practice is committed. The ethical principles, rules, and values to which a professional practice is committed by virtue of its professional role is its *role morality*. So, for example, the police are, by virtue of their professional role, committed to the principles of justice and the rule of law. The principles of justice and the rule of law, among other things, constitute, therefore, the role morality of policing. Similarly, the media as professional disseminators and communicators of information to the public and more generally as mediators of information are committed by their professional role to certain ethical, epistemic and eudaimonic principles of conduct as per the Dual Obligation Information Theory (DOIT) which include or should include the principles of truthfulness, reliability, objectivity, independence and trustworthiness, among others.

The role morality of a profession sets, in turn, its own internal rules and codes of conduct for the normative regulation of that profession, and in the case of the media, includes or should include epistemic, ethical and eudaimonic principles in its code of conduct. *Media Ethics Codes* in general such as those of media companies such as *The Guardian*, the *New York Times*, *The Times, The Washington Post*, and the *Sydney Morning Herald*, among others, do include such epistemic and ethical principles even if those principles are not always complied with. Thus, typically, the code of ethics of a profession, would reflect and be constitutive of the role morality of that profession. To the extent that a profession's code of ethics does not reflect or is not constitutive of that profession's role morality, that code of ethics is normatively inadequate. It is therefore of paramount importance that before establishing a profession's code of ethics, the role of the profession, determined by the ultimate goals and objectives of that profession, are well understood, and accurately described. Let us now examine what the professional role of Facebook is with regard to its activities and objectives.

5.2.2 Facebook's Primary Role

Facebook is the medium through which approximately 2.2 billion people worldwide (Galloway 2017: 90) disseminate and communicate text and visual information, using *Facebook*, *WhatsApp,* and *Instagram.* Facebook likes to think of and define itself as a *platform*, but as we saw calling itself a platform does not absolve that company of any normative responsibility but merely obfuscates what Facebook's actual role is, which if examined carefully in terms of what Facebook actually does, is that of a *media company*. For Facebook collects, stores, curates, mediates, as well as moderates the information of its users, not unlike what newspapers such as the *Times* and *The Guardian* do with information provided by their subscribers through comments posted on their respective newspaper 'platforms'. The extra activity that Facebook engages in is to sell its users' information for profit to advertisers and other information contractors, often without the knowledge and consent of its users, as in the case of *Cambridge Analytica*. However, that is also not entirely new, as some traditional media companies in the form of newspapers, commercial radio and TV stations, have done something similar by presenting paid-for-ads and PR media releases disguised as editorial comment to its audiences, generally known in the industry as advertorials (Spence 2008; Spence et al. 2011). As we saw in Chap. 4 such advertorials not only violate epistemic and ethical principles but area also conducive to media corruption.

Similar in kind but expressed differently in practice and to a much greater extent, that is what Facebook's business model essentially is: collecting and selling their users' information to advertisers and other information brokers for profit, often without the explicit knowledge and consent of their users, as in the case of *Cambridge Analytica*. The main difference between what Facebook does and how traditional media use advertorials, is that the content used by Facebook is provided by its users and surreptitiously sold to advertisers. Both, however, the media audiences and the Facebook users are used as advertising target practice.

On the above analysis so far, Facebook appears for all intents and purposes to operate as a *media company* for which its 2.2 billion users provide the content. A very valuable content, which Facebook sells to advertisers and other information brokers to make Facebook, along with Apple, Amazon, Microsoft, and Google, one of the wealthiest companies in the World. In 2018 Facebook had a $US534 billion Market Capitalisation (Galloway 2017: 7). Nice work if you can get it and get away with it.

So, having established that Facebook in virtue of its primary role of collecting, storing, curating, and mediating information content generated by its users is a Media Company, if not by name by activity at least, it should be held to the same normative standards and responsibilities as other media companies are. Let us not forget that as we saw earlier in this chapter, the Convergent Media comprising the fourth and fifth Estates is also normatively held to account for user-generated content in its publications. By parity of argument, Facebook as part of what is referred to in this Chapter as the *sixth Estate*[5]should also be held to the same normative media standards. That requires Facebook to act responsibly in monitoring and editing information disseminated on its platform by its users as other media companies and publishers do, *Wikipedia*, for example. Though the information comes from its

[5]The term, sixth Estate, is a neologism I introduced in this book to distinguish the media role of Tech companies such as Facebook and Google from that of the fourth and fifth Estates.

users, that does not alleviate Facebook of its primary responsibility of checking the normative quality and integrity of that information. Especially, regarding *fake news, misinformation, and disinformation.*

Let us now examine more specifically what those normative standards, principles and responsibilities are vis-a- vis Facebook's Role Morality based on the *Dual Obligation Information Theory* (DOIT).

5.3 Facebook's Normative Commitments as a Media Company

As a media company Facebook is committed, like all other media companies, to the fundamental principles of truth, trust and the public's right to be informed truthfully, reliably and transparently, based on those principles. This is simply because if Facebook is a media company that collects, curates and mediates communication of information then it is bound to the normative commitments that emanate from within the inherent normative structure of information as demonstrated by the Dual Obligation Information Theory (DOIT), which was examined in Chap. 2.

Having established, in accordance with the normative requirements of DOIT, that Facebook as a media company, bound by the same normative principles and responsibilities as other media companies, Facebook's normative violations against the requirements of DOIT generally, express themselves in at least two primary ways in practice:

First, it violates the normative requirements of DOIT as a media company by its failure of not adequately monitoring and editing through prevention and correction, misinformation, disinformation, and fake news on its platform. Facebook has denied that it has any normative responsibility for monitoring, fact-checking and editing political advertising content placed by rival political parties on its platform (Milkman 2019), thus, conveniently shirking any of its normative responsibilities as a media company, as required by DOIT. However, following Mark Zuckerberg's pronouncements on Facebook in 2019 (Zuckerberg 2019) and in an op-ed article in the *Financial Times* in 2020 that "Big Tech needs more regulation" (Zuckerberg 2020), that might change. We shall examine the topic of regulation in more detail in Chap. 7.

The second way in which Facebook's violates the normative requirements of DOIT as a media company, is by its harvesting of users' information with the aid of opaque algorithms and its business model, which it sells to advertisers and other information brokers for profit. And as we shall see in the case of Cambridge Analytica, it does so without the users' informed consent. This general practice, which as we shall examine in more detail in Sect. (5.9), involves a *conflict of interest* between its role as a media company and its business model whose overarching goal is to sell user's information for advertising profit, without its users' informed consent, as illustrated in the Cambridge Analytica case. This conflict of interest lies at the heart of Facebook's operations and as we shall examine in more detail in Sects. (5.9 and 5.10) is conducive to systemic media corruption. Suffice to say in this section, that this second expression of Facebook's systemic violation of its normative responsibilities as a media company, as required by DOIT, also reflects a form of media corruption also present, as we saw in Chap. 4, in the traditional media companies representative of the fourth Estate as well as the fifth Estate. The type of media corruption is in the form of *advertorials*: the practice of presenting paid-for-content in the form of advertisements or press-release material deceptively, as editorial or news content (Spence 2008).

In the case of traditional advertorials by the media companies of the fourth and fifth Estates, the content is generated by those companies in partnership with the advertisers or PR companies and presented to their audiences as credible and objective journalistic content or editorial comment, without the users being aware of the deception and manipulation. In Chap. 4 that practice was referred to as an "unholy alliance" or "media corruption by collusion" between journalism, advertising, and public relations (Spence 2008, 2014, 2017, 2018; Spence et al. 2011). Interestingly, in the case of Facebook, this process is reversed. The 'advertorials' are created through users' content without their knowledge or informed consent, and then sold to advertisers, who in turn, target the users with advertisements, tailored specifically to the users' individual profiles created by Facebook's algorithms. As we shall see in Sect. (5.5) in the case of Cambridge Analytica, a similar advertising technique was used in 2016 to influence the U.S. Presidential Elections as well as the Brexit referendum in the UK.

Although the process involving traditional advertorials in the media of the fourth and fifth Estates, and Facebook's surveillance advertising practice based on its business model are different in type, they are similar in kind. Both are designed to deceive, manipulate, and exploit their users through misinformation. Another characteristic they both have in common is a *conflict of interest*. A conflict between a media company's professional role morality of disseminating and communicating information to the public, and in Facebook's case, its role morality as a media company of mediating and curating its users' information, held for them in trust, and on the other side of the conflict, Facebook's financial interest in the form of advertising profits,; specifically in situations when the latter interest is allowed to come into conflict and take priority, over the former interest. As we shall examine in more detail in Sect. (5.9) such conflicts of interest involving a conflict of roles, expressed either in the form of advertorials, or in the form of surveillance targeted advertising via profiling, as in the case of Facebook and analogously Google, are conducive to media corruption as well as violate the epistemic and ethical principles required by DOIT. As we can see, there is clearly a close conceptual relationship between the normative requirements of DOIT and those of the Media Corruption model that is explained by a common normative denominator they share, that of morality. This helps explain why media corruption and corruption generally, is *fundamentally a moral problem* (Miller 2018; Miller et al. 2005).

Having examined Facebook's two general types of normative violations with regard to the normative principles required by DOIT, and initially at least with regard to the Media Corruption model; and having established the close conceptual normative link between the two, we shall now examine more specifically Facebook's normative violations and failures in the Cambridge Analytica case. The purpose is to determine through an analysis of that case study, whether any of those normative failures also constituted media corruption and more generally, systemic media corruption.

5.4 The Cambridge Analytica Case

One of the biggest and most controversial cases involving Facebook was the Cambridge Analytica case[6] that exposed the sale of millions of users' data to third party information- brokers without the users' knowledge or consent. As a result of that exposure Facebook was fined $US5 billion as part of a settlement with the Federal Trade Commission (USA Today: 2019) and £500,000 GBP by the UK Information Commissioner's Office (ICO). What is of interest about this case and other similar cases involving both Facebook and Google as well as other tech companies is the role the fourth and fifth Estates played in exposing the unethical and illegal practices of those companies. It is a case of the Convergent Media of the fourth and fifth Estates keeping a check on the sixth Estate that comprises these new Tech Media Companies.

In summary, as described in Wikipedia (see note 47) the Cambridge Analytical case is as follows:

> In March 2018, multiple media outlets broke news of Cambridge Analytica's business practices. *The New York Times* and the *Observer* reported that the company had acquired and used personal data about Facebook users from an external researcher who had told Facebook he was collecting it for academic purposes.[18] Shortly afterwards, the BBC Channel 4 aired undercover investigative videos showing Nix [Cambridge Analytical CEO Alexander Nix] boasting about using prostitutes, bribery sting operations and honey traps to discredit politicians on whom it conducted opposition research, and saying that the company "ran all of (Donald Trump's) digital campaign". In response to the media reports, the Information Commission of the UK pursued a warrant to search the company's servers. Facebook banned Cambridge Analytica from advertising on its platform, saying that it had been deceived. On 23 March 2018, the British High Court granted the Information Commissioner's Office a warrant to search Cambridge Analytica's London offices. The personal data of up to 87 million Facebook users were acquired via the 270,000 Facebook users who used a Facebook app called "This Is Your Digital Life". By giving this third party app permission to acquire their data, back in 2015, this also gave the app access to information on the user's friends network; this resulted in the data of about 87 million users, the majority of whom had not explicitly given Cambridge Analytica permission to access their data, being collected. The app developer breached Facebook's terms of service by giving the data to Cambridge Analytica. On 1 May 2018, Cambridge Analytica and its parent company filed

[6] For details of that case see Cambridge_Analytica. (Wikipedia. Accessed: 19 September 2019).

for insolvency proceedings and closed operations." (https://en.wikipedia.org/wiki/Cambridge_Analytica).
Accessed: 19 September 2019.

A key question of this case and other similar cases involving the collection and distribution of users' data to unknown third parties to be used for unknown purposes, was whether Facebook had obtained *informed consent* from its 87 million users whose data they collected and passed on to Cambridge Analytical. It transpires that only 270, 000 Facebook users gave their consent by installing an app that allowed Facebook to collect information from their Facebook profiles and those of their friends' profiles, which they then provided to the makers of the app who in turn passed it on to Cambridge Analytical. But apart from the 270, 000 Facebook users who had installed the app and thus could be presumed to have given their consent, though not necessarily for the purpose for which it was used, most of the remaining 87 million Facebook users whose information was harvested for use by Cambridge Analytical, were unaware their data had been collected in this way and that it would be used to form voter targeting for Trump's Presidential election campaign (Tufekci Zeynep 2018a). So, most of those Facebook users not only did not give consent for the harvesting of their information by Facebook, but moreover did not provide consent for the purpose of its use, that is, to target voters in the Trump Presidential election. Because of those reasons Facebook was found guilty of breach of user's privacy and fined by the Federal Trade Commission, as well as by the UK Information Commissioner's Office (ICO).

5.5 The Normative Violations by Facebook in the Cambridge Analytical Case

Having determined the key facts of the Cambridge Analytical case let us now examine the specific normative issues of this case by application of the Dual Obligation Information Theory (DOIT).

Facebook's part in allowing the harvesting of its user's information for use by Cambridge Analytica was an epistemic and ethical violation of their *right to informed consent*, their *right to privacy* and crucially, by implication, their *right to autonomy*, as they were offered no knowledge that their information was collected and sent to a third party, and furthermore this was done without their knowledge of the purpose for which their information was to be used by Cambridge Analytica. In doing so, Facebook violated the fundamental communication principles of trust, reliability, and truthfulness, as well as its users' rights to freedom and wellbeing, which supports their fundamental right to autonomy as informational communicative agents.

Moreover, as we examined previously in Sect. (5.4) Facebook's actions in the form of an 'advertorial' of selling users' information for advertising profit without their knowledge and consent, similarly as in the case of traditional advertorials used by the legacy media, Facebook's use of 'advertorials' not only constituted normative violations of the requirements of DOIT, but in addition, constituted media corruption, a topic we shall examine in more detail in Sects. (5.8 and 5.9). In order, to distinguish the type of advertorials used in legacy media from the type used by Facebook, I shall refer to Facebook's use of their type of 'advertorials' as *advert-facetorials*.

In sum, Facebook's actions in this case at least, both by omission and by commission, were unethical. To further investigate how Facebook's actions in the case of Cambridge Analytica, constituted media corruption, and whether this was a one-off instance of corruption or a case of systemic corruption, we will now examine if and how the characterizing features of corruption as well as the necessary and sufficient conditions of corruption generally and media corruption specifically apply to Facebook in its part in the Cambridge Analytica case.

5.6 Did Facebook's Part in the Cambridge Analytica Case Constitute Media Corruption?

As we examined in Chap. 3 regarding general corruption and in Chap. 4 regarding media corruption, the six characterizing features of corruption are almost always present and accompany acts of corruption. Let us recall what these are: the *possession of power*, *disposition* to exercise that power, *opportunity* to exercise that power, *invisibility* or *concealment*, self-*regarding gain*, and a pre-existing *fiduciary duty of trust*.

As explained in Chap. 4, *possession of power* is the ability or capacity to act in a manner capable of bringing about a certain intended desired outcome; a *disposition to exercise that power* is the possession of a predisposition, pro-attitude or willingness to purposefully exercise that power; *opportunity* is having the opportunity, either presented to oneself or engineered by oneself, to engage in some activity for which one has the power and the predisposition in which to engage; *invisibility* or *concealment* is the ability or quality an agent has for keeping the motives and the identity of the agency of his actions invisible, concealed, or hidden from the gaze of others; *Self-regarding gain* is any gain, not necessarily financial, that accrues to the agent personally or to a group of which he is a member, as a result of his or the group's actions; fiduciary duty of trust is a socially pre-established and widely acknowledged fiduciary relationship of trust that exists between the corrupt person or corrupt group and the person or group of persons who are harmed in some way by the corrupt person's or the corrupt group's actions. With regard to the condition of invisibility, while the actions themselves would be visible at least with regard to their effects and consequences, the identity of their agency is invisible. Or at least the corrupt agent's intention is to keep his agency invisible or concealed. Those six features are are almost always present and accompany acts of corruption. For without power, one cannot commit a corrupt act. Possessing power is not enough; one must have the disposition to exercise that power willingly. Similarly, through lack of opportunity, one cannot engage in corrupt activity, even when one has both the power and the disposition to act corruptly. Invisibility seems to also be a characterizing feature of corruption that is usually, if not always, present in instances of corrupt activity.

All six features and their enabling conditions that characterize corruption and media corruption specifically seem to be present in the way that Facebook acted in the Cambridge Analytica case. Namely, *possession of power*, a *disposition* to exercise that power, an *opportunity* to exercise that power, *invisibility* or *concealment*, and *self-regarding gain* and abuse of a *fiduciary relationship of trust*. Facebook had the power as well as the disposition and opportunity to exercise that power and with the exception of 270, 000 people, did so under concealment without informing 87 million other users and without obtaining their informed consent, for the purpose of collecting and passing on those users' information to Cambridge Analytica for a self-regarding gain and by doing so, violating the fiduciary duty of trust owed to and expected by their users. As such, we can conclude that Facebook's actions by commission and omission in the case of Cambridge Analytica, had all the six characterizing features of media corruption.

This assessment also supports our earlier analysis in Sect. (5.4) where we discussed the practice of advertorials as a form of media corruption. In the Cambridge Analytica case, Facebook's role in allowing the harvesting of users' content to be used for targeted political advertising, as in the 2016 Presidential Elections and similarly in the Brexit referendum in the UK, constituted media corruption in the form of *advertorial*. As mentioned earlier in Sect. (5.4) this is a Facebook-type of 'advertorial' based on users' content served to them in the form of 'surveillance targeted advertising', without the users' knowledge and informed consent. Notice how an advertorial, has all the characterizing features of media corruption and corruption generally, and as we shall examine in Sect. (5.9) it involves also a conflict of interest, which is in most cases, conducive to media corruption and corruption generally. This further illustrates that such conflicts of interest are particularly ethically problematic as they tend to give rise to Systemic Corruption, as in the case of Facebook, which we will examine in more detail in Sect. (5.9). Another observation worth reiterating at this point is that Facebook's role in the Cambridge Analytica case also illustrates the close conceptual and normative relationship between DOIT and Media Corruption model used in this book. Namely, that Facebook's normative violations against the requirements of DOIT were pre-conditions for further violations in the form of media corruption. That is because media corruption, as in the case of Facebook's violations of DOIT as canvassed above, is also fundamentally an epistemic and ethical problem, a problem of trust.

Facebook may raise the objection that they did not know that the 270,000 users who gave their consent would pass on the information to their friends and so on. Even if that were the case, doubtful as that might seem, given that Facebook has a good knowledge of how their system works and how it is used (the more clicks by more users the better financially it is for Facebook) then at the very least Facebook acted negligently. That still amounts to media corruption by negligence as it involves a failure of the normative responsibilities they owed to their users and a failure of the fiduciary duty of trust to their users, as a media company. By analogy it would be similar if a patient was harmed by the negligence of his medical doctor who negligently administered the wrong treatment, when the doctor knew or should have known what the correct treatment was.

5.7 The Corrupting Effects of Facebook's Violation of Its Normative Media Responsibilities

What remains for us to examine now in this section more specifically, is what were the actual *corrupting effects* of Facebook's unethical and corrupt behavior and who and what was corrupted and in what way, and what are the moral implications of that corruption? As the corruption involved is institutional corruption what we need to determine is what the corrupting effects were (a) on the institution itself by virtue of its role as a media company, (b) the institutional persons qua *institutional role occupants* or *participants*, in this case Facebook's users, (c) the other institutional actors involved, in this case the clients of Facebook, in their capacity as advertisers and other third parties, for example, Cambridge Analytica, to whom the users' information was sold, and finally (d) the corrupting effect it had on democratic political institutions. Before we do, let us recall what constitutes corruption in terms of its *causal corrupting effects*.

As in the case of the characterizing features of corruption referred to above, it would also be useful to recall the necessary and sufficient conditions of corruption, with regard to corruption generally and as they specifically apply to media corruption that we examined in Chaps. 3 and 4 (Miller 2018; Spence et al. 2011, chapter 6).

1. An instance of institutional corruption is an instance in which an action or joint action or set of actions performed by an agent or set of agents undermines or has a tendency to undermine or contribute to the undermining of a legitimate institutional role, process, goal(s) or purpose(s) (understood as a collective good) of that institution and/or an effect of the despoiling of the moral character of an institutional role occupant (s), qua role occupant of that institution. This is the *Institutional Actor Condition*.
2. An action or set of actions is corrupt only if it corrupts something or someone. This is the *Cause and Effect Condition*.
3. An action or set of actions is corrupt only if the role occupant(s) who performs that action(s) intended it or foresaw the corrupting effects of that action(s) – or at the very least, could and should have foreseen the corrupting effects – or could have reasonably avoided the action(s). This is the *Moral Responsibility Condition*.

A common trait of institutional corruption that is not, however, a *necessary condition,* is its predominantly *systemic* nature. It is not a necessary condition for even if the corruption as illustrated by the Cambridge Analytica was a one-off case, it would still count as corruption because of its high impact and wide unethical repercussions and damage to public trust.

Another general feature of corruption is that all forms of corruption are immoral, though not all forms of immorality constitute corruption. Many forms of corruption, such as political bribery, are illegal, though some, like fabricating stories in journalism and advertorials, are not (Spence et al. 2011, chapter 6). Corruption as understood and explained in this book and in this chapter specifically, is therefore fundamentally a matter of morality (Miller 2018; Spence et al. 2011, chapter 6). This is further illustrated by the close conceptual connection between corruption and unethical conduct as illustrated by the application of DOIT to the Cambridge Analytical case.

Three distinct types of institutional corruption we can identify with regard to Facebook's part in the Cambridge Analytical case, arising directly from its surveillance business model are, *information and communication corruption*, *democratic political corruption*, and *citizenry corruption*, the latter being a type of *institutional personal corruption*.

5.7.1 Information and Communication Corruption

Applying the three conditions of the definition of corruption above we can now demonstrate that Facebook's part in the Cambridge Analytica had a corrupting effect on its institutional media role in undermining the information and communication processes and purposes of the collection, mediation, curation and management of the information and its communication placed in trust on Facebook's site by its users, and as required by its fiduciary duty of trust as a media company (i.e., its *role morality*) and the normative requirements of DOIT that apply to the communication of information. This also demonstrates that corruption generally and media corruption specifically is fundamentally a moral problem, as demonstrated by the close conceptual relationship referred to above that holds between the Dual Obligation Information Theory (DOIT) and the Media Corruption model.

Another aspect of Facebook's media corruption as illustrated by the Cambridge Analytica case is its use of an *advert-facetorial*, a neologism I use in this chapter to distinguish Facebook's surveillance type of 'advertorial' from traditional advertorials by legacy media. In the case of Facebook's use of advert-facetorials, users' information was harvested and used in political advertising in the 2016 U.S. Presidential Elections and also in the UK Brexit Referendum to influence voters. In addition, as previously canvassed, the use of advert-facetorials by Facebook, generated by its business model through non-transparent algorithms, which metaphorically, at least, parallel the 'ring of invisibility' in Gyges Myth, further demonstrates that this form of media corruption that involves the selling of users' information to advertisers and other information contractors for profit without the users' informed consent, constitutes more generally, *systemic media corruption*.

5.7.2 Democratic Political Corruption

Applying the three conditions of the definition of corruption as above, we can demonstrate that Facebook's part in allowing Cambridge Analytical to target and use its 87 million users' profiles in Donald Trump's 2016 presidential campaign, had the effect of undermining the electoral process, which had the effect of also undermining the political institutions that comprise the democratic system itself. Even if Facebook had not intended their act of giving unauthorized access to their users' information for voter-profiling as used by Cambridge Analytica, they should have foreseen the corrupting effects this may have on the democratic process and taken steps to avoid the distribution of their users' profiles to Cambridge Analytica. As Zeynep Tufekci correctly observed in her New York Times article (March 19, 2018),

> A business model based on vast data surveillance and charging clients to opaquely target users based on this kind of extensive profiling will inevitably be misused. The real problem is that billions of dollars are being made at the expense of the health of our public sphere and our politics, and crucial decisions are being made unilaterally, and without recourse or accountability.

Tufecki's astute observation also seems to confirm our concern regarding Facebook's inherent and generic conflict of roles, to which, as discussed earlier, its surveillance business model gives rise and is thus conducive to systematic media corruption. We shall examine that conflict of roles to which Facebook's business model gives rise in Sect. 5.7.

With regard to institutional political corruption as illustrated by the joint actions of Facebook and Cambridge Analytica, Dennis Thompson makes a point that is in keeping and lends support to our analysis on institutional corruption above. According to Thomson's understanding of institutional political corruption,

> The fact that an official [for our purposes, Facebook and Cambridge Analytica corporate actors] acts under conditions that tend to create improper influence is sufficient to establish corruption, whatever the official's motive. (Thompson 2013: 13 in in Miller 2018).

As in our analysis of conflicts of interest and conflicts of roles earlier, it is not the motive that is decisive in determining acts of corruption or at least acts and roles conducive to corruption but the *tendency to corrupt* in undermining a legitimate institutional purpose or role. According to Thompson, [a practice] is corrupt if it is of a type that tends to undermine [core] processes and thereby frustrate the primary purpose of the institution (Thompson 2013: 7 in Miller 2018).

A general conclusion we can derive from the above analysis so far is that the inherent conflict between Facebook's two roles that of the their surveillance business model and their role as a media company, has a tendency to undermine their media role by corrupting the purposes and processes of the information and communication of its users, as well as having a tendency to undermine the legitimate purposes and roles of the democratic political institutions, which those informational processes are meant to support. The result is a *perfect storm* and of great concern as the damage of corruption to our systems of information and communication, as well as to our democratic political institutions that are closely related through the power of social media, is substantial and ongoing.

Referring back to Plato's Myth of Gyges we can now see more clearly that Facebook, as illustrated by the Cambridge Analytica case, acts like Gyges under a cloak of invisibility, acting corruptly for its self-interest and profit while simultaneously maintaining a superficial public profile of probity and legitimacy for the common good of humanity. What Plato refers to as the phenomenon of "perfect injustice, appearing just when you are not".

According to Seumas Miller, Mark Warren describes the connection between corruption and democracy, as one of "duplicitous exclusion" (Warren 2006: 803–807 in Miller 2018) and Ceva and Ferreti as the 'bending of public rules in the service of "surreptitious agendas" (Ceva and Ferretti 2017: 6 in Miller 2018). Echoing the Myth of Gyges, Warren, according to Miller, claims that corruption in democracies takes place under two conditions; (1) the norm is violated; and (2) violators claim to be complying with the norm (Warren 2004: 337 in Miller 2018). As Miller astutely observes "the duplicity condition – and the related surreptitious agenda of Ceva and Ferretti – is reminiscent of Plato's Ring of Gyges". Indeed. For typically, corrupt persons or corporations avoid the ethical obligations of contractual and fiduciary relationships based on trust by operating under conditions approaching those of perfect injustice. They do so by committing their corrupt deeds under a cloak of invisibility that allows them to avoid the social disapproval and retribution of socially recognized unethical and illegal conduct, whilst at the same time securing the social approbation of recognized ethical conduct by wearing the dissembling mask of morality; at least in the negative sense of not appearing to be acting immorally. It is a case of having your civic cake and eating it too.

In conclusion of this section, Facebook appears by the above analysis and as illustrated by the Cambridge Analytica case, to have operated corruptly under Gygean conditions of invisibility, aided by the opacity of its business model and algorithms, by breaking the rules and violating the civic and moral rights of its users for profit, and simultaneously appearing to be acting ethically, when they were not.

5.7.3 *The Collective Moral Responsibility of Citizens*

If we know or suspect that our information is harvested by Facebook to build virtual profiles of us that are then sold to advertisers and/or other third parties such as information brokers or political actors without our informed consent, as in the case of Cambridge Analytica, are we ourselves as users in some way and to some degree ethically responsible for the corrupt ways in which our information is applied by Facebook? Especially as in the Cambridge Analytica case where the corruption involved was institutional political corruption that undermined the democratic system? Specifically, by undermining public trust and in turn damaging the democratic system itself.

In answering that question let us first examine in what different ways, directly or indirectly, fully, or partially, our own ethical responsibility or lack of, as users, might be explained. In doing so it may be helpful first to apply the features and conditions of corruption we applied to Facebook in the Cambridge Analytica case to determine whether those features and conditions of corruption also applied to Facebook's users in that particular case

In the absence of informed consent by most of Facebook's users and on the assumption that even those users who gave consent might not have known of the specific purpose for which their information and profiles were being used by Cambridge Analytica, we can conclude that both the features and conditions of corruption we examined above do not apply to the users and therefore they are not responsible for Facebook's corruption. As explained above, institutional corruption presupposes intent or at least foreknowledge and ability to avoid the corruption which Facebook's users did not have in that particular case.

However, given our retrospective knowledge of the Cambridge Analytica case and the ensuing fallout from the loss of public trust in the democratic political institutions and the resulting damage to those institutions, do we as Facebook's users have an ethical responsibility to exercise more vigilance and take more care in ensuring the privacy and security and overall the integrity of our shared information, which in turn, should reciprocally be respected and protected by Facebook? Moreover, are we collectively responsible as users, that our shared information is not abused and undermined by being used for unethical and illegitimate purposes by Facebook and by the third parties to which it sells our information as illustrated by the Cambridge Analytica case? For as we saw in the Cambridge Analytica case, Facebook's actions have the tendency of undermining and corrupting the normative integrity of users' information, as well as the normative and legitimate roles of the media, and moreover, the social, financial, and political institutions that together comprise our democratic system. The answer to the above questions is clearly yes. Facebook's users do have those ethical responsibilities by virtue of being *institutional role occupants* of a media company, bound by the normative requirements of DOIT.

The shared and joint normative responsibilities of Facebook's users is of particular interest and importance in our present enquiry; for the users of Facebook provide the content on which Facebook trades. It is this most valuable resource that Facebook sells to advertisers and third parties to generate its huge profits for which its users receive no financial benefit, apart from a free service provided by Facebook to its users. Which, in itself, is a very valuable service as relationships with friends, colleagues and family, are important and a common social good, from which society benefits, as illustrated currently across the world, as a result of the Covic-19 pandemic.

That institutional role that Facebook's users occupy, *qua institutional role occupants*, raises an interesting analogy between journalists and other professional media professionals such as PR consultants and advertisers, and Facebook users. Whereas the former, communicate information as part of their paid employment for their respective media companies and institutions, Facebook's users provide informational content to be shared by their friends and for use by advertisers and other communication brokers for a free service by Facebook. In both cases, however, both the media professionals as members of the fourth and fifth Estates and the Facebook users as members of the sixth Estate, are bound by the same normative principles as demonstrated by DOIT. That is, they are bound by principles of transparency, truthfulness, reliability, trustworthiness, and respect for the informational rights of all communicators, as equal members of the infosphere. A consequence of living in the infosphere is that the normative responsibilities and commitments of informational agents as demonstrated by DOIT are not less but more. And given the global nature of the infosphere and the World Wide Web, also global and universal.

Another consequence, is that the corruption of information and its communication processes and the resulting corruption of democratic political institutions as illustrated by the Cambridge Analytica case, is a global concern, one that should also be shared by Facebook's users worldwide, as *global citizens of the infosphere*. Just as climate change affects everyone globally, so does the misuses and abuses of information and its communication, as well as the corrupting effects it has on the infosphere including those on the democratic political institutions it also tends to corrupt. We are, therefore, jointly, and collectively normatively responsible for the wellbeing and integrity of the infosphere just as we are of our shared ecosystem.

Given that Facebook users are also bound, as institutional role occupants, by the normative requirements of DOIT, are they also in any way responsible for any of Facebook's actions that may constitute corruption, as in the Cambridge Analytical case? Is there some degree of distributed normative responsibility, moral and epistemic that can be attributed to Facebook's users qua institutional role occupants for Facebook's corrupt actions? Here is an argument that at first blush appears to lend support to an affirmative answer to that question.

Insofar as Facebook's users have or ought to have some knowledge concerning:

1. Facebook's part in the Cambridge Analytica case and similar other cases that led to corruption; and
2. Knowledge of the generic conflict of interest at the heart of Facebook's surveillance business model conducive to such corruption; and
3. That as users of Facebook there is a reasonable presumption that they are expected as institutional role occupants of a media company for which they provide and share informational content, to have such knowledge.
4. Then, it is reasonable to conclude that the users of Facebook bear some partial joint and collective normative responsibility pertaining to them as institutional role occupants, for any present and/or future unethical and or corrupt practices that Facebook engages in, through the misuse and abuse of their information. Being a distributed normative responsibility shared jointly and collectively by Facebook's users, such normative responsibility would be minimal for each of its 2.2 billion Facebook users.

Of course, this would also depend on how much knowledge the users of Facebook have concerning Facebook's operations and financial media activities, especially when often those activities are opaque and shrouded under a cloak of invisibility and concealment. However, despite that limitation or because of it, in the age of information, ignorance, of how one's information is being used and for what purposes by media tech companies such as Facebook and Google, is no bliss and no longer morally excusable. Just as drivers of vehicles are expected to have essential knowledge of traffic laws when using their vehicles, analogously Facebook users, as information agents and institutional role occupants, should have the essential normative knowledge required for the communication of their information and its use. This also entails a normative education of using and communicating information so as to ensure or at least minimize the unethical and corrupt uses and applications of our shared and collective information on Facebook and by extension on the infosphere.

Referring to Lawrence Lessig's *Dependence Corruption,* Seumas Miller (2018) points to Lessig's distinction between "The responsibility for changing individual behavior within the system and responsibility for changing the system itself" (Lessig 2013: 15).

Although according to Miller (2018: 14) Lessig is applying his notion of dependence corruption to the U.S. democratic political processes, Lessig's notion of dependency corruption can also be usefully applied to our present discussion of the normative responsibility of Facebook users concerning Facebook's unethical and corrupt practices, as illustrated in the Cambridge Analytica case.

With regard to Lessig's distinction between the two types of responsibility, we can say with some justification, that although Facebook's users cannot be held responsible for changing Facebook's system vis-à-vis its surveillance business model, which as we saw earlier creates the conflict of roles that are conducive to media corruption, they can be held partly responsible to some degree for changing their individual behavior within Facebook's system; on the reasonable assumption that Facebook's users have or ought to have some basic knowledge of Facebook's system, just as one is presumed to have some basic knowledge of the traffic system and its governing laws when driving a vehicle on the road. Knowledge such as how Facebook collect users' information and sells it to advertisers and third parties, and in some cases does so, as in the Cambridge Analytica case, without their informed consent.

Although Facebook had full moral responsibility for their corruption in the Cambridge Analytica case, its users did not have any responsibility if they had no knowledge and did not give their informed consent that their information was to be used by Facebook in that corrupt manner. However, given the justifiable ensuing loss of trust in Facebook vis-à-vis the Cambridge Analytica case, its users as institutional role occupants share some partial joint and collective responsibility if Facebook is found to engage in ongoing instances of systemic media corruption.

As a consequence, Facebook's users have, as Lessig suggests vis-à-vis his notion of dependence corruption, a responsibility of changing their individual behavior *within the Facebook system* (Lessig 2013: 15; Miller 2018). To that end, Facebook's users share a collective responsibility to take appropriate precautionary measures and exercise vigilance and due care to how Facebook collects and uses their information and for what purposes. Referring to Lessig's dependence corruption as it applies to the US democratic political system, Seumas Miller makes the correct observation that,

> It is the combined effect of the many individual actions of a large number of legislators (and funders and lobbyists) that does the institutional damage. Therefore, each only makes a small causal contribution and each, therefore, only has a small share in the moral responsibility for the outcome. (Miller 2018: 14)

Applying Miller's argument to Facebook, we can analogously say that the many individual users of Facebook, 2.2 billion of them, only has a small share in the normative responsibility for the outcome of institutional corruption. Miller makes the further correct observation, vis-à-vis political corruption in the US democratic system that,

> Moreover, changing the system, there is a need for joint action; it is a joint moral responsibility involving shared *partial individual* responsibility. Thus, legislators could, and they could, jointly act…….to address the problem of dependency …the moral responsibility in play is a species of collective responsibility; specifically, a moral responsibility (Miller 2018: 15).

Analogously, applying Miller's further observation above to Facebook, we can say that insofar as Facebook's users bear some partial moral responsibility as institutional role occupants of Facebook, they also have some partial individual moral responsibility for changing Facebook's system; especially as content producers and providers of that system that creates vast profits each year for Facebook through the sale of user's content to advertisers and other information contractors, such as Cambridge Analytica. That responsibility, as Miller correctly argues, is a collective moral responsibility they share jointly.

One way they can do so, is to bring collective pressure to bear on Facebook as content producers, to render that system more transparent and accountable by being compliant with the normative requirements and moral responsibilities that Facebook is required to comply with and uphold by virtue of operating as a media company. That collective intervention has two aspects.

The first, concerns the conflict of roles between Facebook's role as a media company and Facebook's surveillance business model that as we saw earlier in this chapter is conducive to media corruption both actual (as in the case of Cambridge Analytical) and potential corruption in the future. Regarding that concern, the users are entitled to collectively request Facebook to normatively resolve that conflict.

The second concern relates to Facebook's misuse and abuse of its users' privacy and the integrity of its users' information and communications. As producers of Facebook content, which is one of Facebook's most valuable monetary resource, Facebook's users can, therefore, collectively request Facebook to apply more transparent and accountable normative controls and care of their data.

5.8 The Conflict of Interest at the Heart of Facebook's Business Model Conducive to Media Corruption

The core normative problem for Facebook's operations that encompasses ethical, epistemic and eudaimonic requirements and responsibilities in accordance with the Dual Obligation Information Theory (DOIT), is a *conflict of interest* between the financial interests of Facebook given its business model on the one hand, and the normative interest of its users, given Facebook's role morality as a media company, on the other. Conflicts of interest, as we saw in our analysis above, can be conducive to corruption.

Facebook's conflict of interest arises out of its business model that is based primarily on surveillance, the watching, tracking and collection of vast amount of its users' data through sophisticated AI algorithms for the overarching purpose of selling their users' content to advertisers, political actors and other information brokers, such as in the Cambridge Analytica case. But as in the case of Cambridge Analytica, however, the normative interests of Facebook's users, epistemic, ethical and eudaimonic, are not only not served but undermined and violated. Facebook's users are merely the human resource in this unequal and seemingly unfair deal, which ironically provide the content that make Facebook so successful and enormously wealthy.

5.8.1 What Is a Conflict of Interest?

According to the "standard view" (Davies 1998: 590),

> A conflict of interest is a situation in which some person *P* (whether an individual or corporate body) has a conflict of interest. *P* has a conflict of interest if and only if (1) *P* is in a relationship with another requiring *P* to exercise judgement in the other's behalf and (2) *P* has a (special) interest tending to interfere with the proper exercise of judgement in that relationship. The crucial terms in this definition are 'relationship', 'judgement', 'interest' and 'proper exercise'.

The "relationship" required must be fiduciary, that is, it must involve one person trusting another, to exercise judgement in his service. "Judgement" is the ability to make certain kinds of decisions that require knowledge or skill, correctly and reliably. "Interest" is any influence, loyalty, concern, emotion, or other feature of a situation tending to make *P*'s judgement (in that situation) less reliable than it would normally be. "Proper Exercise" of judgement is normally a question of social fact and includes what people ordinarily expect, what *P* or the group *P* belongs to invites others to expect, and what various laws, professional codes, or other regulations require (Davies 1998: 590).

What is generally wrong with a conflict of interest is that it renders one's judgement less reliable than what normally it should be and results in a failure or abuse of a fiduciary duty. Generally, a conflict of interest can arise in at least one of two ways:

(A) One has a self-regarding interest that is in conflict, at least potentially so, with one's fiduciary duty, having the tendency to interfere with the proper exercise of one's judgement regarding that duty.
(B) One has two potentially competing fiduciary duties or roles that are in conflict with each other, at least potentially so, having the tendency to interfere with the proper exercise of one's judgement with regard to one or the other of the two competing duties or roles so that one is not able to properly exercise both duties or roles.

So, for example, there is a clear conflict of interest in the case of an accountant who is also the manager of a football club and audits the financial statements of his club. For his special interest in the club as manager would tend to make his judgement as auditor less reliable than what it ordinarily should be because it would be less objective and independent that what would normally be expected from a disinterested auditor. The conflict of interest arises as a direct result of the conflict between the two competing roles in which the accountant/manager-of-football-club is engaged in, such that it has a tendency to interfere with one or the other of those two competing roles and the respective fiduciary duties associated with each of those roles.

Crucially for the purpose of this chapter, conflicts of interest are conducive to corruption.

The above examples illustrate that although a conflict of interest might not in the first instance necessarily involve or result in corruption, it can nevertheless provide the conditions which might facilitate corruption. Thus, it is better for all concerned if the conflict of interest is avoided. In cases in which the conflict of interest is not too severe and is not avoidable, it may be possible for the person with the conflict of interest to carry on, if the conflict is disclosed and managed in an apparent and accountable way.

Facebook's conflict of interest is of the second type described above and arises as a direct result of a conflict between two seemingly conflicting roles: (a) The role based on their surveillance business model of collecting users' information for profiling and selling to advertisers and other clients thereby opaquely targeting users for vast amount of profits, and (b) the role they have as a media company of facilitating and mediating the sharing of digital information by users. As we saw in the case of Cambridge Analytica these two roles can and do come into conflict that result in the violation of the users' legal and normative informational rights.

As we saw earlier, such a conflict of interest also arises in the form of *advertorials* in the legacy media, and as *advert-facetorials* in Facebook's business operations, as the role of being a media company conflicts with the role of advertising when the latter is given priority over the former. Moreover, the advertising is disguised as journalistic content in the case of traditional advertorials used by legacy media, and in the case of Facebook, what is disguised through concealment, is that the targeted advertising is generated by concealed appropriation of users' content through profiling, produced by Facebook's non-transparent algorithms, without the users' knowledge and informed consent. In both cases, the role of being a media company is fundamentally undermined and usurped by concealed advertising for profit in violation of fundamental normative principles (as required by DOIT), which results in *media corruption* when the media company's *fiduciary duty of trust* owed to its users, is further undermined, as illustrated in Facebook's role in the Cambridge Analytica case.

What becomes clear from our analysis of the Cambridge Analytica case above is that those two roles are in an *inversely proportional conflict of interest*, which means that Facebook makes more profits even as it behaves badly. The profit motive of its voracious business model is inversely proportional to its ethics. Acting unethically and illegally, as in the paradigmatic Cambridge Analytica case, pays more than had they acted ethically, even after paying a five billion-dollar fine. When the primary motive of Facebook's business is to make as much profit as possible ethics takes a back seat at best.

The *inverse proportionality of this conflict of interest* marks it as an *inherently generic feature* of what is fundamentally epistemically and ethically wrong with Facebook's business model and its application. For the model is *designed* to generate profits by increasing its user base and time spent on the site (Galloway 2017: 105). That involves sharing user data with third party apps without the user's knowledge and without their consent. Despite warnings from the FCC against this ongoing practice and a promise from Facebook to comply with FCC's request for obtaining users' consent for their information being accessed by third party apps, that promise remains unfulfilled (Galloway 2017: 106). Basically, because it is time consuming and costly to police and will cost Facebook money to implement and will result in loss of revenue. When profit is the primary objective and ethics interferes with that objective, ethics takes a walk.

We can now conclude from the above analysis that Facebook's conflict between its two diametrically opposed roles of harvesting and selling its users' information to third parties for profit, and its curating, facilitating, managing, and mediating the sharing of information by its users, is conducive to media corruption as illustrated in the Cambridge Analytical case. It remains an ongoing conflict of roles because that conflict is a generic and inherent feature of Facebook's business model that motivates and fuels Facebook's media corruption and is conducive to it. This makes Facebook's media corruption a systemic ongoing problem.

5.9 The Systemic Problem of Harvesting and Marketing Information

The problem of the collection and harvesting of users' information via opaque algorithms that is then sold for profit to advertisers, often without the users' knowledge and informed consent, is not limited to Facebook. Insofar as Google, like Facebook, operates as a media company in its information practices through its *search* function and its communication and curations practices that involve the collection, profiling and harvesting of users information via its Apps such as Gmail for example, which like Facebook sells to advertisers for profit; as well as its YouTube practices that have been partly shown to be responsible for the spread of misinformation, fake news and deep fakes, on the internet generally and specifically during the US Presidential elections of 2016[7]; then Google's media role also places Google like Facebook, within the parameter of the sixth Estate. Therefore, some of the *types* of normative issues examined in this chapter with regard to Facebook, apply equally to Google; for example, its selection, collection, and harvesting of users' information via its opaque algorithms, which then sells for profit to advertisers without their knowledge or informed consent. As in the case of Facebook, that problem is systemic: A conflict of interest between the collection and curation of users' information in its role of a media company, and its business model that is specifically designed and geared to generate massive profits through the sale of users' information to advertisers. And as in the case of Facebook, the more time users spend on Google search and more clicks on its other apps and more watch time on You Tube, the more money Alphabet-Google makes. That in itself is not a problem. The problem is the monetization and weaponization of the information of its users that gives Google enormous power and control to influence every aspect of our lives.

Operating like Gyges both within and outside the Social Contract for the common good,[8] Google operates under the concealment of its opaque AI-driven algorithms in near-monopolistic manner that allows it to evade and avoid the epistemic and ethical responsibilities of transparency, accountability, truthfulness and trustworthiness by which other media companies are bound. As in the case of Facebook' operations, illustrated by the Cambridge Analytica case, Google's operations undermine citizens' democratic rights to privacy, autonomy, and wellbeing, as well as the democratic system and its associated institutions. The real problem of Google's and Facebook's method and practices is their invasive and non-transparent collection of users' data and its unfair and unaccountable and non-transparent use (Pasquale

[7] See, for example, Zeynep Tufekci (2018). You Tube, The Great Radicalizer, The *New York Times*, March 10, 2018; Christopher Mims (2018). Who has more of your personal data than Facebook, The Australian and Wall St Journal, April, 23, 2018; Frank Pasquale (2015) *The Black Box Society: The Secret Algorithms That Control Money and Information*, Cambridge, Massachusetts: Harvard University Press, pp. 50–51;66;78–79;96;185;190–191. 214–215; and for a more comprehensive account of the problem, see, Shoshana Zuboff (2019) *The Age of Surveillance Capitalism: The Fight for a Human Future at the New Frontier of Power*, Profile Books; Webb, Amy (2019). *The Big Nine: How the Tech Titans and Their Thinking Machines Could Warp Humanity*, Hatchet Books; Foroohar, Rana (2019); Galloway, Scott (2017). *The Four: The Hidden DNA of Amazon, Apple, Facebook and Google*. London, Great Brittain: Bantam Press; Van Dijck, Poell and De Waal (2018), *The Platform Society: Public Values in a Connected World*. Oxford: Oxford University Press; and Lynch, Michael P. (2016) The Internet of Us: Knowing and Understanding Less in the Age of Big Data, Penguin Random House.

[8] The Social Contract referred to here is based on the philosophical ethical theories of Thomas Hobbes, John Locke and John Rawls that will be examined in more details in Chap. 7. Although different in their approach and articulation those social contract theories counsels every citizen and corporations to act for the common good of society as whole and not for their own exclusive self-interests in violation of the common good.

2015: 55). The blurring and blending of their information practices with advertising, just as in the case of cash-for-comment and advertorials in some of the practices of the fourth and fifth Estates, a topic examined earlier in Chap. 4, becomes a much bigger and uncontrollable epistemic and ethical problem when it is done at the unprecedented stratospheric global level and scale in which both Google and Facebook now operate. As Frank Pasquale poignantly puts it in regard to Google, but equally applicable to Facebook, "Don't Be Evil" is a thing of the past; you can't form a trusting relationship with a black box" (Pasquale 2015). Referring to the Myth of Gyges on which the *model of media corruption* presented in this book is based (see Chap. 4) Frank Pasquale correctly observes (2015: 190) that,

> Black box insiders are protected as if they are wearing a Ring of Gyges – which grants its wearer invisibility but, Plato warns us in *The Republic,* is also an open invitation to bad behavior.

He goes on to ask the very crucial question that philosophers since Plato have been asking, and a question Shoshana Zuboff also asks in the her book *The Age of Surveillance Capitalism* (2019) and I am now asking in this book, "what kind of society does this create"? Is it one we want and is it fit for human beings? A society in which the primary purpose of most human beings, as Aristotle clearly identified, is a good and worthy life that leads to the attainment of eudaimonia or happiness? Can we be happy in a world dominated and ruled by a handful of Tech Oligarchs, accountable only to themselves and pursuing their own self-interest over that of the common good of society? A world not of our making or design that neither is within our control, nor one that we have chosen. As Frank Pasquale astutely observes (2015),

> Accountability requires human judgement, and only humans can perform the critical function of making sure that, as our social relations become ever more automated, domination and discrimination aren't built invisibly into the [black boxes] code.

The major systemic problem identified in this chapter at the heart of Facebook's operations and analogously at the core of Google's operations, is an inherent conflict of interests between, on the one hand, Facebook's role as a media company and the normative responsibilities and commitments it has for the safeguarding of its users' information, as required by the Dual Obligation Information Theory (DOIT); and on the other hand, Facebook's financial interests that are determined by an invasive and aggressive business model of maximining profits through the sale of users' data to advertisers; a business model that is by design geared to override and exert priority for Facebook's financial interests over the users' rights over their information.

Insofar as a similar systemic problem is evident in Goggle' operations identified also as conflict of interest between its business model that favors Google's financial interests over the normative informational rights of it users, then Google's systemic problem just as in the case of Facebook, as analyzed in this chapter, is conducive to systemic media corruption. Systemic institutional corruption, as we saw in Chap. 3, is particularly problematic and harmful to society overall.

5.10 Conclusion

The overall objective of this chapter has been to demonstrate how some of the information and communication practices of Facebook, constitute media corruption (Spence 2008, 2017). To that end, the chapter examined what the professional and business role of Facebook is regarding its information/communication practices. It then demonstrated that its role of curating and mediating the information and communication provided by its users, which affords them the collective sharing and exchange of knowledge-relevant information on its platform, reveals that Facebook is essentially a *media company*, and not merely a "platform". As such, Facebook is liable to the same normative responsibilities of other media companies based on the Dual Obligation Information Theory (DOIT). As such DOIT commits Facebook to a *normative editing responsibility*, qua media company, to ensure both the preventive detection and corrective editing of fake news, as well as other forms of misinformation disseminated on its platform. Based on DOIT's normative requirements, Facebook is furthermore normatively accountable for the harvesting of users' information, which it collects with the aid of algorithms and sells to advertisers and other information brokers for profit, without the users' informed consent. This general practice involves a *conflict of interest* between its role as a media company, and its selling of users' information to advertisers for profit without the users' informed consent. That conflict of interest lies at the heart of Facebook's operations primarily as a result of its business model and thus, conducive to systemic media corruption.

That type of media corruption referred to in the chapter as *'advert-facetorial'*, is a type of *advertorial,* also present in legacy media. In the case of traditional advertorials by legacy media companies, the content is generated by those companies in partnership with the advertisers and presented to the users as credible and objective independent journalistic content, without the users' awareness of the deception and manipulation. In the case of Facebook, this process is reversed. The *'advert-facetorials'* are created through users' content without their informed consent, and then sold to advertisers, who in turn, target the users with advertisements, tailored specifically to the users' individual profiles created by Facebook's algorithms. Although the process involving traditional advertorials in the legacy media, and Facebook's surveillance advertising practice based on its business model are different in type, they are similar in kind. Both are designed to deceive, manipulate, and exploit their users, through misinformation. Another characteristic these advertorials both share in common is a *conflict of interest.* A conflict between a media company's professional role morality of disseminating and communicating information to the public, and in Facebook's case, its own role morality as a media company of mediating and curating its users' information.

Such conflicts of interest involving a conflict of roles, expressed either in the form of advertorials, or in the form of *advert-facetorials* in the case of Facebook, are conducive to media corruption and violate the epistemic and ethical principles required by DOIT. This clearly demonstrates the close conceptual and normative relationship between DOIT, and the Media Corruption model used in this chapter, and further demonstrates and explains why media corruption and corruption generally, is *fundamentally a moral problem.*

The chapter also demonstrated that Facebook's normative violations with regard to DOIT and its related violations with regard to the Media Corruption model as examined in this chapter, constitute media corruption and more generally, ongoing systemic media corruption. A corruption that manifest itself through its corrupting effects in at least three ways: As *information and communication corruption, political corruption* and because of its corrupting effects on its users qua citizens, *civil corruption.*

Finally, the chapter demonstrated that the problem of the collection and harvesting of users' information via opaque algorithms that is then sold for profit to advertisers, often without the users' knowledge and informed consent, is a *generic systemic problem* not limited to Facebook. Insofar as Google, like Facebook, operates as a media company in its information practices through its *search* function and its communication and curations practices that involve the collection, profiling and harvesting of users information via its apps such as Gmail for example, which like Facebook sells to advertisers for profit; as well as its YouTube practices that have been partly shown to be responsible for the spread of misinformation, fake news and deep fakes, on the internet generally and specifically during the US Presidential elections of 2016[9]; then Google's media role also places Google like Facebook, within the parameter of the sixth Estate. Insofar as a similar systemic problem is evident in Goggle' operations identified also as conflict of interest between its business model that favors Google's financial interests over the normative informational rights of it users, then Google's systemic problem just as in the case of Facebook, as analyzed in this chapter, is conducive to systemic media corruption. Systemic institutional corruption, as we saw in Chap. 3, is particularly problematic and harmful to the whole of society as it undermines the collective common good of society and its underlying democratic system and aligned institutions.

References

Ceva, Emanuela, and Maria Paola Ferretti. 2017. Political Corruption. *Philosophy Compass* 7 (2): 1–10.

Davies, Michael.. 1998. *Encyclopedia of Applied Ethics*, vol 1, A–D, 590. Academic

Elliott, Deni, and Edward Spence. 2018. *Ethics for a Digital Era*. Oxford: Wiley-Blackwell.

[9] See, for example, Zeynep Tufekci (2018). You Tube, The Great Radicalizer, The *New York Times*, March 10, 2018; Christopher Mims (2018). Who has more of your personal data than Facebook, The Australian and Wall St Journal, April, 23, 2018; Frank Pasquale (2015) *The Black Box Society: The Secret Algorithms That Control Money and Information*, Cambridge, Massachusetts: Harvard University Press, pp. 50–51;66;78–79;96;185;190–191. 214–215; and for a comprehensive account of the problem, see, Shoshana Zuboff (2019) *The Age of Surveillance Capitalism: The Fight for a Human Future at the New Frontier of Power*, Profile Books.

Foroohar, Rana. 2019. *Don't Be Evil: The Case Against Big Tech*. London: Allen Lane, Random House.

Galloway, Scott. 2017. *The Four: The Hidden DNA of Amazon, Apple, Facebook and Google*. London: Bantam Press.

Lessig, Lawrence. 2013.Institutional Corruptions. *Edward J. Safra Working Papers* 1.

Milkman, Oliver. 2019. Defiant Mark Zuckerberg defends Facebook policy to allow false ads. *The Guardian*, December 2, 2019.

Miller, Seumas. 2018. Corruption. Stanford Encyclopedia of Philosophy. (Winter 2018 edition), Edward N. Zalta (ed.).

Miller, Seumas, Peter Roberts, and Edward Spence. 2005. *Corruption and Anti-Corruption: An Applied Philosophical Approach*. Upper Saddle River: Pearson/Prentice Hall.

Mims, Christopher. 2018. Who has more of your personal data than Facebook? *The Australian and Wall St Journal*, April 23, 2018.

Pasquale, Frank. 2015. *The Black Box Society: The Secret Algorithms That Control Money and Information*. Cambridge, MA: Harvard University Press.

———. 2008. Corruption in the Media. *International Journal of Applied Philosophy*. 22:2 – Fall 2008: 231–241.

———. 2009. A Universal Model for the Normative Evaluation of Internet Information. *Ethics and Information Technology* 11 (4): 243–253.

———. 2011. Information, Knowledge and Wisdom: Groundwork for the Normative Evaluation of Digital Information and Its Relation to the Good Life. *Ethics and Information Technology* 13 (3): 261–275.

———. 2014. The Advertising of Happiness and the Branding of Values. In *Business Ethics*, ed. Michael Boylan, 2nd ed. Pearson/Prentice Hall: Upper Saddle River.

———. 2017. Corruption in the Media. In *The Handbook of Business and Corruption: Cross-Sectoral Experiences*, ed. Michael S. Aßländer and Sarah Hudson, 453–480. Bingley: Emerald Group Publishing.

———. 2018. Harm in Media Marketing: The Branding of Values. In *The Handbook of Media Ethics*, ed. Patrick Plaisance, 237–251. Walter de Gruyter GmbH.

———. 2020. The sixth estate: Media corruption in the age of information. *Journal of Information, Communication and Ethics in Society*, Emerald Publishing Limited, 1477996X.

Spence, Edward, Andrew Alexandra, Aaron Quinn, and Anne Dunn. 2011. *Media, Markets and Morals*. Oxford: Wiley-Blackwell.

Thompson, Dennis F. 2013. Two Concepts of Corruption: Individual and Institutional. *Edward J. Safra Working Papers* 16.

Tufekci, Zeynep. 2018a. Facebook's Surveillance Machine, *The New York Times*, March 19, 2018.

———. 2018b. You Tube, The Great Radicalizer. The *New York Times*, March 10, 2018.

Warren, Mark E. 2004. What Does Corruption Mean in a Democracy. *American Journal of Political Science* 48 (2): 328–343.

———. 2006. Political Corruption as Duplicitous Exclusion. *PS: Political Science and Politics* 39 (4): 803–807.

Wikipedia. 2019. https://en.wikipedia.org/wiki/Cambridge_Analytica. Accessed 19 Sept 2019.

Zuboff, Shoshana. 2019. *The Age of Surveillance Capitalism: The Fights for A Human Future At The New Frontier of Power*. London: Profile Books Ltd.

Zuckerberg, Mark. 2019. Four Ideas to Regulate the Internet. *Facebook*, March 30, 2019.

———. 2020. Big Tech Needs More Regulation. *Financial Times*, February 18, 2020.

Chapter 6
Investigative Journalism – The Serum Against the Snake's Bite

O my friend, why do you who are a citizen of the great and mighty and wise city of Athens, care so much about laying up the greatest amount of money and honour and reputation, and so little about wisdom and truth ... Are you not ashamed of this? (Plato, Apology, 1952).

6.1 Introduction

We know of the key cases of media corruption and corruption generally referred to in this book, because they were first exposed through the media, and specifically investigative journalists working in conjunction with whistleblowers and citizen journalists. The media and in particular the legacy media of the fourth Estate in the form of investigative journalism working in some cases in conjunction with the fifth Estate that together constitute the *convergent media* (Elliott and Spence 2018, Chapter 6) has proved over a long period of time, to be one of the most consistently effective anti-corruption measure in informing the public of different types of corruption, such as political, financial, sport, and police corruption, as well as corruption in the clergy and the media.

However, although the media reports and exposes cases that have been identified and analysed in this book as types of *media corruption*, such cases though recognized as cases involving unethical and illegal practices, such as the *News of the World* scandal, are not normally referred to or described in those investigations as types of *media corruption*. That might partly explain the plethora of academic books and journal articles on *media ethics* but a distinct lack of books on *media corruption*.

Unlike examples of exposures of political corruption, such as the exposure of the Watergate scandal of the early 1970s by the *Washington Post* journalists, Bob Woodward and Carl Bernstein, the exposure in the 1950s of U.S. Senator Joseph McCarthy's zealous witch-hunts of alleged communists by the legendary journalist Edward R. Murrow, the exposure of police and political corruption in the State of

E. H. Spence, *Media Corruption in the Age of Information*, Library of Public Policy and Public Administration 15, https://doi.org/10.1007/978-3-030-61612-0_6

Queensland in the 1980s, by the Australian veteran journalist Chris Masters, and more recently the reporting of the *Panama Papers* financial and offshore tax corruption by the *International Consortium of Investigative Journalists (ICIJ)* and that of the Cambridge Analytica case in 2016 by *The Guardian* and *New York Times*, as well as the exposure of the Commonwealth Bank corruption by the *Sydney Morning Herald* in Australia in 2014, media corruption by contrast although often exposed and reported by the media, is not presented or understood by the public, the media and media academics, as another form of *corruption*. This is largely because the concept of media corruption as such has not received the philosophical attention it deserves.

Using the metaphorical analogy of Socrates as the first investigative journalist (Spence et al. 2011), the chapter will demonstrate the crucial importance that investigative journalism still plays in the exposure of corruption. This chapter will also examine how the symbiotic relationship between the fourth and fifth Estates working together in conjunction expose and report on global corruption. This is a welcome and major development and paradigm shift on how that symbiotic relationship between the corporate investigative journalists of the fourth Estate and the citizen journalists of the fifth Estate, as well as whistleblowers, such as Julian Assange, Chelsea Manning and Edward Snowden, and before them many others such as Daniel Ellsberg, Frank Serpico and Katharine Dunn, together with the collective voices of social media in their role of *bearing witness*, valiantly expose major and worldwide instances of corruption.

If corruption exists in the media the media itself in the form of the fourth and fifth Estates can be an effective anti-corruption measure in exposing media corruption, as *corruption,* as it does with other forms of corruption, be it police, financial or political corruption. This is of crucial importance at a time when, as we examined in Chap. 5, very powerful and influential tech companies such as Facebook and Google operating in essence as media companies, under the guise of a normatively neutral 'platform', engage in media corruption.

6.2 Key Cases of Corruption Exposed and Reported by Investigative Journalists

Two notable cases of corruption that attracted worldwide attention in 2016 and continue to do so in 2020, were those of the *Panama Papers* and *Cambridge Analytical*. Both were exposed and reported by investigative journalists. The first involved widespread financial and offshore tax corruption on a global scale. The second, as we examined in Chap. 5, constituted information and media corruption, which extended to political and civic corruption. This section of the chapter will highlight some of the most notable and impactful cases of institutional corruption exposed and reported by investigative journalists across a span of more than seventy years: from the *Edward R. Murrow v. Senator McCarthy* case of the 1950's and the *Serpico* case of the 1960's involving police corruption, to the *Panama Papers* and the *Cambridge Analytical* cases of 2016 and their ongoing repercussions in 2019–2020. One of those repercussions in the case of the Panama Papers investigation, was the murder of Malta's celebrated investigative journalist, Daphne Caruana Galizia, in 2017, which led to the resignation of Malta's Prime Minister Joseph Muscat in January 2020. Described as a "one-woman WikiLeaks" Daphne Caruana Galizia's investigative blog had alerted the Panama Papers investigation by the *International Consortium of Investigative Journalists (ICIJ)*, of corruption in Malta (Juliette Garside 2017).

6.3 2016–2020

6.3.1 Panama Papers

The following is a documented summary of the case from information obtained from *Wikipedia* (https://en.wikipedia.org/wiki/Panama_Papers – accessed 12 February 2020), and corroborated by various articles from *The Guardian* (2016–2019), which played a key part in the investigation of that case by the *International Consortium of Investigative Journalists (ICIJ)* and its subsequent exposure and reporting (Garside et al. 2016a, b).

6.3.1.1 Summary

The Panama Papers comprise leaked documents that provide details of financial information of offshore entities created in tax havens across the world. The documents were created by Mossack Fonseca, a law firm operating out of Panama. The documents contain personal financial information about wealthy individuals and public officials that had previously been kept private. Although offshore business entities are legal, journalists who viewed the leaked documents found that some of the shell corporations created by Mossack Fonseca were used for illegal purposes that included fraud, tax evasion, and the avoidance of international sanctions. The documents comprising the Panama Papers were leaked by the whistleblower 'Joe Doe', to the German journalist Bastian Obermayer from the newspaper Suddeutsche Zeitung (SZ). 'Joe Doe' remains anonymous, even to the journalists who worked on the investigation. The documents comprising the Panama Papers were posted in full on its website by the *International Consortium of Investigative Journalists* (ICIJ) that carried out the investigation. *SZ* sought help from the ICIJ due to the large amount of data involved. Journalists from 107 media organizations in 80 countries analyzed the documents detailing the operations of the law firm. The first news stories about the Panama Papers were published in April 3, 2016, along with 150 of the documents themselves, after more than a year of investigation.

6.3.2 Cambridge Analytica

Having examined in some detail the normative issues of that case in Chap. 5, and in particular Facebook's involvement in that controversy, this section will only describe in outline the crucial role of investigative journalists and whistleblowers in its exposure.

6.3.2.1 Summary

For over a year, beginning in 2017 *The Guardian* and the *Observer* with information provided by insider whistleblowers employed by Cambridge Analytica, published a series of articles titled the *Cambridge Analytica Files* documenting in great detail how Cambridge Analytica harvested the profiles of 87 million Facebook users, which then used to target voters with personalized political advertisements, in both the 2016 U.S. Presidential election and the UK Brexit Referendum. Central to that investigation was *The Guardian* investigative journalist Carole Cadwalladr and the insider whistleblowers, Christopher Wylie and later Brittany Kaiser, who starred in a Netflix documentary *The Great Hack*, which aired in 2020. The investigation led to the closure of Cambridge Analytica (Carole Cadwalladr 2018).

6.3.2.2 Analysis

The key features of the aforementioned two cases relevant to all the other key cases that follow, are:

1. The crucial role of the *investigative journalists* of the legacy media of the fourth Estate and citizen journalists of the fifth Estate, in exposing and reporting unethical and illegal practices, involving corruption.
2. The role of *whistleblowers*, in the case of the Panama Papers "John Doe" who leaked the documents to the journalist, Bastian Obermayer from the newspaper *Suddeutsche Zeitung* (*SZ*), and in the case of Cambridge Analytica, Christopher Wylie and later Brittany Kaiser, who provided inside information to *The Guardian*.
3. As in the Cambridge Analytica case and other cases of institutional corruption cited in this section, sometimes the corruption consisted of *corruption by collusion* and a *conflict of interest*, expressed as we saw in Facebook's part in the Cambridge Analytica controversy, as a *conflict of roles*. A simple example we saw earlier in Chap. 4 is that of advertorials that involves media corruption by collusion between advertisers, public relations consultants, and journalists. In the Panama Papers case, it involved a collusion of political and financial corruption in the form of fraud, tax evasion, evasion of international sanctions, and money-laundering. In the case of Cambridge Analytica, it involved collusion between a Big Data science company, Cambridge Analytica, a media company,

Facebook, and political campaign actors in the U.S. Presidential Elections, and the UK Brexit Referendum.

4. The publication of a book on the Panama Papers titled *The Laundromat* by two-time Pulitzer Prize–winning investigative reporter Jake Bernstein, in 2019. A feature film by the same title, based loosely on the book and starring Meryl Strip, Gary Oldman, and Antonio Banderas, that was also screened on *Netflix* in the same year. This is an important feature shared by most of the key cases relating to the exposure and reporting of corruption by investigative journalism as cited in this chapter. It is the exposure of corruption to a much larger worldwide audience through the *creative arts* in the form of feature films, documentaries, and books. The exposure of corruption through the creative arts is significant and important as it has a greater distribution and reach to wider public audiences globally, with extended social impact on crucial matters of public interest. Together with the exposure of corruption by investigative journalists, the creative arts in the form of books, documentaries, and feature films provide a most valuable service to society by informing citizens on issues of public interest, such as corruption, that they might otherwise not have been aware of.

6.3.3 Timeline of Other Notable Cases of Corruption Exposed by Investigative Journalists (1950s–2020s)

In addition to the *Panama Papers* and *Cambridge Analytica* cases examined above, the following is a timeline of other key cases of investigative journalism that illustrate in chronological order, across a span of over seventy years, the exposure and reporting of corruption, including media corruption, by investigative journalists. The purpose of presenting such a timeline is to highlight the continuing importance and significance of investigative journalism as a powerful and effective public measure against institutional corruption, including political, police, judicial, financial, clergy, and media corruption.

Recent efforts of worldwide political manipulation in countries such as the U.S., the UK, the EU, Brazil, the Philippines, and Turkey, to subvert, and in some cases as in Turkey, suppress the media that comprises the fourth and fifth Estates, calls for an urgent and timely reminder why investigative journalism and the media generally is as much needed now as it has been in the past. Given the unprecedented, unequal and unaccountable power of Tech Giants such as Facebook and Google, referred to in this book as the "sixth Estate", the role of investigative journalism in the exposure of corruption, including media corruption, is even more crucial now in the Age of Information and Big Data, dominated by Big Tech companies whose prime aim is amassing profits for themselves at the expense of the common good of society. The attempted political manipulation and control of the media in some Western countries, resembles the tactics employed in countries such as Russia, China, North Korea, and Turkey presently. On occasions, it involves not only the imprisonment but the murder of journalists, as illustrated in the recent cases of Daphne Caruana Galizia in Malta (2017) and Lyra McKee in Northern Ireland (2019). The diachronic timeline of the following key cases, spanning a period of more than seventy years, from the 1950's to the present (2020), emphasizes the crucial importance investigative journalism still plays as an effective accountability and anti-corruption measure; a role it continues to play today, in safeguarding our democratic system and its associated institutions. We begin the timeline with the story of the legendary investigative journalist Edward R. Murrow and his exposure of Senator Joseph McCarthy's witch-hunting tactics, that led to McCarthy's downfall.

6.3.4 Edward R. Murrow (1950s)

6.3.4.1 Summary

"On March 9th, 1954, Murrow—who was then perhaps the country's most highly revered journalist—devoted an entire episode of his CBS program "See it Now" to the words and deeds of Senator Joseph McCarthy, who had already done much to earn his notorious place in history. Using McCarthy's own statements, Murrow painted a picture of a man whose recklessness with the truth and ugly attacks on his critics had contributed to a climate of deep fear and repression in American life. At the end of the show, Murrow turned to the camera and delivered a long monologue, which read, in part:

> *This is no time for men who oppose Senator McCarthy's methods to keep silent, or for those who approve. We can deny our heritage and our history, but we cannot escape responsibility for the result. There is no way for a citizen of a republic to abdicate his responsibilities. As a nation we have come into our full inheritance at a tender age. We proclaim ourselves, as indeed we are, the defenders of freedom, whatever it continues to exist in the world, but we cannot defend freedom abroad by deserting it at home*. (Mirkinson 2014).

The above quoted passage describes one of the most celebrated cases of investigative journalism in the U.S. and more widely across the world by the legendary investigative journalist Edward R. Murrow who spoke up in defense of the truth and what is right, at a time when most people were afraid to do so in case they brought the unfavorable attention of Joseph McCarthy upon themselves. At the present time when investigative journalism has come under attack in countries not guided by ethical principles and the rule of law but political leaders who consider themselves to be above and beyond morality and the law, and equate the truth with 'fake news' that they themselves create and perpetuate, this is a cautionary tale for citizens that still value and care for the truth and for what is right, regardless of their own political affiliations. Socrates who can, at least by analogy, also be considered an investigative journalist, "a gadfly", as he referred to himself, facing death by hemlock, also chose truth and what was right over convenience or fear. Few today, unless they are historians or philosophers, would recall, let alone celebrate, the political leaders of

Socrates' time, but they would know of Socrates, and celebrate his achievements, largely through the dialogues of Plato.

6.3.4.2 Analysis

At least two of the aforementioned four features associated with the public exposure of corruption, in this case political corruption, is the reporting by an investigative journalist, Edward R. Murrow, and the feature film *Good Night and Good Luck* (2005)[1] directed by George Clooney, starring David Strathairn, as Edward R. Murrow. Films, whether documentaries or features, as previously suggested, are an important media vehicle for informing the public of important historical events concerning matters of public interest, especially as in this case, bringing to the attention of contemporary audiences a significant journalistic investigation into political corruption that occurred almost seventy years ago. It is important, for it helps inform and shape our shared and collective historical memory as a society.

6.3.5 Frank Serpico (1970s)

6.3.5.1 Summary

Frank Serpico was a New York City Police officer, best known for his role as a whistleblower in exposing police corruption in the late 1960s and early 1970s. In 1967 he provided credible evidence of widespread systematic police corruption, which was exposed and reported by a *New York Times* front-page article, to which he contributed, and was published on April 25, 1970. It led to an investigation panel known as the *Knapp Commission* that investigated the accusations of police corruption, resulting in reform of the police force.

6.3.5.2 Analysis

The Serpico case into police corruption has three of the aforementioned features associated with the public exposure of corruption. A whistleblower, Frank Serpico, the investigative journalists of the *New York Times*, the feature film *Serpico* of 1973, based on a biography of Frank Serpico by Peter Mass (1973), and the 2017 documentary, *Frank Serpico*, by writer and director Antonio D'Ambrosio, starring Frank

[1] For a critical review of the film see Alex von Tunzelmann (2015) Good Night, and Good Luck: attack on McCarthyism simplifies but satisfies, The Guardian, March 30, 2015. https://www.theguardian.com/film/filmblog/2015/mar/30/ggod-night-and-good-luck-george-clooney-edward-murrow-reel-history. Accessed: April 8, 2020.

Serpico himself. Serpico's fame came largely after the release of the 1973 film *Serpico,* starring Al Pacino in the title role.[2]

6.3.6 *Pentagon Papers (1970s)*

6.3.6.1 Summary

"The Pentagon Papers was the name given to a top-secret Department of Defense study of U.S. political and military involvement in Vietnam from 1945 to 1967. As the Vietnam War dragged on, with more than 500,000 U.S. troops in Vietnam by 1968, military analyst Daniel Ellsberg—who had worked on the study—came to oppose the war, and decided that the information contained in the Pentagon Papers should be available to the American public. He photocopied the report and in March 1971 gave the copy to *The New York Times*, which then published a series of scathing articles based on the report's most damning secrets.

Beginning on June 13, 1971, the *Times* published a series of front-page articles based on the information contained in the Pentagon Papers. After the third article, the U.S. Department of Justice got a temporary restraining order against further publication of the material, arguing that it was detrimental to U.S. national security... In the now-famous case of *New York Times Co. v. United States*, the *Times* and the *Washington Post* joined forces to fight for the right to publish, and on June 3, 1971, the U.S. Supreme Court ruled 6–3 that the government had failed to prove harm to national security, and that publication of the papers was justified under the First Amendment's protection of freedom of the press".

History.com Editors, https://www.history.com/topics/vietnam-war/pentagon-papers. Accessed: 17 February 2020.

6.3.6.2 Analysis

The Pentagon Papers case has at least three of the aforementioned general features of the public exposure of corruption including: the investigative journalists of the *New York Times and the Washington Post*; an insider whistleblower, Daniel Ellsberg; and the wider public exposure of the case through the feature film *The Post* (2017) directed by Steven Spielberg and starring Tom Hanks and Meryl Streep; *The Most Dangerous Man in America*: *Daniel Ellsberg and the Pentagon Papers*, a 2009 documentary directed by Judith Ehrlich and Rick Goldsmith; and *The Pentagon Papers* a 2003 television historical film about Daniel Ellsberg and the events leading up to the publication of the Pentagon Papers in 1971. The film was directed by Rod Holcomb and stars James Spader as Ellsberg.

[2] See the entry on Wikipedia https://en.wikipedia.org/wiki/Frank_Serpico. Accessed: March 17, 2020.

As in the Serpico and Edward R. Marrow cases we examined earlier, as well as most of these illustrative cases of corruption examined in this section, the role played by the *creative arts* in bringing to public attention those cases to international audiences worldwide, was significant. Without it, the exposure of corruption to wider international public audiences, especially subsequently to those events, the wider public might have remained uninformed of such important matters of public interest; matters of crucial importance, which continue to have a lasting significance today in shaping our shared and collective historical memory as citizens, lest we forget. That is the main purpose of including this diachronic timeline of those cases in this chapter: to remind us of the continuing important role that investigative journalism, together with the creative arts, align to inform and guide our collective historical consciousness as a society.

6.3.7 *Watergate (1970s)*

6.3.7.1 Summary

> The Watergate scandal began early in the morning of June 17, 1972, when several burglars were arrested in the office of the Democratic National Committee, located in the Watergate complex of buildings in Washington, D.C. This was no ordinary robbery: The prowlers were connected to President Richard Nixon's re-election campaign, and they had been caught wiretapping phones and stealing documents. Nixon took aggressive steps to cover up the crimes, but when *Washington Post* reporters Bob Woodward and Carl Bernstein revealed his role in the conspiracy, Nixon resigned on August 9, 1974... Their reporting won them a Pulitzer Prize and was the basis for their best-selling book *All The President's Men*. Much of their information came from an anonymous whistleblower they called *Deep Throat*, who in 2005 was revealed to be W. Mark Felt, a former associate director of the FBI.

History.com.au https://www.history.com/topics/1970s/watergate. Accessed: 14 February 2020.

6.3.7.2 Analysis

The Watergate case of political corruption also highlights some of the features of the public exposure of corruption referred to above, namely, a whistleblower, William Mark Felt (known before his real name became known as *Deep Throat*); the role of investigative journalists of the *Washington Post*, Bob Woodward and Carl Bernstein; and a feature film, *All The Presidents Men* (1976) directed by Alan J. Pakula, starring Robert Redford as Bob Woodward and Dustin Hoffman as Carl Bernstein, based on the book, *All The President's Men*: *The Greatest Reporting Story of All Time*, by Carl Bernstein an Bob Woodward (1974). As in the Serpico and Edward R. Marrow cases, as well as the Pentagon Papers case analyzed above, the role played by the *creative arts* in bringing to public attention those cases was significant. Reiterating for emphasis what was said earlier, such important matters of public interest are of crucial importance and continue to have a lasting significance today in shaping our shared and collective historical memory and our collective responsibility as citizens.

6.3.8 The Moonlight State and Police Corruption (1980s)

6.3.8.1 Summary

The Moonlight State was the title of an *ABC Four Corners* program in Australia, screened on the ABC TV Channel in 1987 on the investigation and exposure of police corruption in Queensland, by the legendary Australian investigative journalist, Chris Master that initiated the Fitzgerald Inquiry into police corruption.

Four Corners (1987) https://www.abc.net.au/4corners/the-moonlight-state%2D%2D-1987/2832198. Accessed; April 8, 2020.

6.3.8.2 Analysis

Central to this case as with the other key cases outlined in this section, is the role of investigative journalism and its effectiveness in exposing and reporting corruption; in this case police corruption.

6.3.9 The Boston Globe's Exposure of Church Abuse (2002)

6.3.9.1 Summary

This case is about the exposure of the sexual abuse of children by Catholic priests, by The *Boston Globe's* investigative journalism team, *Spotlight*. The public exposure by *Spotlight* in 2002 led to the expulsion of several priests charged with sexual abuse of children in their care and the resignation of the head of the Boston Archdiocese, Cardinal Bernard Law. The *Spotlight* team with *The Boston Globe* were awarded the 2003 Pulitzer Prize for Public Service (Bradlee 2002).

6.3.9.2 Analysis

Just like the other key cases highlighted in this section, this case concerns the crucial and critical work conducted by investigative journalists in exposing corruption, in this case, corruption of the clergy. This case as in some of the other cases examined earlier, highlight the important contribution of the creative arts in the exposure of corruption to wider international audiences. A feature film, *Spotlight,* of The Boston Globe investigation into sexual abuse of children within the Catholic Church, was screened in 2015. The film was directed by Tom McCarthy and written by McCarthy and Josh Singer, starring Mark Ruffalo, Michael Keaton, Rachel McAdams, John Slattery, and Stanley Tucci. It won several international film awards including the Academy Award for Best Picture and Best Original Screenplay.

6.3.10 Katharine Gun v. UK Government (2003)

6.3.10.1 Summary

This case concerns Katharine Gun, a UK *Government Communications Headquarters (GCHQ)* translator who leaked a secret document of an American plan from the *National Security Agency (NSA)* in 2003 to bug phones and emails of the UN Security Council members in an effort to win votes for a UN resolution in favor of waging war against Iraq. Britain at the time under the leadership of the then Prime Minister, Tony Blair, was in favor of war. As a result, Katharine Gun who confessed to her role in leaking the document was arrested and charged with breaking the Official Secrets Act. The case against her at the trial that followed at the Old Baily in London was eventually dropped by the prosecution representing the UK Government. It prompted speculation that the UK Government wished to avoid its own role in the affair concerning the leaked document being revealed. (Oliver Burkenman and Richard Norton-Taylor (2004); Martin Bright, Ed Vulliamy and Peter Beaumont 2003).

6.3.10.2 Analysis

At least three of the aforementioned features of the public exposure of corruption are present in this case: the exposure conducted by investigative journalists (The Guardian), a whistleblower (Katharine Gun) and not least the wider exposure of the corruption, in this case institutional political corruption, by the feature film *Official Secrets*, a 2019 British-American docudrama based on the life of the whistleblower Katharine Gun. The film was directed by Gavin Hood and starred Keira Knightley as Gun. The other actors were Matt Smith, Matthew Goode, Adam Bakri, Indira Varma and Ralph Fiennes.

6.3.11 News of the World Scandal (2006–2011)

6.3.11.1 Summary

A decade before the hacking scandal involving Cambridge Analytica and Facebook came to light in 2016 through its initial exposure by *The Guardian*, another infamous hacking scandal was exposed in several investigative articles by *The Guardian* and *New York Times* over the period from 2006 to 2011. It concerned the secret hacking of people's mobile phones by staff of the *News of the World* (NOW) newspaper owned by Rupert Murdoch's *News Limited*, who also owns *Fox News* in the USA. The people whose phones conversations were secretly hacked included members of the Royal family, celebrities, actors, and politicians and that of the murdered girl Milly Dowler, that shocked the nation and prompted Rupert Murdoch to close down the newspaper in 2011. The final front-page of the paper declared, "Thank you and goodbye" (The BBC, 4 August 2012).

The investigations of the phone-hacking scandal raised critical questions in the press and parliament about the close relationship of the Metropolitan Police handling the criminal investigation and the journalists of *News of the World*, which led to the resignation of the Metropolitan Commissioner, Sir Paul Stephenson, as well as that of the Assistant Commissioner, John Yates. The editor of the *News of the World*, Andy Coulson who also quit his post following the investigation of the hacking scandal was later employed by the Prime Minister, David Cameron, as his media advisor, for which he faced some question concerning his judgement over Coulson's appointment. Another major repercussion that followed the closing down of the News of the World was the *Leveson Inquiry*, conducted by Lord Justice Leveson that examined "the culture, practices and ethics" of the UK press and its relationship with police and politicians (The BBC, 4 August 2012).

6.3.11.2 Analysis

This case, as the other cited key cases in this section, highlight the common features they all have in common: the public exposure of corruption by the media, and in particular the legacy media in the form of the fourth Estate. The primary role as usual in all those key cases is that of the investigative journalists, in this case of *The Guardian* and the *New York Times*. Fist to expose the *News of the World* phone-hacking scandal was Nick Davies, an investigative journalist of *The Guardian*. According to an interview of Nick Davies by the *Yorkshire Post* on the occasion of the publication of his book *Hack Attack: How the Truth Caught Up with Rupert Murdoch* (2014), the investigation into the News of the World Scandal took up six years of his life (The Yorkshire Post 2014). In that interview Davies refers to "an unhealthy alliance between certain sectors of the press, the police and Westminster". He went to conclude that he is,

> 'not optimistic about the future, and part of the problem is that we have allowed democratic power to move away from the people and into the hands of small groups who have tremendous financial and political power'.

It would be interesting to hear what Nick Davies has to say about the events that occurred in the Cambridge Analytica scandal and Facebook's part, and how that might have influenced the U.S. Presidential elections and the UK Brexit Referendum to leave the EU, in 2016.

6.3.12 Banking Bad: Banking Misconduct Investigation (2014–2019)

6.3.12.1 Summary

This is a case involving financial corruption by one of the biggest banks of Australia, the *Commonwealth Bank of Australia (CBA).* The case was first exposed and reported by the Fairfax investigative journalist Adele Ferguson on May 5, 2014 on the *ABC Four Corners*, weekly investigative journalism program, and presented by the journalist Kerry O'Brien. It tells the story of how many ordinary Australian citizens took legal action against the CBA and won. It led to a *Royal Commission into Misconduct in the Banking, Superannuation and Financial Services Industry* in Australia. The case concerns the financial planning division of CBA that has been described as "a profit at all cost – a culture that has been built on commissions". The Four Corners investigation exposed the rogue practices of CBA financial planners whose profit-motivated advice to their CBA retiree clients resulted in the loss of their life savings (*Banking Bad*, a joint Four Corners Fairfax investigation reported by Adele Ferguson and presented by Kerry O'Brien, May 5, 2014).

6.3.12.2 Analysis

Just as the other cases cited in this chapter, this case into financial corruption by one of the leading banks of Australia, the Commonwealth Bank of Australia (CBA), highlights the common features of its public exposure. The leading role of investigative journalists, Adele Ferguson, in her reporting in the *ABC Four Corners* program; the role of an insider whistleblower; and the wider publicity of the case through a publication of a book by Adele Ferguson, *Banking Bad* (2019) by ABC Books. Echoing Edward R. Murrow' words from the past, of speaking up for the truth and what is right, Ferguson's dedication in her book is particularly poignant and significant: *To those who choose not to stay silent.* At a time when political leaders around the world attempt to silence journalists, Adele Ferguson's words, jut as those of Edward R. Murrow's seventy years ago, are a timely reminder to those who still value truth and what is right in accordance with public ethical principles and values and the rule of democratic laws, not to remain silent.

6.4 Conclusion

This chapter has sought to demonstrate the crucial importance investigative journalism plays as an effective *anti-corruption* measure in exposing and reporting corruption, including media corruption, and how the symbiotic relationship between the fourth and fifth Estates contributes to the exposure and reporting of global corruption. This is a welcome and major paradigm shift on how this symbiotic relationship between the legacy investigative journalists of the fourth Estate and the citizen journalists of the fifth Estate, as well as whistleblowers, such as Julian Assange, Chelsea Manning, and Edward Snowden, and before them many others such as Daniel Ellsberg, Frank Serpico and Katharine Dunn. Together with the collective voices of social media in their role of *bearing witness*, they have valiantly exposed major and worldwide instances of corruption, as the historical timeline of key cases in this chapter, spanning a period of over seventy years, illustrates.

If corruption exists in the media, the media itself in the form of the convergent media of the fourth and fifth Estates can also become an effective regulative measure in exposing media corruption, as it does with other forms of corruption, such as political, financial, sports corruption etc. This is of crucial importance when very powerful and influential tech companies such as Facebook and Google, operating in essence as a media companies, under the guise of normatively neutral 'platforms', engage in media corruption.

Aligned closely to the public's right to information is the role of investigative journalists. Socrates, a philosopher from Athens (469–399 BCE), was probably the first investigative journalist. Socrates, just as contemporary investigative journalists, sought diligently to uncover the truth. According to the Oracle of Delphi he was also the wisest. Being accused of "being irreverent to the gods and corrupting the youth of Athens," he told the court at his trial that like a "gadfly," his mission was to engage his fellow citizens in debate on matters of virtue, truth, and wisdom. He was sentenced to death by hemlock for his troubles. In his closing speech to the jurors, he reprimanded his fellow citizens for caring more about money and reputation than about morality and knowledge:

> O my friend, why do you who are a citizen of the great and mighty and wise city of Athens, care so much about laying up the greatest amount of money and honour and reputation, and so little about wisdom and truth … Are you not ashamed of this? (Plato 1952)

Since Socrates, many good and worthy journalists have followed in his footsteps. These include, among many others, the legendary U.S. journalist Edward R. Murrow who took on Joseph McCarthy in the 1950s and won at a time when most walked in fear of McCarthy; the respected Australian journalist Chris Masters, who exposed wholesale police corruption in Queensland in the 1980s; and journalists who, like Socrates, paid with their lives for informing the public of what they thought the public had a right to know: Irish journalist Veronica Guerin (1958–1996) and Russian journalist Anna Politkovskaya (1958–2006); and more recently (1964–2017) Daphne Caruana Galizia the Maltese blogger-journalist murdered for her part in the Panama Papers investigation of corruption in Malta (Garside, Juliette, 2019a, b), as well as Lyra Catherine McKee (1990–2019) a journalist from Belfast, Northern Ireland, whose investigation of the "Troubles"[3] concerning the violent sectarian inter-communal conflict between the Protestants and the Catholics during that led to her murder.

Those journalists, whether consciously or not, shared Socrates's unshakeable conviction that truth and what is right is the bloodline of a free democracy. Just as for present-day democracies, the dissemination of information to the public on matters of public interest, espoused in journalistic codes of ethics, as the right of the public to know, was seen to be essential. It provides justification for the claim that the public has a right to know what the government is doing in its name.

Members of the public have that right in view of the fact that citizens are part of the democratic process and must therefore have the necessary information to enable them to participate, at least in principle if not always in practice, in the deliberations carried out on *their behalf* by their elected representatives. That conviction is also expressed in Australia's *Media and Entertainment Arts Alliance* (MEAA) journalism code of ethics, which states that,

> "respect for truth and the public's right to information are fundamental principles of journalism." Similar principles are also enunciated by the code of ethics of the International Federation of Journalists (IFJ), which declares that "respect for truth and for the right of the public to truth is the first duty of the journalist". https://www.meaa.org/meaa-media/code-of-ethics/

The following quoted passage, mentioned earlier in this chapter, is worth repeating in full as an appropriate statement to the conclusion of this chapter. As we saw earlier, it describes one of the most celebrated cases of investigative journalism in the U.S. and more widely across the world by the legendary investigative journalist Edward R. Murrow who spoke up in defense of the truth and what is right, at a time when most people were afraid to do so in case they attracted the unfavorable attention of Joseph McCarthy upon themselves. Similarly, Socrates' quoted passage above also exemplifies the same defiant spirit of Edward R. Murrow in the relentless pursuit of the truth and what is right without fear or favor. Although Socrates lived almost 2500 years ago in the City of Athens, described as the cradle of democracy, his defiant spirit for what is right and true while facing death, still survives and persists to this day through the tireless work of investigative journalists, as illustrated in this chapter.

> This is no time for men who oppose Senator McCarthy's methods to keep silent, or for those who approve. We can deny our heritage and our history, but we cannot escape responsibility for the result. There is no way for a citizen of a republic to abdicate his responsibilities. As a nation we have come into our full inheritance at a tender age. We proclaim ourselves, as indeed we are, the defenders of freedom, whatever it continues to exist in the world, but we cannot defend freedom abroad by deserting it at home (Mirkinson, Jack 2014).

---

[3]The "Troubles" concerns a violent sectarian conflict from 1968 to 1998 in Northern Ireland between the Protestant unionists or loyalists who wished the province to remain part of the United Kingdom and the Roman Catholic nationalists or republicans who wanted Northern Ireland to become part of the Republic of Ireland.

At the present time when investigative journalism has come under attack in countries not guided by ethical principles and the rule of law, at least not in practice, but by the self-interests of political leaders who consider themselves to be above and beyond morality and the law, this is a cautionary tale for citizens that still value and care for the truth and what is right, regardless of their own political affiliations. Adele Ferguson's dedication "*To those who choose not to stay silent*" in her book *Banking Bad* (2019), is a worthy and appropriate acknowledgement to all those courageous and dedicated investigative journalists referred to in this chapter as well as many others, who chose not to remain silent but speak out for what is truthful and right even, like Socrates, at the cost of their own lives.

References

ABC, Four Corners. 1987. *The Moonlight State*. https://www.abc.net.au/4corners/the-moonlight-state%2D%2D-1987/2832198. Accessed 8 Apr 2020.

BBC. 2012. *Q&A: News of the World phone-hacking scandal.* 4 August 2012. https://www.bbc.com/news/uk-11195407. Accessed 2 July 2020.

Bernstein, Carl, and Bob Woodward. 1974. *All The President's Men: The Greatest Reporting Story pf All Time*. New York: Simon & Schuster Paperbacks.

Bradlee B. Jr. 2002. Deputy Managing Editor. Betrayal: The Crisis in the Catholic Church, by the investigative staff of The *Boston Globe*, May 10, 2002.

Bright, Martin, Vulliamy, Ed., and Beaumont, Peter. 2003. Revealed: U.S. dirty tricks to win vote on Iraq War. *The Guardian*, 2 March 2003.

Burkenman, Oliver, and Norton-Taylor, Richard. 2004. The spy who wouldn't keep a secret. *The Guardian,* 26 February 2004.

Cadwalladr, Carole. 2018. 'I made Steve Bannon's psychological warfare tool': meet the data war whistleblower. *The Guardian, March* 18: 2018.

Davies, Nick. 2014. *Hack Attack: How the Truth Caught Up with Rupert Murdoch*. New York: Farrar, Status and Giroux.

Elliott, Deni, and Edward Spence. 2018. *Ethics for a Digital Era*. Oxford: Wiley-Blackwell. Chapter 6.

Ferguson, Adele. 2014. Banking Bad, a joint *Four Corners Fairfax* investigation reported by Adele Ferguson and presented by Kerry O'Brien, May 5, 2014.

———. 2019. *Banking Bad: Whistleblowers. Corporate cover-ups. One journalist's fight for the truth*. ABC Books.

Garside, Juliette. 2017. Malta car bomb kills Panama Papers journalist. *The Guardian*, October 17, 2017.

———. 2019a. Maltese businessman charged over murder of investigative journalist, *The Guardian*, December 1, 2019.

———. 2019b. How a dog called Peter sparked Malta's political crisis. *The Guardian*. November 30, 2019.

Garside, Juliette, Harding, Luke, Watt, Holly, Pegg, David, Bengtsson, Helena, Bowers, Simon, Gibson, Owen and Hopkins, Nick. 2016a. Mossack Fonseca: inside the firm that helps the super-rich hide their money. *The Guardian*, April 8, 2016.

Garside, Juliette, Watt, Holly, and Pegg, David. 2016b. The Panama Papers: how the world's rich and famous hide their money offshore. *The Guardian*, April 4, 2016.

History.com Editors. 2020. *The Pentagon Papers*. https://www.history.com/topics/vietnam-war/pentagon-papers. Accessed 17 Feb 2020.

History.com.Editors. 2020. *Watergate*. https://www.history.com/topics/1970s/watergate. Accessed 14 Feb 2020.

Media and Entertainment Arts Alliance (MEAA). 2020. *Journalism Code of Ethics, Australia*. https://www.meaa.org/meaa-media/code-of-ethics/. Accessed 29 Mar 2020.

Mirkinson, Jack. 2014. 60 Years Ago, Edward R. Murrow Took Down Joseph McCarthy. *The Huffington Post*, March 11, 2004. https://www.huffingtonpost.com.au/entry/edward-murrow-joseph-mccarthy-60-years-later_n_4936308?ri18n=true. Accessed 8 Apr 2020.

Plato. 1952. *Apology, translated, Benjamin Jowett*. Chicago: Encyclopedia Britannica, Inc. and University of Chicago.

Spence, Edward, Andrew Alexandra, Aaron Quinn, and Anne Dunn. 2011. *Media, Markets and Morals*. Oxford: Wiley- Blackwell.

The Newsroom, *Yorkshire Post*. 2014. Reporter who exposed the phone-hacking scandal. 15 October 2014.

Tunzelmann Alex von. 2015. Good Night, and Good Luck: attack on McCarthyism simplifies but satisfies. *The Guardian*, March 30, 2015. https://www.theguardian.com/film/filmblog/2015/mar/30/ggod-night-and-good-luck-george-clooney-edward-murrow-reel-history. Accessed 8 Apr 2020.

Wikipedia. 2020a. *Panama Papers*. https://en.wikipedia.org/wiki/Panama_Papers. Accessed 12 Feb 2020.

———. 2020b. *Frank Serpico*. https://en.wikipedia.org/wiki/Frank_Serpico. Accessed 17 Mar 2020.

Chapter 7
Public Policy and Regulative Change to Combat Media Corruption

People need to feel that global technology platforms answer to someone, so regulation should hold companies accountable when they make mistakes.

Mark Zuckerberg (2020). Big Tech Needs More Regulation, Financial Times.

7.1 Introduction

In this chapter questions of systemic changes in policy and legislation as well as issues of self-regulation and government regulation in combating corruption and media corruption specifically, will be examined and anti-corruption solutions explored in effectively responding to the challenge of media corruption in the information age.

In Chap. 6, we examined how investigative journalism has proved an effective anti-corruption measure in exposing and informing the public of corruption, such as political, financial, corporate, police and not least, media corruption. The outline of the role of investigative journalists and whistleblowers in the exposure and reporting of corruption has been demonstrated in that chapter by illustrative key cases spanning a period of over seventy years. As a vital part of the media in the form of the fourth and fifth Estates, investigative journalism continues its vital mission as the vanguard of democracy of holding governments, institutions, and corporations, both private and public across a wide spectrum of society, to account.

It is no exaggeration to say that without a free and accountable media, democratic states with a longstanding tradition of respect for the law and ethical principles and values, would not be able to function effectively for the common good of citizens. If the first casualty of war is the truth, the media, in the form of the fourth and fifth Estates, perceived and expected to be the champions of truth, is the second casualty. We have witnessed throughout history as well as currently in some seemingly democratic countries, how powerful politicians or 'strongmen' while

E. H. Spence, *Media Corruption in the Age of Information*, Library of Public Policy and Public Administration 15, https://doi.org/10.1007/978-3-030-61612-0_7

appearing to act for the common good of their countries, act more like oligarchs or despots, in pursuit of their own self-interests. To that end, they have vigorously attacked and tried to subdue and silence any criticism by the media, often through outright lies and misinformation in total disregard for the truth.

As we saw in Chap. 6 the exposure and reporting of corruption by investigative journalists, often with the help of whistleblowers and citizen journalists, has led in some instances to government investigations resulting in regulation, as illustrated by the following key cases examined in Chap. 6:

- *The Serpico* case led to the *Knapp Commission* in 1970 and the investigation of corruption within the New York City Police Department following the testimony of police detective, Frank Serpico, and the exposure of the corruption by the *New York Times*. The commission confirmed the existence of widespread police corruption and made a number of recommendations that resulted to changes within the police force.
- *The Moonlight State* case involving the exposure of police and political corruption in Queensland, Australia, by the investigative journalist Chris Masters in 1987 on the *ABC Four Corners* program led to the *Fitzgerald Inquiry* into police corruption. That inquiry also resulted in recommendations and changes within the Queensland police force.
- *The Boston Globe's Exposure of Church Abuse* case in 2002 that following the exposure and reporting by the *Spotlight* investigative journalism team of The *Boston Globe* led to wide-ranging changes within the Catholic Church in Boston.
- *The Newbs of the World Scandal* that as a result of the investigation and exposure of media corruption by investigative journalists of *The Guardian*, led to the *Leveson Inquiry* in 2011, a judicial and public inquiry into the culture, practices and ethics of the British press.
- Last but not least, the *Banking Bad: Banking Misconduct Investigation* case, that following the exposure of financial and banking corruption in Australia by the Fairfax journalist Adele Ferguson on *ABC Four Corners* in 2014, led to the *Royal Commission into Misconduct in the Banking, Superannuation and Financial Services Industry* in 2017–2019, that resulted in regulative changes in the banking industry in Australia.

The aforementioned examples, spanning a period of over fifty years, demonstrate the effectiveness and crucial importance of a free and independent media for exposing and bringing corruption to public notice through investigative journalism. As a result, it has informed and motivated the instigation of government intervention through judicial and public inquiry, resulting in measures against institutional corruption, including regulation.

7.2 The Regulation of Media Corruption and Other Normative Misdemeanors

Following the exposure of Facebook's part in the Cambridge Analytica hack by *The Guardian,* Facebook was fined £500,000 GBP by the *Information Commissioner's Office (ICO)*, which Facebook agreed to pay in 2019.

Because Cambridge Analytica's data protection violations occurred in 2015, before the implementation of the EU's *General Data Protection Regulation* (GDPR) in 2018, the ICO was only able to impose the maximum fine of £500,000 GBP. Had the data breach occurred after the implementation of GDPR by the EU in May 2018, the potential fine would have been much higher, of up to 4% of Facebook's annual turnover. In imposing the fine, ICO's deputy commissioner, James Dipple-Johnstone stated that ICO's main concern was that 'UK citizen data was exposed to a serious risk of harm' and that,

> Protection of personal information and personal privacy is of fundamental importance, not only for the rights of individuals, but also as we now know, for the preservation of a strong democracy....with this strong commitment to protecting people's personal information and privacy, we expect that Facebook will be able to move forward and learn from the events of this case. (Hern 2019).

Following the ICO ruling, Harry Kinmonth, the lawyer representing Facebook, confirmed the ICO's concerns about privacy and data protection by saying that,

> Protecting people's information and privacy is a top priority for Facebook, and we are continuing to build new controls to help people protect and manage their information (Hern 2019).

As we saw in Chap. 6, Facebook was also imposed a record-breaking $US5 billion fine by the U.S. *Federal Trade Commission (FTC)* the largest penalty ever imposed on a company for violating consumers' privacy rights, eclipsing the $US22 million fine imposed on Google in 2012. Under the settlement, after an investigation prompted by the Cambridge Analytica scandal that was exposed and reported by The *Guardian* and the *New York Times*, Facebook agreed to expand its privacy protections across Facebook, as well as on Instagram and WhatsApp. Facebook must also maintain a data security program, which includes protections of users' information (Snider and Baig 2019; Kang 2019).

More recently in 2020, the information and privacy commissioner of Australia has launched legal action against Facebook over Facebook's part in the Cambridge Analytica scandal, for breaching Australian law in compromising the personal information of more than 300, 000 Australian users. In a statement, the commissioner Angelene Falk of the *Office of the Australian Information Commissioner* said that 311,127 Australian users of Facebook had their data "exposed to be sold and used for purposes including political profiling, well outside users' expectations". In support of the commissioner, Rod Sims the chair of the *Australian Competition and Consumer Commission* (*ACCC*) acknowledged that the Cambridge Analytica breach was a "major problem" and welcomed the commissioner's action (Hunter and Samios 2020). As we shall see later in this chapter, the *Australian Competition and Consumer Commission* (ACCC) took its own court action against Google in October 2019 for misleading customers about its use of personal data. That case is still pending.

Fast-forward to 2020, and Mark Zuckerberg has announced that Facebook will not ban political ads, defending his decision on the grounds that Facebook will 'stand up for free expression', defending that decision "because in order to be trusted, people need to know what you stand for" (Helmore 2020). Free expression and free speech are indeed valuable features of democracy with the crucial proviso, however, that free expression does not cause harm and is always balanced with the moral right to *freedom from harm*; a harm that, as in the Cambridge Analytica case, comes through misinformation, disinformation and disregard for the truth in violation of the privacy and autonomy as well as the wellbeing of Facebook's users; and generally, the infringement of the democratic rights of citizens that are also undermined, as illustrated in Chap. 5 when examining the epistemic, ethical and eudaimonic violations by Facebook in the Cambridge Analytica case.

As examined in the normative analysis of Facebook's part in the Cambridge Analytica case in Chap. 5, the problem with Facebook's position of not adequately and effectively gatekeeping and monitoring misinformation and fake news on its platform, is the conflict of interest that lies at the heart of its operations: the inherent conflict between its role as a media company and its business model of making huge profits from advertising revenue, and in this case, political advertising. Given that for every 'click' Facebook makes money, and the more user clicks the more money Facebook makes, then from a purely financial consideration, it would seem not to matter much to Facebook if the information on which those 'clicks' and 'likes' is based, is true or false. As Rana Foroohar correctly observes (2019: 235),

> Their [Facebook's] model dictated that whatever content resulted in the most clicks, and thus the most revenue, for the platform would win the day, even if that content was designed to manipulate voters or fan flames of racism and hate. It speaks to how much Facebook—as well as the other major platform firms—has to lose.[1]

Instrumentally at least, but of course not ethically, misinformation or disinformation is just as profitable for Facebook as reliable and true information. As in the case of advertorials and political propaganda we examined in Chap. 4, falsehoods can be financially more profitable when *persuasion* for self-interest is perceived to be more effective than *factual information*. If Facebook's priority is to maximize profits, and the monetization of information is at the core of its business model, ethical consequences resulting in harm to its users and society generally through misinformation as well as the users' violation of privacy rights, takes second place at best. Fines

[1] Interestingly, and perhaps not unexpectedly, having perhaps learned their ethical lesson from their role in the Cambridge Analytica scandal, Facebook, following Twitter's example of censoring some of President Trump's tweets on the basis that they constituted misinformation, Facebook has also recently (June 2020) removed certain of Trump's political ads on the basis that they contained symbols used by the Nazis and as such constituted organized hate that violated Facebook's policies (Tucker and Ortutay 2020).

alone cannot fix the problem. Facebook and the other tech companies such as Google, need to adopt an ethical culture *proactively* and openly within their corporate structures that respects peoples' rights to privacy and autonomy through transparent and accountable measures that protect users' data.

As illustrated by the Cambridge Analytica case examined in Chap. 5, misinformation through fake news and fake videos, as well as violations of citizens' privacy and autonomy undermine democracy itself. For that reason the responsibility of ensuring the epistemic, ethical and eudaimonic integrity of users' data collected and mediated through the tech companies' platforms and the various apps attached to those platforms, is a *collective responsibility* that should be shared by the whole of society: The tech companies, especially the Big Tech companies such as Facebook, Alphabet-Google, Amazon, Apple and Microsoft, the government and its agencies as both regulators and users and developers of information platforms, the market actors with access to platform users' information for commercial purposes, and importantly, civil society actors who disseminate and communicate information on platforms such as Facebook and Google.

As in the case of climate change that affects all of us as a global community, and to which we all contribute to various degrees by our consumer practices and choices and should therefore share a common responsibility, we are analogously equally responsible for protecting and safeguarding the epistemic, ethical and eudaimonic integrity of the infosphere. As demonstrated in Chap. 6, the normative principles and requirements of the Dual Obligation Information Theory (DOIT) apply universally and globally to all disseminators and users of information and its communication. As examined earlier, investigative journalism whose role is the exposure and reporting of media corruption and corruption generally, has proved an effective measure against corruption in informing the public of its occurrence as well as motivating its ongoing regulation. In this section of the chapter, we will examine the shared responsibility all stakeholders have in protecting and safeguarding the normative integrity of information and its communication on the internet that includes Tech companies, Government, Market Actors, and Citizens as users and contributors of information.

In a recent book, *The Platform Society: Public Values in a Connected World* (Van Dijck, Poell and De Waal 2018), the authors argue persuasively that the 'platformization' of society, especially through the activities of the Big Tech companies, 'requires an integral approach in defending consumers' and citizens' rights'. They correctly observe that "the current platform ecosystem is predicated on an architecture that is primarily staked in, and driven by, economic values and corporate interests" (Chap. 7, p.139). This observation confirms and further highlights the basic normative problem with Facebook's role in the Cambridge Analytica case that we identified in Chap. 5; namely, as an inherent conflict of interest between its business model and its role as a media company that renders that conflict conducive to systemic media corruption. For it tends to favor Facebook's economic interests over those of its users' rights to the privacy and security of their data. Such a conflict of interest can also be generalized to apply, in principle at least, to all tech companies, such as Google, for example, whose economic interests also tend to override at times the ethical and legal rights of users, competitors and society generally. In 2017, for example, the European Union's antitrust regulator fined Alphabet-Google a record €2.42 billion ($US2.71 billion), for unfairly favoring, through its search engine, its own services (i.e. Google Shopping) over those of rivals (Drozdiak and Schenchner 2017).

The fundamental problem of the global platformization of societies by the Big Tech companies such as Facebook, Google, Amazon, Apple and Microsoft, is that their significant monopolistic power spreading across most public and market sectors of society and the infrastructural services they offer, makes our societies increasingly dependable on those tech companies and their platforms (Van Dijck, Poell, and De Waal 2018, p.147). As we saw in the Cambridge Analytica case such power when is not adequately transparent, accountable and responsive to ethical principles and social values, nor adequately regulated by government and its subsidiary professional and legal agencies and institutions, democracy itself is at risk of being undermined and citizens harmed. Adequate regulation of the Big Tech companies is therefore of paramount importance to ensure that risk is minimized by making the Big Tech complies more transparent, accountable and ethically and legally responsible for their policies and practices.

Central to the economic dominance exercised by the platforms of the Big Tech companies over society, especially our informational and social transactions, such as those we share daily on Facebook and Google, is the business models of those tech companies. The clickbait of users generates billions of dollars annually for companies such as Facebook and Google but with little or no transparency of the underlying business models and the algorithms that run them. The capture, storage and selling of user's data, often without their consent occurs without transparency and public accountability resulting as we saw in the case of Facebook's role in Cambridge Analytica, to media corruption, to which Facebook's business model was conducive. Given the *information asymmetry* that exists between the tech companies and their users,[2] it wouldn't be unreasonable to expect the tech companies to be more transparent and accountable to their users on how, in general, on the basis of their business models and opaque algorithms, their monetization schemes of capturing, storing and selling of users' data work. That might also help explain to their users how fake news and misinformation arrives in their information streams (Van Dijck, Poell, and De Waal 2018, p. 144).

[2] For a more extensive discussion of *information asymmetry* and its causes and contexts see Pasquale (2015), Zuboff (2019) and Foroohar (2019).

7.3 The Articulation and Rationale of Public Ethical Principles and Values

Just as technology shapes society, society can and ought to shape technology. After all technology has been created and advanced for the good of humanity. Underlying the political, economic, the market and media institutions of society, is the *Social Contract*, that at least since Plato (*Republic*, 359a and 359b), and later in the 17th and 18th centuries, Thomas Hobbes (*Leviathan*, 1651), John Locke (*Two Treatises of Civil Government*, 1689), Jean-Jacques Rousseau (*The Social Contract*, 1762) and more recently in the twentieth century, David Gauthier (*Morals by Agreement*, 1986) and John Rawls (*A Theory of Justice*, 1971), counsels us through rational arguments to strive for the common good of society as a whole. Although expressed differently by those philosophers the central idea all share in common, is that of the moral equality as individuals. As individual citizens, presumed to have equal rights, we should therefore constrain our self-interests for the collective common good of society and the state. The argument equally applies in principle to institutional groups, such as corporations, institutions, and professions.

According to John Rawls's influential version of the social contract theory, the problem with the idea of a theoretical contractual agreement between self-interested contractors in "a state of nature",[3] such as that of Thomas Hobbes' social contract theory, is not the agreement itself as such, but the *conditions* under which the contractual agreement is determined. According to Rawls a contract can only give equal consideration to each contractor if it is negotiated from a position of equality – in Rawls' theory that original position of equality is called the "original position". For Rawls it corresponds to the *state of nature* in the traditional theory of the social contract as articulated in Thomas Hobbes' equally influential theory. To provide conditions of equality in the "original position", according to Rawls, contractors must agree to principles of justice, conceived as *fairness,* behind a *veil of ignorance* without knowing their talents or infirmities and without knowing what position they occupy in society. In summary that argument is as follows:

1. It is assumed that each contractor is *instrumentally rational* and so would attempt to do as best for oneself as possible. That is, utilize the best means to maximize one's ends.
2. But since no one knows what position they occupy in society behind the assumed veil of ignorance, asking people to decide what is best for themselves has the same consequence as asking them to decide what is best for everyone considered impartially.

---

[3] The idea of a *State of Nature* that features in the Social Contract theories, should be understood not in terms of a historical or anthropological account of the origins of society in terms of some pre-social existence of human beings, nor in terms of actual historical agreements concerning the obligations of governments and individuals but as an abstract theoretical model of explaining and articulating the moral equality of individuals (Kymlicka 1990, p.60).

3. For in order to decide, behind a veil of ignorance, which principles will promote my own good as an individual, I must put myself in the shoes of every person in society and consider what promotes their good, since I may end up being one of those persons.
4. Through the "veil of ignorance" device, Rawls' contract theory substitutes a *moral equality* in place of a physical, economic, political or social inequality. An inequality, which contrary to moral equality, tends to favor the interests of some individuals or groups over those of others and over the collective common good of society as a whole. This was illustrated by the examples of corruption, including media corruption, in the case studies of *News of the World* and *Cambridge Analytica* that we encountered earlier in Chap. 6.

The attraction of Rawls' "veil of ignorance" device in the social contract theory, is that it offers a principled and structured method for removing bias and partiality for obtaining impartiality, at least in principle, which is definitive of the moral point of view. Rawls' contract device illuminates in a clear manner the basic idea of morality as impartiality, equality, and fairness. The principles of impartiality, equality, and fairness are also highlighted by the Dual Obligation Information Theory (DOIT) and relatedly by Alan Gewirth's Rationalist Ethical theory of universal rights, based on his argument for the *Principle of Generic Consistency (PGC)* (Gewirth 1978, 1996; Spence 2006).

Another influential contemporary ethical theory is that of *Utilitarianism* also referred to as *Consequentialism,*[4] as the ethics of any action is measured primarily by its consequences. According to Utilitarianism, an action is moral if it promotes overall happiness or wellbeing and reduces overall suffering or harm in society. Thus, the *standard* of moral action is the increase of happiness or wellbeing or reduction of suffering or harm as much as possible for as many people as possible – "*the greatest happiness for the greatest number*". The attraction of Utilitarianism is that it is simple. What could be simpler than basing morality on that which increases the overall happiness or wellbeing of most people in society. It is also intuitive and appealing as it seeks to maximize what we all ultimately value – happiness or well-being, or general preference satisfaction for most people, in a non-arbitrary and impartial manner. Just as the Social Contract theories of Thomas Hobbes and John Rawls, as well as the Ethical Rationalist theory of Aland Gewirth, Utilitarianism also recognizes and supports the ethical principles of impartiality, equality, and fairness.

In sum, all four of those influential contemporary ethical theories, the Social Contract theories of Hobbes' and Rawls', Utilitarianism, and Gewirth's Ethical Rationalist theory, as well as Immanuel Kant's moral theory (*Groundwork for the*

[4]Some of the well-known proponents of Utilitarianism are the English philosophers, Jeremy Bentham (1748–1832), John Stuart Mill (1806–1873) and R.M. Hare (1919–2002), and the Australian philosopher Peter Singer (1946-present). Peter Singer is also known, somewhat controversially, for extending his Utilitarian theory to include the rights of animals; on the basis that as sentient entities animals can also suffer pain and should, therefore, be included into the Utilitarian calculation of maximizing wellbeing and reducing suffering.

Metaphysics of Morals (1785)[5] that resembles in certain key features, Rawls' and Gewirth's theories, although different in their theoretical approaches and detail, share the fundamental key ethical principles of equality, equal mutual respect of persons' rights, and the common good of society. That should provide us with some confidence that the ethical principles of equality, impartiality, and fairness for the common good of society are universal principles of ethics supported by most if not all contemporary ethical theories.[6]

In addition to impartiality, equality and fairness, and the common good, other important ethical principles and values in relation to the dissemination and communication of information, are *privacy*, *transparency*, *accuracy*, *trustworthiness*, *responsibility* and *accountability,* principles which as we saw earlier in in Chap. 2, are also advocated and supported on the basis of the *Dual Obligation Information Theory (DOIT)*. Together those principles constitute the public societal repertoire of ethical principles and values that underpin our democratic system, and which are overall, supported by the ethical theories cited above. However, those principles and values are not always clearly articulated and not inculcated within the corporate structures of the Big Tech companies, such as Facebook and Google, which, through their substantial global financial power and clout, exert a significant influence over all aspects of society at present. Though appearing, like Gyges, to act for the common good of society, the Big Tech companies, as we saw in Facebook's part in Cambridge Analytica, and analogously in some of the informational practices of Google, sometimes at least, act in ways that, far from promoting the common good, undermine it. They do so, under a cloak of invisibility provided by their non-transparent business models and opaque algorithms that primarily favor their commercial interests over the common good of society. As an additional measure of regulation, the aforementioned public ethical principles and values should be clearly articulated and included as part of good governance guidelines, applicable to all tech companies and other corporate market institutions, including the media.

---

[5] Immanuel Kant's celebrated argument referred to as the *Categorical Imperative* counsels us to "Act only on the maxim through which you can at the same time will that it be a universal law." This is the keystone of Kant's ethics. "Promising falsely" for example, could not be a universalizable maxim for no one would ever take promises seriously. Another formulation of the Categorical Imperative known evocatively as the "Kingdom of Ends" states that we should "Treat humanity in your own person or in the person of any other never simply as a means but always at the same time as an end". So, for example, when someone says to you disapprovingly, "I feel as if you are using me", they are in effect invoking Kant's categorical imperative.

[6] For a comparative analysis of those ethical theories see Will Kymlicka (1990), *Contemporary Political Philosophy: An Introduction*. Oxford: Clarendon Press, 9–94; as well as Michael Boylan (2000), *Basic Ethics*: *Basic Ethics in Action*. Upper Saddle River, New Jersey: Prentice Hall.

7.4 The Necessary Alignment of Public Ethical Principles and Values with Regulation

Although different in their theoretical approach, two overarching necessary conditions all ethical theories, as those referred to above, have in common for their practical application and rational assent, are *justification* and *motivation*. Justification is necessary in providing good reasons why any putative rational agent should accept, at least theoretically, the rational validity of an ethical theory and the principles and values it advocates and supports. Motivation is also a necessary condition, as any ethical theory that although rationally justified, offers no adequate motivation for its rational acceptance, because let us say, it is too abstract and not adequately action-guiding, and would therefore be impractical. Most rational ethical theories, such as Utilitarianism, Social Contract theories, Kantian Ethical theories, and Ethical Rationalist theories, such as that of Alan Gewirth's, seem to provide adequate rational justification and motivation. However, what ethical theories cannot provide, in our less than ideal world, is *compliance*. This is simply because rational justification and motivation even when adequate, cannot *guarantee* practical compliance. As the saying goes, 'you can lead a horse to water, but you can't make it drink'.

Rational agents acting as individuals or as groups out of self-interest might recognize and theoretically at least accept the rational justification and motivation to act morally in accordance with ethical principles and values but choose not to comply with those principles and values, out of self-interest. As in the case of Gyges, they may think and convince themselves that they can evade detection and avoid social disapproval by merely appearing to be ethical and just, but under a veil of invisibility, created by their position of power and entitlement, choose not to act ethically if they consider that it is not in their self-interest to do so. But even in situations in which Gygean conditions don't fully apply, a person might choose to act against their own rational moral judgement if they are convinced that their self-interest or that of their group in a certain situation takes priority over their required moral judgement.

This illustrates that there exists a *motivational gap* between a rational agent's normative reasons for acting and their psychological motives that can be narrowed and bridged through moral education but cannot be entirely closed. The creation story in the book of *Genesis* in the Bible, even if interpreted as merely an instructive myth or an allegory, shows how compliance is not guaranteed even if commanded by God. Anticipating the practical possibility of non-compliance with the Social Contract, Hobbes stipulated that external regulation through the legitimate sovereign authority of a King was therefore necessary to ensure its compliance. In contemporary society of course, the equivalent authority for imposing external compliance is the democratic government and its supporting institutions.

The discussion in this section, so far, demonstrates that a close normative alignment between ethical principles and values on the one hand, and compliance with those principles and values on the other, is not only desirable but essential for the common good of society. Especially so in the case of Big Tech companies, such as Facebook and Google, that at times seek to advance their own financial interests at the expense of the common good of society. Given the ongoing systemic conflict of interest between the tech companies' business models that predominantly favors their financial interest over their users' epistemic and ethical interests and rights, and those of society generally, government regulation is therefore necessary.

In a recent op-ed article by Mark Zuckerberg, "Big Tech Needs More Regulation" published in the *Financial Times* (February 16, 2020) the Facebook CEO argues for more regulation along similar lines as his previous article published on *Facebook* in March 30, 2019. This is a welcome initiative by Facebook and in keeping with the suggestion canvassed above in this section, that the protection and safeguarding of the normative integrity of information and its communication on the infosphere, especially its dissemination through the Big Tech platforms, such as those of Facebook and Google, should be a shared responsibility: a collective normative responsibility, epistemic, ethical, and eudaimonic, shared collectively by all relevant key stakeholders, including Tech companies, Government, Market actors, the Media, and Citizens as users and communicators of information. As Mark Zuckerberg correctly states,

> People shouldn't have to rely on individual companies addressing these issues [regulation issues] by themselves. We should have a broader debate about what we want as a *society* [emphasis added] and how regulation can help…It's time to …define clear responsibilities for people, companies and governments going forward. (Zuckerberg 2019).

This is a belief also expressed persuasively by the authors of *The Platform Society* (Van Dijck and De Waal 2018:139), who claim that,

> Creating public value for the common good should ideally be the shared responsibility of market, state, and civil society actors. The Big Five [Facebook, Google, Amazon, Apple and Microsoft], as major shapers of the ecosystem, can rewrite the rules for democratic societies; but how can they act responsibly in a new global world order? …Public institutions have a special function as *guardians* [emphasis added] of social trust and a democratic common.

The three authors go on to correctly suggest that, "platformization requires an integral approach rather than just a sectoral one when it comes to defending consumers' and citizens' rights" (2018:139).

The comments of Mark Zuckerberg and those of the authors of *The Platform Society* cited above, provide further support for a shared and integral global approach to the normative regulation of the Internet as argued for in this chapter. It should include the adoption and inculcation of public ethical principles and values and in addition, government regulation to ensure compliance with those principles and values. The Dual Obligation Information Theory (DOIT), examined in Chap. 2, was designed specifically for the purpose of providing an information-communication normative model that could apply globally; especially, in the Age of Information. For the normative principles applicable to the Internet, being a global network, requires a normative model that has global applicability.

Four areas of regulation that Mark Zuckerberg highlights in his article "Four Ideas to Regulate the Internet" (Mark Zuckerberg 2019) are:

- Harmful content, for which 'internet companies should be accountable for enforcing standards on harmful content'.
- Protection of elections, for which 'he believes legislation should be updated to reflect the reality of the threats and set standards for the whole industry'. According to Zuckerberg, 'Facebook's systems would be more effective if regulation created common standards for verifying political actors.
- Effective privacy and data protection, which according to Zuckerberg 'needs a globally harmonized framework, citing the EU *General Data Protection Regulation* (GDPR) as a possible common global framework for adoption. According to Zuckerberg, a global framework such as the GDPR, 'should establish a way to hold companies such as Facebook accountable by imposing sanctions when Facebook makes mistakes.'; and finally,
- Regulation guaranteeing the principle of data portability that 'requires clear rules about who is responsible for protecting information when it moves between services.

According to Mark Zuckerberg (2019), Facebook has a responsibility to help address those issues… and that there 'should be a broader debate about what we want as a society and how regulation can help'. He concludes that 'the rules governing the internet need to be updated so as to define clear responsibilities for people, companies and governments.'

Mark Zuckerberg's four ideas for regulating the internet and repeated in his op-ed article in the *Financial* Times (2020) are important, at least as a first step, in recognizing and publicly acknowledging and articulating, as CEO of one of the largest tech companies, the need for regulation and putting forward some general ideas of how regulation could be accomplished. Another important public principle that Mark Zuckerberg highlights with regard to regulation in his 2020 follow-up article in the *Financial Times*, is *transparency*. This is a welcome and important addition, for without transparency there can be no effective accountability.

Interestingly, but perhaps not surprising, the four ideas of Mark Zuckerberg's concerning regulation, those of *harmful content*, *protection of elections*, *effective privacy and data protection*, as well as *transparency*, are five key areas of Facebook's normative failures highlighted in the Cambridge Analytica case, as demonstrated in Chap. 5. For as we saw in the normative analysis and assessment of that case, Facebook's collection, and dissemination of users' data without the users' informed consent, was used by Cambridge Analytica to exert influence on both the 2016 US Presidential Elections and the UK Brexit Referendum. The harmful content comprised fake news and misinformation that targeted individual voters to sway their electoral choices, thus undermining the democratic electoral system itself, and in the process, undermined the privacy and security of the data of Facebook's users. And all was done with the aid of Facebook's invisible algorithms and motivated by its opaque business model, with a total lack of transparency and consequently lack of accountability.

As demonstrated in Chap. 5, Facebook's actions by commission and omission in the Cambridge Analytica case, constituted institutional media corruption. In light of that, Zuckerberg's call for more external regulation in those five key areas is an important step forward as an acknowledgement of the problem and its suggested solution through government regulation.

7.5 Oversight and Accountability by Proactive Regulation

Another important area concerning regulation that Mark Zuckerberg highlights in his *Financial Times* co-ed article (2020), is *oversight* and *accountability* that goes beyond mere self-regulation and clearly and unambiguously introduces the need for *external* government regulation. As he states in that article,

> people need to feel that global technology platforms answer to someone, so regulation should hold companies accountable when they make mistakes.

He goes on to say,

> that if we don't create standards that people feel are *legitimate* [emphasis added], they won't trust institutions or technology (Mark Zuckerberg 2020).

This statement by Zuckerberg is significant for at least two important reasons:

1. The statement suggests not only retrospective regulation through substantial fines imposed on tech companies such as those imposed on Facebook and Google for their past 'mistakes', as examined earlier in this chapter, but crucially, *prospective regulation* through regular and ongoing 'oversight'. The term "oversight" suggests proactive ongoing regulation, just as, for example, in the case of annual independent auditing of financial statements, and tax returns.
2. Zuckerberg, in fact, suggests this interpretation of proactive regulation through oversight in his 2019 article cited earlier, "Four Ideas to Regulate the Internet", in which he highlights the 'need for a more active role for government and regulators'. Later in that article he refers to the *transparency reports* Facebook publishes on its effectiveness of removing harmful content on its platform, which he believes every internet service should provide, and which he considers "just as important as financial reporting".

As a professional practicing accountant for many years both in the UK (London) and Australia (Sydney) in my previous working life before becoming an academic philosopher, Mark Zuckerberg's statement above "just as important as financial reporting" caught my immediate attention and interest. For as an independent accountant specializing in auditing, I conducted external audits of many private and public corporate companies, as well as external audits of government departments. This essentially involved examining not only the veracity of the annual financial statements prepared by those companies but also the internal underlying systems of those companies on which the reporting of their financial statements was based. For if, for example, the stock accounting system of a company was faulty or inaccurate, the reported stock value of that company in their financial statements, which determined the annual profit or loss of the company, would also be inaccurate and therefore unreliable and untrustworthy.

Analogously, with regard to the internal systems of tech companies, such as Facebook and Goggle, for example, that collect, commodify, select and monetize user's information that generate their reported profits, an independent external audit would seek to verify that process to ensure it was conducted according to accepted normative public principles, values and standards such as those cited above, namely, *privacy*, *transparency*, *accuracy*, *trustworthiness*, *responsibility* and *accountability*. Principles, which respect their users' epistemic, ethical, and eudaimonic interests, and those interests are fairly balanced with, and not overridden by, the financial interests of the tech companies. Such an independent external *normative audit* of tech companies would provide a reasonably effective oversight in the form of external regulation, which would parallel the existing financial audits of most private and public corporate companies at present.

Referring to the Big Tech companies' opaque algorithms that for the most part remain non-transparent and not subject to public accountability, Frank Pasquale's comment in his book *The Black Box Society* (2015) seems to lend support to my proposal for external platform audits of Big Tech companies such as Facebook and Google. He says that, "far more of their algorithms should be open for inspection – if not by the public at large, at least by some trusted auditor" (Pasquale 2015, p.141). Similarly, Foroohar's suggestion that "Big Tech companies should also be required to keep audit logs of the data they feed into their algorithms. And be prepared to explain their algorithms to the public" (Foroohar 2019, p.277) also appears to lend further support to my argument for external independent audits of Big Tech companies. For given the *asymmetry* of information and *control* that exists between the public and Big Tech companies, such as Facebook and Google, how else can *compliance* by Big Tech, for ensuring adequate *transparency* and *accountability*, be secured? If not by some form of external independent audits?

In his article "Four Ideas to Regulate the Internet" Mark Zuckerberg (2019) also hints at such a possibility by stating that,

> One idea is for third party bodies to set standards governing the distribution of harmful content and measure companies against those standards. Regulation could set baselines for what's prohibited and require companies to build systems for keeping harmful content to a bare minimum.

Although Zuckerberg's statement refers specifically to harmful content, there is no reason, in principle at least, why that could not also be extended to include issues of privacy and data protection, as well as the protection of elections through the monitoring of political ads, which he also refers to in that article. The general ideas that Mark Zuckerberg expresses in that article, is also in keeping with the overarching *normative* statement he makes in his 2020 *Financial Times* article, that "tech companies should serve society'. This is an important and significant statement by the CEO of Facebook as it emphasizes and acknowledges, by implication at least, the normative priority of the common good of society over the narrower financial interests of tech companies, which as illustrated by the Cambridge Analytica case, do not always serve the common good of society.

Lending theoretical and normative support to Mark Zuckerberg's statement that technology should serve society, I have argued in an earlier published paper that technology is not good in itself but only good if it serves the collective common good of societies and humanity at large (Spence 2011).

The idea of an independent audit of tech companies to assess compliance with common standards comprising public normative principles and values, as proposed above, faces, however, the challenge of adequate expertise and professional competence by the external regulators (to whom I will refer to here as *platform auditors*) in carrying out such a demanding role. Although not referring to independent external auditors as I have done above, the authors of the *Platform Society* (2018:158) outline some of the problems that enforcement agencies in general would face in carrying out such a regulatory role. They claim, not unreasonably that,

> Enforcement agencies that are assigned to execute regulation are *insufficiently equipped to* administer even the most basic form of accountability. Regulatory fixes require detailed insights into how technology and business models work, how intricate platform mechanisms are deployed in relation to user practices, and how they impact social activities. .... platform mechanisms are very difficult to control because they play out across infrastructural and sectoral platforms. Moreover, they pertain simultaneously to constantly changing algorithms, obscure business models, and incomprehensible terms of service. Government regulators need specialized digital teams equipped with combined technical and legal knowledge to probe these complex mechanisms.

Although the challenge as described above for introducing external regulation of tech companies through external compliance audit is difficult, it is not insurmountable. Large traditional financial audits of national and international companies conducted by independent external auditors, working for professional accountancy firms, such as those of the Institutes of Chartered Accountants in the UK and Australia, for example, and their equivalent bodies in the USA and the EU, are not without complexity and also do require specialist adequate knowledge of the systems of the companies audited. My own experience as audit manager, working with a team of auditors, required us to liaise closely with the managers and staff of the various sections within each company we audited, so as to first determine what the systems of each section of the company were and how those systems functioned. Once we acquired an overall understanding of a company's systems, which included its computer systems, we would then devise audit checks and controls to test those systems for their functionality, veracity, and adequacy. Admittedly the systems of tech companies, such as those of Facebook and Google, might be much more complex but auditors in the future conducting regulatory audits of tech companies would be expected and specifically trained to have a basic knowledge of how the computer systems of tech companies function so as to enable them to test them. This might require the platform audit teams in the future to include auditors that have adequate knowledge of computers and their AI systems, including their algorithms.

If compliance with public normative principles and values as those cited above by the Big Tech companies is essential for the common good of society and its underlying democratic system, as well as its political and civil associated institutions, then some government external regulation whether conducted through independent external auditors as suggested above, or some other effective way, is not only desirable but necessary. Mark Zuckerberg's acknowledgement of the necessity of external government regulation is therefore a significant first step in motivating such a system of external government regulation.

As argued above, good governance of the Internet requires a joint collective effort by all stakeholders in society, including tech companies, market actors, and citizens, and all the users of the Internet in fact. Historically, governments through the political power assigned to them on the basis of the social contract for the common good of society, have the authority and jurisdiction to introduce regulatory systems to protect the rights of citizens and consumers. As we saw earlier in this chapter, the Information Commissioner's Office (ICO) in the UK, the Federal Trade Commission (FTC) in the USA, as well as the European Union through the introduction of the *General Data Protection Regulation* (GDPR) have all imposed hefty fines on both Facebook and Google for their misconducts. In October 2019, the *Australian Competition and Consumer Commission* (ACCC) took Google to court for misleading customers about its use of personal data. According to the ACCC Chairman Rod Sims, the ACCC was,

> Taking court action against Google because we allege that as a result of these on-screen representations, Google has collected, kept and used highly sensitive and valuable personal information about consumers' location without them making an informed choice (Hunter 2019).

The court action emerged from the ACCC's released digital platforms inquiry in July 2019, proposing drastic changes to regulation of the Big Tech companies, including stronger protection for consumer data. This is how the Treasurer of the Australian Government Josh Frydenberg described the proposed regulation of the ACCC,

> Make no mistake, these companies [Facebook and Google] are among the most powerful and valuable in the world and they need to be held to account and their activities need to be more transparent (Ferguson Hunter 2019).

Such government legislation at least across the three continents, United States, the European Union, and Australia is a significant step forward in the regulation of the Big Tech companies, especially Facebook and Google, which between them, through the various activities of their platforms, exert enormous near-monopolistic global power over all sectors of society, social, political and financial. Bringing the Big Tech companies under institutional oversight for accountability through government regulation is a positive measure for ensuring the public common good of society is protected and promoted, as acknowledged by Mark Zuckerberg in his two cited articles above.

In addition to government regulation, civil society actors as citizens have a collective shared responsibility to protect and promote the normative integrity of the infosphere just as they do or ought to do, of the biosphere. This as we saw earlier in Chap. 2 as well as in Chap. 5, is also normatively required by the *Dual Obligation Information Theory* (DOIT) which demonstrates that the dissemination and communication of digital information in the infosphere commits all us globally, as disseminators of information, to epistemic and ethical principles and values. The platformization of society has introduced, according to Helbing et al. (2017, 12), a "new social contract, based on trust and cooperation, which sees citizens and consumers not as obstacles or resources to be exploited, but as partners" working together for the common social good of society. As the authors of the *Platform Society* (Van Dijck, Poell, and De Waal 2018, 151) correctly observe,

> Digital platforms can empower individual citizens to unite and to rally behind public advocacy efforts in order to influence democratic processes….individuals can muscle up collective power and become a force to be reckoned with because user metrics are one of the biggest currencies of the platform economy.

The empowerment of citizens to collectively protect the privacy and integrity of their information and its use by tech companies such as Facebook and Google is not only desirable, but moreover, as we examined in Chap. 5, a *normative responsibility* to be shared collectively by the users of platforms such as those of Facebook and Google, in order to safeguard the integrity of their information and prevent its misuse. For as we saw, in the Cambridge Analytica scandal, users' information can be misappropriated by the actions of tech companies such as Facebook and Google, which in some cases, have been shown to be conductive and result in systemic media corruption. Such actions not only undermine the users' informational rights as individuals, but moreover, also undermine our collective rights as citizens, which also in turn, undermine democracy itself and its associated and supportive institutions.

Tim Berners Lee, one of the early pioneers of the Internet and creator of the *Open Society Foundation*, has supported a democratic, fair, and secure Internet where citizens can exercise democratic control over information and data flows. When presenting the goals of the *Open Society Foundation* in 2017, he raised three key concerns regarding the future of the World Wide Web (Web) as a tool in the service of humanity. Those were: The loss of control over our personal data; how easily misinformation can spread on the Web; and the opaque ways political advertising campaigns are directly targeted at users, as illustrated by the Cambridge Analytica case (Van Dijck et al. 2018, 153). Tim Berners Lee's three key concerns for the Internet provides further motivating reasons for civil society actors, together with public and government institutions, to collectively work together towards a more effective regulation of the Big Tech companies for the common social good of society. To that end, the participation of the tech companies themselves, as suggested by the CEO of Facebook Mark Zuckerberg, is also vital. As Van Dijck et al. (2018, 162) correctly argue,

> A digital world in which large corporations have both an overwhelming market presence and the leverage to influence political actors gives rise to highly unbalanced *polities*. For democracies to work in the age of platformization, they need the concerted efforts of all

actors – market, state, and civil society – to build a sustainable and trustworthy global platform ecosystem, a system that come equipped with distributed responsibilities as well as with checks and balances.

7.6 The Market Good vs The Public Good

The Big Tech companies such as Alphabet-Google, Amazon, Facebook, Apple and Microsoft, have created if not by intention at least by effect, a sharp divide between the *Market Good* and the *Public Good* of society through their command and control over our collective information that has impacted all areas of social, political and economic activity. As Rana Foroohar aptly puts it (2019: 116) "we might think we are in control, but in fact, we are being manipulated by the attention merchants [Foroohar's reference to Big Tech]. It has resulted through the complexity of their algorithms and opacity of their business models, in an unequal power between the financial interests of those companies and the public common good of society as was illustrated in the Cambridge Analytica case examined in Chap. 5. George Dyson in his book *Turing's Cathedral* alluding to this command and control by the Big Tech companies over society, described it thus: "Facebook defines who we are, Amazon defines what we want, and Google defines what we think" (Dyson 2012, quoted in Pasquale 2015).

It is the complexity and opacity of the Big Tech companies' algorithms and business models that create, as we saw in Facebook's part in the Cambridge Analytica controversy, a *conflict of interest* between the *normative obligations* those companies have as corporate institutions expected to serve the public good, and their *financial interests* that have a tendency to favour the later over the former, undermining the *common good* of society and the underlying *democratic system* that supports and sustains it. Such conflicts of interest, as we saw in Chap. 5, can be conducive to corruption and specifically in the case of Facebook and Google, systemic media corruption.[7]

The authors of the *Platform Society* (Van Dijck, Poell, and De Waal 2018,165) refer to the divide between the market good and the public good as a, "tipping point" that tilts the "private-public divide" toward data-driven high-tech companies, hence derailing the power of national governments and institutions". They refer to this, as a,

> "Postdemocratic" scenario: the nexus of political-corporate-media elite empowered by globalization creates political regimes that overemphasize economic growth and corporate-friendly priorities. Although these societies continue to use all the institutions of democracy, they become no more than a formal shell.... they cannot expect markets to regulate themselves while also being protectors and promoters of the public good. Local, national, and

[7] For a further detailed discussion of the conflict of interest between the Market Good V. The Public Good, see Spence et al. (2011), Chap. 3. For how Big Tech promotes 'consumer welfare over citizen welfare', which ultimately promotes and favors not the common good of society but that of the financial good of Big Tech, and consequently results in the "corruption of the political process", see Foroohar (2019:183–190).

> supranational bodies will need to be both protectors and promoters of public values and the common good.

As we have seen in this chapter there has been a significant willingness by government bodies such as the *Information Commissioner's Office (ICO)* in the UK, the *Federal Trade Commission (FTC)* in the US, the European Union (EU) under the provisions of the *General Data Protection Regulation* (GDPR), and the *Australian Competition and Consumer Commission* (ACCC) to hold tech companies to account by imposing unprecedented substantial fines against tech companies, such as Facebook, Google and Apple, for various breaches of undermining citizens' information and data protection rights as well as market competitor' trading rights. Just recently Apple was fined €1.1 billion by the antitrust competition regulator in France, the *Autorité de la Concurrence*, for conspiring with wholesalers *Tech Data* and *Ingram Micro* to align prices. Tech Data was fined €76 million and Ingram Micro €63 million for their part in the conspiracy. According to Isabelle de Silva, head of the French competition watchdog (Monaghan, Angela 2010),

> Apple and its two wholesalers agreed to not compete against each other and prevent resellers from promoting competition between each other, thus sterilising the wholesale market for Apple products.

Although this willingness by Governments to regulate tech companies through the imposition of hefty fines is a welcome first step it is by itself not enough. As argued earlier, what is needed in addition to *retrospective* regulation of tech companies through fines, is *prospective* regulation of those companies through external *platform audits* conducted by independent Government sponsored agencies to ensure compliance with professional standards that align with public ethical principles and values. To that end, those public ethical principles and values as well as being protected through external regulation, should also be promoted, and encouraged by their inculcation within the corporate structures of the tech companies through appropriate education and training programs.

7.7 Conclusion

This chapter has examined questions and issues of government regulation concerning the Big Tech companies such as Facebook, Google, Amazon, Apple, and Microsoft, and explored what systemic changes in policy and legislation are needed in combating corruption and media corruption by the Big Tech companies, as well as explored possible anti-corruption solutions in effectively responding to the challenge of corruption and media corruption especially, in the Age of Information.

The chapter examined how investigative journalism has proved an effective anti-corruption measure in exposing and informing the public of corruption, such as political, financial, corporate, police and not least, media corruption. The role of investigative journalists and whistleblowers in the exposure and reporting of corruption, first demonstrated in Chap. 6 through an analysis of illustrative key cases spanning a period of over seventy years, was revisited in this chapter to illustrate the ongoing significance of investigative journalism in the regulation of corruption including media corruption, as well as other ethical misdemeanors, manifested in some of the practices of the Big Tech companies. As a vital part of the media in the form of the fourth and fifth Estates, investigative journalism continues its vital mission as the vanguard of democracy of holding governments, institutions, and corporations, including tech companies, both private and public across a wide spectrum of society, to account.

The chapter then argued for the necessity of a clear public articulation of the rationale of public ethical principles and values through an examination of their historical justification and motivation on the basis of several contemporary ethical theories such as Social Contract theories, Utilitarian theories, Ethical Rationalist theories such as those of Immanuel Kant and Aland Gewirth, and not least, the Dual Obligation Information Theory (DOIT), that applies specifically to the normative evaluation of information (analogue and digital) and its impact on society.

The chapter then examined and argued for the necessary normative alignment of public ethical principles and values with government regulation comprising both retrospective regulation through penalties such as fines as well as prospective regulation through external and independent audits of the Big Tech companies by the government and its associated agencies. As well, the chapter argued for the inculcation of public ethical principles and values within the corporate structures of the tech companies through education and training programs.

Finally, the chapter concluded with revisiting the key normative problem at the heart of the unethical practices of some of the tech companies such as Facebook and Google; namely, that of a conflict of interest between their public corporate role, and specifically their media role, which commits them to the common good of society, in contrast to their opaque business models and algorithms that tend to primarily favor their financial interests, at the normative expense of the common good of society; thus, undermining the underlying *democratic system* itself.

It is the complexity and opacity of the Big Tech companies' algorithms and business models that create such a conflict of interest, as we saw in the analysis of Facebook's part in the Cambridge Analytica controversy, in Chap. 5. Such conflicts of interest can be conducive to corruption and specifically in the case of Facebook's part in the Cambridge Analytica case, to systemic media corruption. Analogously, insofar as Google, like Facebook, is essentially a media company, as argued in Chap. 5, some of the practices of Google in the harvesting of user' information for advertising revenue without the users' informed consent, are also conducive to systemic media corruption.

Oversight and accountability through prospective regulation of tech companies as proposed in this chapter, through external *platform audits* conducted by independent Government sponsored agencies, can ensure compliance with professional standards that align with public ethical principles and values for the common good of society. This would mitigate if not entirely remove the harmful normative effects of those conflicts of interest within the corporate structures of the Big Tech companies.

References

Bentham, Jeremy. 1823. *An Introduction to the Principles of Morals and Legislation*. https://oll.libertyfund.org/titles/bentham-an-introduction-to-the-principles-of-morals-and-legislation. Accessed 3 July 2020

Boylan, Michael. 2000. *Basic Ethics: Basic Ethics in Action*. Upper Saddle River: Prentice Hall.

Drozdiak, Natalia, and Schenchner, Sam. 2017. Google Slapped With $US2.7 Billion EU Fine Over Search Results. *The Wall Street Journal*, June 27, 2017.

Dyson, George. 2012. *Turing's Cathedral: The Origins of the Digital Universe*, 308. New York: Pantheon.

Foroohar, Rana. 2019. *Don't be Evil: The Case Against Big Tech*. London: Allen Lane, Random House.

Gauthier, David. 1986. *Morals by Agreement*. Oxford: Oxford Scholarship Online, 2003. https://www.oxfordscholarship.com/view/10.1093/0198249926.001.0001/acprof-9780198249924. Accessed 3 July 2020.

Gewirth, Alan. 1996. *The Community of Rights*. Chicago: University of Chicago Press.

———. 1978. *Reason and Morality*. Chicago: University of Chicago Press.

Helbing, D., B.S. Frey, G. Gigerennzer, E. Hafen, M. Hagner, Y. Hofsstertter, J. Vn den Hoven, R.V. Zicari, and A. Zwitter. 2017. Will Democracy Survive Big Data and Artificial Intelligence? *Scientific American*, February 25, 2017. https://www.scientificamerican.com/article/will-democracy-survive-big-data-and-artificicial-intelligence/.

Helmore, Edward. 2020. Facebook commitment to free speech will 'piss people off' Zuckerbrg says. *The Guardian*, February 2, 2020.

Hern, Alex. 2019. Facebook agrees to pay fine over Cambridge Analytica scandal. *The Guardian*, October 30, 2019.

Hobbes, Thomas. 1651. *Leviathan*. http://www.gutenberg.org/ebooks/3207. Accessed 3 July 2020.

Hunter, Fergus. 2019. Consumer watchdog takes legal action against Google for 'misleading' conduct. *The Sydney Morning Herald* and *The Age*, October 29, 2019.

Hunter, Fergus, and Samios, Zoe. 2020. 'Systemic failures': Facebook facing legal action over Cambridge Analytica Scandal. *The Sydney Morning Herald and The Age*, March 9, 2020.

Kang, Cecillia. 2019. F.T.C Approves Facebook Fine of About 5 Billion. *The New York Times*, July 12, 2019.

Kant, Immanuel. 1785. *Groundwork for the Metaphysics of Morals*. http://www.gutenberg.org/ebooks/5682. Accessed 3 July 2020.

Kymlicka, Will. 1990. *Contemporary Political Philosophy: An Introduction*. Oxford: Clarendon Press.

Locke, John. 1689. *Two Treatises of Civil Government*. http://www.gutenberg.org/ebooks/7370. Accessed 3 July 2020.

Mill, John Stuart. 1863. *Utilitarianism*. http://www.gutenberg.org/ebooks/11224. Accessed 3 July 2020.

Monaghan, Angela. 2010. Apple fined record 1.1bn by French competition regulator. *The Guardian*, March 17, 2020.

Pasquale, Frank. 2015. *The Black Box Society: The Secret Algorithms That Control Money and Information*, 15. Cambridge, MA: Harvard University Press.

Plato. *The Republic*: 359a and 359b.

Rawls, John. 1971. *A Theory of Justice*. Cambridge, MA: Harvard University Press.

Rousseau, Jean-Jacques. 1762. *The Social Contract*. http://www.gutenberg.org/ebooks/46333. Accessed 3 July 2020.

Snider, Mike, and Baig, Edward C. 2019. Facebook fined $5 billion by FTC, must update, and adopt new privacy, security measures. USA *Today*, Jul 24, 2019.

Spence, Edward. 2011. Is Technology Good for Us? A Eudaimonic Meta-Model for Evaluating the Contributive Competence of Technologies for a Good Life. *Nanoethics* 5: 335–343.

———. 2006. *Ethics Within Reason: A Neo-Gewirthian Approach*. Lanham: Lexington Books (a division of Rowman and Littlefield).
Spence, Edward, Andrew Alexandra, Aaron Quinn, and Anne Dunn. 2011. *Media, Markets and Morals*. Oxford: Wiley-Blackwell.
Tucker, Eric, and Barbara Ortutay. 2020. *Facebook removes Trump ads with symbols once used by Nazis*. Australia: ABC News.
Van Dijck, Poell, and De Waal. 2018. *The Platform Society: Public Values in a Connected World*. Oxford: Oxford University Press.
Zuboff, Shoshanna. 2019. *The Age of Surveillance Capitalism: The Fight for A Human Future At The New Frontier of Power*. London: Profile Books Ltd.
Zuckerberg, Mark. 2020. Big Tech Needs More Regulation. *Financial Times*, February 18, 2020
———. 2019. Four Ideas to Regulate the Internet. *Facebook*, March 30, 2019.

Epilogue – Knowledge to Wisdom in the Age of Information

Where is the Life we have lost in living?
Where is the wisdom we have lost in knowledge?
Where is the knowledge we have lost in information?
T S Eliot *Choruses from The Rock* (1934).

By way of summing up as well as looking forward to the future, this Epilogue introduces the notion of *wisdom.*[1] As a *meta-type of knowledge*, knowing how to understand and use information upon reflection and with good judgement for the benefit of oneself and the common good of society, wisdom can provide practical "know-how" for applying information to improve our lives and that of others. It is also a *reflective virtue* in the form of practical prudence, which can teach us how to create and use information to live good and meaningful lives in the infosphere – lives that are capable of leading to self-fulfilment, eudemonia or happiness for us and others. What wisdom requires is that we learn the husbandry of information. How to reflect upon it, how to understand it, how to control it so it does not control us, how to judge its implications, so we can foresee its consequences, whether they are good or bad, for us and others. How to use it in ways that enhance our well-being and promote and protect our rights to freedom, privacy, security, and autonomy, both as individuals, and collectively for the common good of society.

Things happen unexpectedly as so painfully demonstrated by the recent Covid-19 pandemic that has locked down the world and has so far claimed the lives of millions of people worldwide. Our normal lives have been upended. The media has responded to the crisis as they have done on so many other occasions in the past, by providing a continuous stream of information in their avowed professional role of keeping the public informed. Interestingly, the Spanish Flu pandemic of 1918 to which the present Covid-19 pandemic has been compared did not start in Spain and neither was it more deadly there. It was named the Spanish flu because the press coverage of the pandemic came from Spain being a neutral country in World War I

[1] See also Spence (2013; 2011a, 2011b; and Elliott and Spence 2018).

E. H. Spence, *Media Corruption in the Age of Information*, Library of Public Policy and Public Administration 15, https://doi.org/10.1007/978-3-030-61612-0

and was free of the wartime censorship, in contrast to countries that took part in the war such as Germany, Britain, France and the USA. Censorship of the media in those countries was in place so as not to lower moral (Taylor 2018). Once again, this demonstrates the ongoing importance and crucial role that a free and unencumbered media plays in times of crisis especially, in informing the public, truthfully, reliably, and in a trustworthy manner without fear or favour, on matters of public interest for which citizens have a right to know. Political manipulation and prevarication in attempts to muffle and obstruct the media, as witnessed recently in some purportedly democratic countries with a robust tradition of a free press, is regrettable and contrary to ethical principles and values in violation of the citizens' right to know the truth. However, not to be outdone, the obstruction of the media, has been matched by a viral flood of misinformation in the form of conspiracy theories, fake news, 'alternative facts' pedalled by social media 'influencers', TV hosts and 'celebrities' without any corroborating and reliable scientific evidence or the testimony of reliable expert witnesses in the field. In the world of social media, where anyone can express an opinion, intended as information, credible or not, justified, trustworthy and reliable information based on knowledge, often counts for much less that the unaccountable personal opinions of the communicators themselves. Fatuous comments and opinions are given more prominence than plain facts. Especially, when the medium of such misinformation is channelled primarily through the platforms of Big Tech companies such as Facebook, Google and YouTube, whose finance-driven business models and opaque algorithms, geared by their overarching directive of making large profits by advertising through users' clickbait, overrides the users' informational rights and the common social good of society. As Frank Pasquale astutely observes with a touch of Juvenalian satiric touch, "Silicon Valley giants are looking less like romantic heroes and more like "Wall Street West" – in groups driven by lust for the quick payday" (Pasquale 2015, 2012).

A recent example of such misinformation is an Instagram video the Australian celebrity chef Pete Evans shared about the BioCharger NG, a "hybrid subtle energy revitalisation platform" that claims to "optimise and improve potential health, wellness and athletic performance". Evans, a judge on a popular commercial TV program *My Kitchen Rules* said he used the device and claimed it could help with the coronavirus, saying on the video that "its programmed [the BioCharger] with a thousand different recipes and there's a couple in there for the Wuhan coronavirus". The video has since been taken down, credit to Facebook, and the *Australian Therapeutic Goods Administration* (TGA) has announced an investigation into the $A14,990 devise. In a statement the TGA said that "the TGA is monitoring non-compliance, particularly in relation to the advertising of products that claim to prevent or cure COVID-19". Following the controversy of Evan's video, *Advanced Biotechnologies*, the creators of the BioCharger, released a statement distancing themselves from Evan's claims and added on their website that "the BioCharger NG is not a medical device" not intended for the cure or prevention of diseases including COVID-19. *The Australian Medical Association's (ATC)* president informed the *Australian Broadcasting Corporation* (ABC) that he had "significant concern about any person promoting a product which claims to be curative of COVID-19" (Butterworth, 2020).

Another example of misinformation through the legacy media this time, came from comments made by the co-host of *This Morning* news program by Eamon Holmes on ITV, a British free-to-air commercial television network. His controversial comments that sparked a backlash from viewers, was his suggestion that it may "suit the state narrative" to dismiss claims, linking 5G technology to the coronavirus, as false. He reportedly criticised the mainstream media for saying that any connection between 5G and the coronavirus was not true "when they don't know it's not true". His comments were made in response to the dismissal by scientists of any link between 5G and the coronavirus, which the Cabinet minister, Michael Gove, had previously criticised the conspiracy theory spread via YouTube linking the two, as "dangerous nonsense". Following the spread of that conspiracy theory through social media, at least twenty phone masts in the UK have been set on fire or vandalised according to government and industry sources (Robinson 2020).

Although there is nothing wrong with expressing doubt and being sceptical, in fact the French philosopher Rene Descartes (1596–1650) based his search for epistemic certainty on his rational "method of doubt".[2] Holmes, however, had no evidence or credible reason for his implied suggestion that the claim of a link between the 5G and the coronavirus, contrary to scientific evidence, could be true. His doubt was based on a simple epistemic confusion of asking for evidence of why the link between the 5G technology and the coronavirus was not true, instead of asking for evidence supporting the truth of the conspiracy theory that produced the claim of a link, in the first place. By analogy, it would be like asking why an epistemic claim that 'the moon is made of cream cheese' is not true, when one should be asking for evidence for the truth of that claim. The onus of proof falls in the first instance on those making an epistemic claim or expressing an opinion.

Those two examples illustrate the problem of spreading misinformation on the Internet through social media networks channelled through the platforms of Tech companies such as Facebook and Google, that Chap. 5 identified as media companies of the 6th Estate, bound by the same epistemic and ethical responsibilities and commitments as other media companies of the 4th and 5th Estates are. Arguably, as discussed in Chap. 7, the informational integrity of the infosphere, just like that of the biosphere, is a collective global responsibility to be shared by the Big Tech companies, governments and their associated institutions and professions, market actors, and the media, and not least, citizens who not only use the Internet for accessing and sharing information but contribute to it as disseminators and communicators of information. That places on everyone who uses and disseminates information, a collective distributed epistemic and ethical shared responsibility in ensuring the informational integrity of the infosphere.

---

[2] For more information on Rene Descartes' "method of doubt" see his *Meditations On First Philosophy*, *Meditations* I and II.

In my academic experience of teaching media ethics and the ethics of information to undergraduate and postgraduate students over a span of 20 years, the first question in the first lecture I would ask students was "what is information?". To my surprise, as far as I recall, students were unable to answer that question. Some would quickly go to Google for an answer. As a trained philosopher I knew of course the importance of asking questions especially, as Socrates did almost 2500 years ago, questions concerning the definition of terms, such as, what is courage, what is virtue, what is truth, what is love, what is beauty, what is knowledge etc.,? The importance of asking students about what information is, made me realise then as now the crucial importance of epistemology or theory of knowledge regarding the media, manifested in all its different forms and types, through the 4th Estate, 5th Estate and the 6th Estate of the Big Tech companies, such as Facebook and Google. Though ethics is widely taught to media and communication students, much less so is epistemology, which is as crucial as the study of ethics, especially in the Information Age. For unless we know what information is and its underlying inherent epistemic characteristics in its communication, such as truth, justification, reliability, credibility, and trustworthiness, how can we possibly determine what are our ethical responsibilities and commitments in its dissemination as individuals, groups, professional institutions, and the Big Tech Media companies? Unless we know, then like some of our present political leaders, we won't know the difference between what is true and what is false, and why it matters, labelling the facts we don't like as "fake news" or "alternative facts", because they do not conform to our pre-existing biases and generally don't serve out own self-interests. That, however, like the anarchic denizens of a Hobbesian State of Nature, devoid of any ethical principles and values, undermines our common social good as a society, when the powerful few do as they please at the expense of the disempowered majority of citizens.

Another crucial question we need to ask in an Age of Information dominated by the five Big Tech companies in Silicon Valley, Alphabet-Google, Amazon, Apple, Facebook and Microsoft and at least three in China, Alibaba, Tencent, and Baidu,[3] is "what kind of a society do we really want?" (Pasquale 2015, 216). It is a question, directly or indirectly, several other authors have recently been asking,[4] including this book. It is partly an existential question as well as a question of orientation and direction for the future of humanity. It is an important and crucial question to ask, at a time when our lives are increasingly dominated in every social, political and financial sphere of society, by the Big Tech Companies, that through the opacity of their business models and complex driven AI algorithms, are powerful, non-transparent and unaccountable, not unlike, as this book has explored, Gyges in Plato's Myth in *The Republic*.[5] As aforementioned, the authors of *The Platform Society*, Van Dijck,

[3] Interestingly, the authors of *The Platform Society*, Van Dijck (2018) compare by analogy the five Big Tech companies of Silicon and Valley with the three Big Tach companies in China.

[4] See, for example, Shoshana Zuboff (2019); Jose Van Dijck, Thomas Poell, and Martijn De Waal (2018); Amy Webb (2019); Scott Galloway (2017); Michael P. Lynch (2016) and Rana, Foroohar (2019).

[5] See Appendix 1.

Poell, and De Waal (2018) compare the five Big Tech companies of Silicon Valley with the three equivalent Big Tach companies in China. They astutely observe that,

> Significantly, two of the world's most diverging ideological-political systems have come to rely on digital ecosystems that are remarkably similar in terms of their socio-technical operations and political governance.....the European Union need to respond to urgent questions concerning the viability of its public sphere in face of two platform ecosystems that each in its own way exerts unprecedented power over their societal organisations which happens largely through the internet (2018, 164-165).

The EU has responded, through the establishment of the *General Data Protection Regulation* (GDPR) in 2018, that has already imposed heavy fines on Facebook, Google, and Apple. A similar response outside the EU can be seen in the UK through its *Information Commissioner's Office (ICO)*, and in Australia through its *Office of the Australian Information Commissioner,* as well as the *Australian Competition and Consumer Commission* (*ACCC*) who have put Facebook and Google on notice and have taken court action, concerning their breaches of privacy and security of users' information. Just recently (20 April 2020), the Australian Government in a landmark decision, has announced that Facebook and Google will be forced to share advertising revenue with Australian media companies, through a mandatory code to be developed by the ACCC. According to the treasurer, Josh Frydenberg, this will create a 'level playing field', and only fair that the media companies that created the content should get paid for it (Taylor, Josh 2020; SBS News, 2020). The Australian media has welcomed the government initiative. The News Corp Australia executive chairman, Michael Miller, reportedly commented that,

> Google and Facebook had built trillion-dollar businesses by using other people's content and refusing to pay for it, and said that... "the decisive move by the government to go directly to a mandatory code of conduct between the international tech giants and Australian news media companies is a vital step that can help secure the future of Australian journalism" (SBS News, 2020).

More like a trickle at present but could quickly turn into a flood of litigations and regulation against the Big Tech companies of Silicon Valley, especially Facebook and Google, which in this book have been identified as essentially media companies. Signs are that the US *Federal Trade Commission (FTC)* might follow suit, as well as other regulatory actions that might follow in the UK and the EU.

However, as pointed out in Chap. 7, retrospective regulation alone through fines is not enough. In addition, what is urgently required, is proactive government regulation comprising the normative alignment of public ethical principles and values and external oversight and accountability through external *platform audits* conducted by independent Government sponsored agencies, that can ensure compliance with professional standards that align with public ethical principles and values for the common good of societies and the inculcation of those principles and values within the corporate structures of the Big Tech companies, through education and training programs.

Anticipating perhaps such a scenario, the CEO of Facebook, Mark Zuckerberg, has signalled such a proposed solution in his two recent articles in 2019 and 2020, examined in Chap. 7. He *wisely* observes that,

> People shouldn't have to rely on individual companies addressing these issues [regulation issues] by themselves. We should have a broader debate about what we want as a *society* [emphasis added] and how regulation can help…It's time to …define clear responsibilities for people, companies and governments going forward. (Zuckerberg, 2019).

In his Financial Times article (2020), he emphasizes that "people need to feel that global technology platforms answer to someone, so regulation should hold companies accountable when they make mistakes". He goes on to say, "that if we don't create standards that people feel are *legitimate* [emphasis added], they won't trust institutions or technology" (Mark Zuckerberg, 2020).

In reference to Mark Zuckerberg's quotation above, I have intentionally used the word "wisely" in order to introduce the notion of wisdom as another important and essential value to the normative evaluation and management of information for the common good of society, and humanity generally. Why is wisdom essential to the normative evaluation of information you ask? Because wisdom as a type *meta-information* can provide us with knowledge of how to live good lives for the attainment of eudaimonia or happiness for ourselves and for the common good of society (Spence, 2011a).

The age of abundant information is paradoxically marked by a deficit of wisdom. It seems the more information we have the less wise we are in managing and controlling it for our individual and collective well-being. The problem is that there is too much information and not enough time to absorb it, understand its implications and judge the best way to use it for our individual and common good. The glut of information has created gluttony for information, which can lead us to behave unwisely and sometimes foolishly. Examples of online and unwise and foolish online behaviour abound. People, for example, undermine their privacy and chances of future employment by placing compromising photos of themselves and friends on Facebook and engage in cyber bulling that has driven some young people to suicide.[6] The problem is widespread and global (Spence, 2013; 2011b).

The Internet is by its very nature a boundary-free public space not well suited to private conversations and secrets and what is more to the point, informational indiscretions. The digitization of information has fundamentally changed not only the way we disseminate information but the way we live. We are becoming informational beings increasingly spending our lives in the infosphere, where we play, pray, download and upload recipes, music and movies, buy and sell, chat and live in other virtual worlds, and make and break 'friendships' at a click. The internet just like the natural environment cannot be neatly constrained and controlled by any one group of individuals, conglomerates, or nations. And like the biosphere of the natural environment, the infosphere of the Internet is capricious and unpredictable and only

[6] For some examples, see Spence, E. (2011b) IT Savvy, But Stupid. *Australasian Science;* May 2011; 32, 4.

favours the uninhibited free dissemination of information by anyone, anytime and anywhere.

If we cannot control or manage the flow of information on the internet just as we cannot control the weather, the next best thing is to control our own online informational behaviour. That is within our control. We must learn how to use and disseminate information wisely in a manner that protects and promotes our individual and collective wellbeing. Wisdom was the core concern of philosophy in ancient Greece and Rome. Plato, Socrates, Aristotle, Zeno the founder of Stoic philosophy, Epicurus, Epictetus, Seneca and Cicero, Confucius in China, and the Budda in India, all provide ready-made models for wisdom.[7]

As a *meta-type of knowledge*, knowing how to understand and use information upon reflection and with good judgement for the benefit of oneself and the common good of society, wisdom can provide practical "know-how" for applying information to improve our lives and that of others. It is also a *reflective virtue* in the form of practical prudence, which can teach us how to create and use information to live good and meaningful lives in the infosphere – lives that are capable of leading to self-fulfilment,[8] eudemonia or happiness for us and others. What wisdom requires is that we learn the husbandry of information. How to reflect upon it, how to understand it, how to control it so it does not control us, how to judge its implications, so we can foresee its consequences, whether they are good or bad, for us and others; and how to use it in ways that enhance our well-being and promote and protect our rights to freedom, privacy, security, and autonomy, both as individuals, and collectively as networks, groups, corporations, and institutions, for the common good of society. In the age of information, it seems we would be better off with more wisdom and a little less information. Switching over from our iPhone and iPad, to Plato or Seneca, may be a good start.

As we saw in Chap. 2 the *Dual Obligation Information Theory (DOIT)* was designed and developed specifically for the purpose of normatively evaluating the dissemination of information at the convergence of the 4th and 5th Estates and analogously that of the 6th Estate, comprising Tech media companies and assessing their normative impact, epistemic, ethical and eudaimonic, on individuals and society.

In summary, the DOIT argument was that the dissemination of information as a process of communication entails a number of general epistemic and ethical values and norms that are necessary and universal for all informational agents in virtue of the inherent normative structure of *Information* and the inherent normative structure of *Action*. The communication of information as *Informational Action* therefore has a dual inherent normative structure that commits all informational agents to general

[7] For a comparative analysis of Western-Eastern Wisdom and its application to the Internet see Hui, Jin. and Spence, Edward (2016). Internet Addiction and Well-Being: Daoist and Stoic Reflections. *Dao: A Journal of Contemporary Philosophy.* Springer.

[8] See Gewirth, Alan (1998), *Self-fulfilment*, Princeton, NJ: Princeton University Press; and Spence, Edward (2006) *Ethics Within Reason: A Neo-Gewithian Approach* (2006). Maryland: Lexington Books (a division of Rowman and Littlefield, USA), Chapter 10.

epistemic and ethical principles and values. The communication of information as *information* commits informational agents to certain communicative epistemic and ethical values such as truth, accuracy, credibility, truthfulness, honesty, reliability, and trustworthiness. As well, the communication of information as informational *action*, commits informational agents to respect the universal rights to freedom and wellbeing of all other informational agents.

Wisdom as a form of knowledge about what a good life is, the value of such a life, and how to actively pursue it, in order to realize its attainment, is also a reflective meta-virtue whose possession enables the identification, evaluation and application of first-order knowledge as information, for the active pursuit of the good life for its attainment. Since wisdom requires information and knowledge oriented towards the realization of a good life for the attainment of eudaimonia, wellbeing, or happiness, and since the acquisition and communication of such knowledge entails epistemic and ethical norms, as well as eudaimonic values, values that relate to the pursuit and attainment of a good life and wellbeing, wisdom is therefore central and crucial to the normative evaluation of information regarding its impact on wellbeing, of individuals and society generally. Hence, the normative structure of information is shown to have a common and essential conceptual connection with wisdom with regard to the promotion of a good life for the attainment of eudaimonia, wellbeing or happiness.

The extension of DOIT to include the notion of *wisdom*, specifically, practical wisdom is the *DOIT-Wisdom* model (Spence 2011a) that allows for the *eudaimonic* evaluation of the impact of information on individuals and society generally. This is particularly useful because *wisdom* being at once an epistemic, ethical and eudaimonic *cluster-concept*, provides a single direct conceptual link between information and its communication on the one hand, and wellbeing on the other. Moreover and relatedly, the DOIT-Wisdom model is also useful as it is capable of providing practical guidance to all informational agents, including the convergent media of the 4th, 5th and 6th Estates, to use and disseminate information wisely, with reflection and good judgement for the good of themselves and that of others, for the common good of society and by extension the global good of humanity.

Returning to the question "what kind of a society do we really want?", which is the question that led to the inclusion of wisdom as an essential concept in evaluating the eudaimonic impact of information on the wellbeing of society and humanity generally, an answer that initially presents itself is: a society in which the wellbeing of individuals and collectively the wellbeing of society and humanity generally, is protected and promoted.

Lee Wilkins correctly points out that in addition to their traditional role of informing the public, journalists should also seek to mitigate harm to the public. To do so, she says, the definition of news should not only include what actually happens but also *what might happen*. As Wilkins eloquently puts it "preventing harm becomes the predominant ethical obligation" of journalists (2010, p.313). Journalists, she argues, should become "mitigation watchdogs". Wilkins argument for "mitigation reporting" in principle if not intent dovetails the argument in this chapter for communicating wisely, for it is through thinking and acting wisely as communicators of information that we not only mitigate harm to ourselves and others but also promote wellbeing for the common good of society. To that end, the media of the convergent media of the 4th and 5th Estates, as well as the Media Tech companies of the 6th Estate, and generally all communicators of information on the Internet, must not only avoid causing harm but also promote the common good of society. Communicators of information in the Information Age of the 21-century and beyond, including possibly autonomous intelligent robots, should not only as Lee Wilkins correctly claims act as "mitigation watchdogs" but moreover, also become "wise watchdogs" in promoting societal wellbeing for the common good of the societies in which they live and the global humanity generally.

Our enchantment[9] with our smart technological devices that we constantly use to get abundant information at a click, fast and offered free from the Big Tech companies is a wonder to behold. And no wonder we are hooked. As Foroohar perceptively observes (2019, p. 119) these technological devices are the 'slot machines' in our pockets the "devil that lives in our phones". But although the service provided is free, the cost is not, and comes at a high price. As it was for Dr. Faust, whose insatiable desire for knowledge unwisely drove him to sell his soul to the Devil. As T.S. Eliot asks with extraordinary prescience in his words quoted above, "where is the wisdom we have lost in knowledge?" Faustus's pact with the devil is metaphorically, at least, analogous to our own present dilemma and brings us back to the question explored in this final chapter and throughout this book: "What kind of a society do we really want?" And as Foroohar correctly observes, it presents us with the paradox of Big Tech (2019, p. 285),

> The good that it does—the information sharing, the relationship building, the productivity enhancing—has been made possible by the bad: the spying the selling, and the utter breaches of truth and public trust. Because the positives have been so divine—the ability to summon a fact or a cab in the twinkling of an eye—the diabolical negatives have been overlooked.

And the "diabolical negatives", as we have explored in this book, are many. In particular, the manipulation, the deceit, the misinformation, the corruption of information, the corruption of the political process and the undermining of the democratic system itself and its institutions, the loss of trust, and crucially, the loss of control over our collective information and data that has unwittingly, ceded control to Big Tech over most aspects of our lives. Is this the kind of life, and the society we wish to live in?

If "in the beginning was the Word, and the Word was with God, and the Word was God" (John 1:1 Gospel of John), can we not in the Age of Information, create a world in which even God (in whichever way we have conceived him) would want to live? Simply, because our information, based not only on knowledge but also guided by wisdom, is trustworthy, honest, true, credible, and just, in accordance with universal ethical principles, virtues, and values.

---

[9] For the enchantment of technology see Foroohar (2019:119–123).

Ironically, some of the characteristics philosophers and theologians have traditionally ascribed to God, such as *omniscience* and *omnipresence* can also be applied analogously to technology, and specifically, the information technologies of Big Tech, such as those of Facebook and Google. Two other godlike characteristics that are not, however, applicable to technology, at least, at the present time, are *omnipotence* and *benevolence*. Certainly not benevolence, for as we examined in this book, Big Tech is primarily motivated through its business model to operate primarily for its own financial gain and not for the common good of society. And though undoubtedly very powerful, Big Tech is not omnipotent. This allows for the timely opportunity to change the game plan by taking back control over our data and how it is used, by making Big Tech, and its associated information brokers, more transparent and accountable through regulation, for the overall benefit of all citizens and the common good of society, as suggested in Chap. 7 of this book. The time is ripe.

Only recently (June 2020) Facebook is again, as in the Cambridge Analytica scandal, plunged into controversy concerning its inadequate policies in regulating hate speech, after several of President Trump's political ads and posts on Facebook were deemed to constitute hate speech. Concerned for their reputations, several big advertisers such as Coco-Cola, Unilever, Honda, Hershey, and at least one hundred other brands, have withdrawn their advertising from Facebook (Kari Paul 2020; Alex Hern 2020a). Given that the highest proportion of Facebook's multi-billion dollar annual revenue comes from adverting, this places enormous financial pressure on the company, which unlike the large fines imposed on the company through regulation, as examined in Chap. 7, strikes at the very heart of Facebook's business model. And which, as we saw in Chap. 5, creates a *conflict of interest* between its role as a media company, and its financial interests that favour its business model over the common good of society. Which has been shown, as in the Cambridge Analytical case, to be conducive to media corruption as well as political corruption.

It is too soon to tell at this juncture what the outcome of the recent controversy facing Facebook will amount to. The pessimistic view is that once the furore subsides, as in the Cambridge Analytica case, it will be back to business as usual. Be that as it may, one thing is certain, however. The commercial pressure exerted on Facebook by advertisers at present that has landed a body blow at the heart of its business model itself, is no small matter. Not when the largest part of its $70bn annual revenue comes from advertising. It adds to the growing backlash against the company and more generally against the other Big Tech companies, such as Google, and further adds to the increasing moral chorus by various citizen groups and institutions, such as the *Common Sense Media*, the *Stop Hate for Profit* coalition, formed in the wake of the killing of George Floyd, and *Change the Terms*, and *Free Press*, that time has come for them to change their ways. Not only for their own financial self-interest but for the common good of a democratic society, of which they are also beneficiaries as citizens and institutions, but also by whose ethical principles, values and laws, they are bound in ensuring that the fundamental rights of all other citizens, less powerful than them, are not violated but protected and promoted. Anything less, not only falls short of ethical standards, principles, and values, but it is also bad for business. In fact, ethical principles and values when perceived to be reflected in the practices of a company might prove to be good for business. Apropos, a Honda Europe spokesperson explained that the company's decision to pause their advertising with Facebook was "in alignment with our company's values, which are grounded in human respect". Similarly, a spokesperson from the Oil group BP informed the *Guardian* (Ales Hern, 2020b) that the reason the company was also halting its advertising with Facebook is because of their belief that,

> "it is critically important for all social media platforms to deploy improved controls to eliminate the distribution of content that is untrue, discriminatory, or intended to incite, raise fear, or fan hate."

Perhaps, just as the advertisers boycotted Facebook,[10] the users themselves, as the other part of Facebook's business model equation, which provide the valuable data that Facebook, and by analogy Google, sells to advertisers for profit, should rise to the occasion and join the moral chorus demanding moral action. After all, they have good reason and the right to demand that the Big Tech companies, and especially Facebook and Google, should respect users' digital rights to their data,[11] on the basis of fundamental ethical principles and values by which those companies, as argued in this book, are bound. This would be both right and wise.

References

Butterworth, Liam. 2020. Coronavirus treatment spruiked by chef Pete Evans criticised by health associations, to be investigated by TGA, *ABC News*, April 12, 2020.

Descartes, Rene. 2018. *Meditations on First Philosophy*, edited and translated by John Cottingham. Cambridge: Cambridge University Press. Online version by Jonathan Bennett (2017). https://www.earlymoderntexts.com/assets/pdfs/descartes1641.pdf: Accessed 3 July 2020.

Eliot, Thomas Stearns. 1934. *Choruses from The Rock*.

Foroohar, Rana. 2019. *Don't be Evil: The Case Against Big Tech*. UK: Allen Lane, Random House.

Fuller, Jack. 1996. *News Values: Ideas for an Information Age*. Chicago: Chicago University Press.

Galloway, Scott. 2017. *The Four: The Hidden DNA of Amazon, Apple, Facebook and Google*. London, Great Brittain: Bantam Press.

Gewirth, Alan. 1998. *Self-fulfilment*, Princeton, NJ: Princeton University Press.

—. 2020b.Third of advertisers may boycott Facebbok in hate speech revolt. *The Guardian*, June 30,2020.Acessed:June30,2020.https://www.theguardian.com/technology/2020/jun/30/third-of-advertisers-may-boycott-facebook-in-hate-speech-revolt.

Hern, Alex. 2020a. How Hate Spech campaingers found Facebook's week spot. *The Guardian*, June 30, 2020. Acessed: June 30, 2020. https://www.theguardian.com/technology/2020/jun/29/how-hate-speech-campaigners-found-facebooks-weak-spot.

Hui, Jin, and Edward Spence. 2016. Internet Addiction and Well-Being: Daoist and Stoic Reflections. *Dao: A Journal of Contemporary Philosophy*. Springer.

Lynch, Michael P. 2016. *The Internet of Us: Knowing and Understanding Less in the Age of Big Data*, Penguin Random House.

---

[10] As at late June 2020.

[11] Rana Foroohar similarly argues in her book *Don't Be Evil* (2019 p. 277) that "individuals should also have their digital rights legalized."

Pasquale, Frank. 2015. *The Black Box Society: The Secret Algorithms That Control Money and Information*. Cambridge, MA: Harvard University Press

Paul, Kari. 2020. Facebook policy changes fail to quell advertiser revolt as Coca-Cola pulls ads. *The Guardian*, June 27, 2020. Accessed 27 June 2020. https://www.theguardian.com/technology/2020/jun/26/facebook-policies-hate-speech-advertisers-unilever

Robinson, Gregory. 2020. Eamon Holmes criticised for giving credence to Covid-19 5G conspiracy theory, *The Guardian*, April 14, 2020.

SBS News. 2020. The government is fat-tracking a code of conduct to force Google and Facebook to pay for news content, *SBS News*, April 20, 2020. Accessed 20 Apr 2020.

Shoshana Zuboff. 2019. *The Age of Surveillance Capitalism: The Fight for a Human Future at the New Frontier of Power*, Profile Books.

Spence, Edward. 2013. Wisdom and Well-being in a Technological Age, *Synesis: A Journal of Science, Technology, Ethics, and Policy* 2013

——. 2011a. Information, Knowledge and Wisdom: Groundwork for the Normative Evaluation of Digital Information and Its Relation to the Good Life, *Ethics and Information Technology*, 13(3):261–275.

——. 2011b. IT Savvy, But Stupid. *Australasian Science;* May 2011; 32, 4.

——. 2011c. Is Technology Good for Us? A Eudaimonic Meta-Model for Evaluating the Contributive Competence of Technologies for a Good Life. *Nanoethics,* 5:335–343.

——. 2006. *Ethics Within Reason: A Neo-Gewithian Approach* (2006). Maryland: Lexington Books (a division of Rowman and Littlefield, USA), Chapter 10.

Taylor, Josh. 2020. Facebook and Google to be forced to share advertising revenue with Australian media companies, *The Guardian*, April 20, 2020.

Taylor, Tegan. 2018. The 1918 influenza pandemic affected the whole world. Could it happen again? *ABC News*, April 13, 2020. https://www.abc.net.au/news/health/2018-04-13/flu-pandemic-1918-what-happened-and-could-it-happen-again/9601986. Accessed 16 Apr 2020.

Webb, Amy. 2019. *The Big Nine: How the Tech Titans and Their Thinking Machines Could Warp Humanity*, Hatchet Books.

Van Dijck, Poell and De Waal. 2018. *The Platform Society: Public Values in a Connected World*. Oxford: Oxford University Press

Zuboff, Shoshanna. 2019. *The Age of Surveillance Capitalism: The Fight for A Human Future At The New Frontier of Power*. London: Profile Books Ltd.

Zuckerberg, Mark. 2019. Four Ideas to Regulate the Internet, *Facebook*, March 30, 2019.

——. 2020. Big Tech Needs More Regulation, *Financial Times*, February 18, 2020.

Appendices

Appendix 1: The Myth of Gyges

The Republic
By Plato
Translated by Benjamin Jowett

Persons of the Dialogue
Socrates, who is the narrator.
Glaucon.
Adeimantus.
Polemarchus.
Cephalus.
Thrasymachus.
Cleitophon.
And others who are mute auditors.

Book II

With these words I was thinking that I had made an end of the discussion; but the end, in truth, proved to be only a beginning. For Glaucon, who is always the most pugnacious of men, was dissatisfied at Thrasymachus' retirement; he wanted to have the battle out. So he said to me: Socrates, do you wish really to persuade us, or only to seem to have persuaded us, that to be just is always better than to be unjust?

I should wish really to persuade you, I replied, if I could.

Then you certainly have not succeeded. Let me ask you now:—How would you arrange goods—are there not some which we welcome for their own sakes, and independently of their consequences, as, for example, harmless pleasures and enjoyments, which delight us at the time, although nothing follows from them?

E. H. Spence, *Media Corruption in the Age of Information*, Library of Public Policy and Public Administration 15, https://doi.org/10.1007/978-3-030-61612-0

I agree in thinking that there is such a class, I replied.

Is there not also a second class of goods, such as knowledge, sight, health, which are desirable not only in themselves, but also for their results?

Certainly, I said.

And would you not recognize a third class, such as gymnastic, and the care of the sick, and the physician's art; also the various ways of money-making—these do us good but we regard them as disagreeable; and no one would choose them for their own sakes, but only for the sake of some reward or result which flows from them?

There is, I said, this third class also. But why do you ask?

Because I want to know in which of the three classes you would place justice?

In the highest class, I replied,—among those goods which he who would be happy desires both for their own sake and for the sake of their results.

Then the many are of another mind; they think that justice is to be reckoned in the troublesome class, among goods which are to be pursued for the sake of rewards and of reputation, but in themselves are disagreeable and rather to be avoided.

I know, I said, that this is their manner of thinking, and that this was the thesis which Thrasymachus was maintaining just now, when he censured justice and praised injustice. But I am too stupid to be convinced by him.

I wish, he said, that you would hear me as well as him, and then I shall see whether you and I agree. For Thrasymachus seems to me, like a snake, to have been charmed by your voice sooner than he ought to have been; but to my mind the nature of justice and injustice have not yet been made clear. Setting aside their rewards and results, I want to know what they are in themselves, and how they inwardly work in the soul. If you, please, then, I will revive the argument of Thrasymachus. And first I will speak of the nature and origin of justice according to the common view of them. Secondly, I will show that all men who practise justice do so against their will, of necessity, but not as a good. And thirdly, I will argue that there is reason in this view, for the life of the unjust is after all better far than the life of the just—if what they say is true, Socrates, since I myself am not of their opinion. But still I acknowledge that I am perplexed when I hear the voices of Thrasymachus and myriads of others dinning in my ears; and, on the other hand, I have never yet heard the superiority of justice to injustice maintained by any one in a satisfactory way. I want to hear justice praised in respect of itself; then I shall be satisfied, and you are the person from whom I think that I am most likely to hear this; and therefore I will praise the unjust life to the utmost of my power, and my manner of speaking will indicate the manner in which I desire to hear you too praising justice and censuring injustice. Will you say whether you approve of my proposal?

Indeed I do; nor can I imagine any theme about which a man of sense would oftener wish to converse.

I am delighted, he replied, to hear you say so, and shall begin by speaking, as I proposed, of the nature and origin of justice.

They say that to do injustice is, by nature, good; to suffer injustice, evil; but that the evil is greater than the good. And so when men have both done and suffered injustice and have had experience of both, not being able to avoid the one and obtain the other, they think that they had better agree among themselves to have neither;

hence there arise laws and mutual covenants; and that which is ordained by law is termed by them lawful and just. This they affirm to be the origin and nature of justice;—it is a mean or compromise, between the best of all, which is to do injustice and not be punished, and the worst of all, which is to suffer injustice without the power of retaliation; and justice, being at a middle point between the two, is tolerated not as a good, but as the lesser evil, and honoured by reason of the inability of men to do injustice. For no man who is worthy to be called a man would ever submit to such an agreement if he were able to resist; he would be mad if he did. Such is the received account, Socrates, of the nature and origin of justice.

Now that those who practise justice do so involuntarily and because they have not the power to be unjust will best appear if we imagine something of this kind: having given both to the just and the unjust power to do what they will, let us watch and see whither desire will lead them; then we shall discover in the very act the just and unjust man to be proceeding along the same road, following their interest, which all natures deem to be their good, and are only diverted into the path of justice by the force of law. The liberty which we are supposing may be most completely given to them in the form of such a power as is said to have been possessed by Gyges, the ancestor of Croesus the Lydian. According to the tradition, Gyges was a shepherd in the service of the king of Lydia; there was a great storm, and an earthquake made an opening in the earth at the place where he was feeding his flock. Amazed at the sight, he descended into the opening, where, among other marvels, he beheld a hollow brazen horse, having doors, at which he stooping and looking in saw a dead body of stature, as appeared to him, more than human, and having nothing on but a gold ring; this he took from the finger of the dead and reascended. Now the shepherds met together, according to custom, that they might send their monthly report about the flocks to the king; into their assembly he came having the ring on his finger, and as he was sitting among them he chanced to turn the collet of the ring inside his hand, when instantly he became invisible to the rest of the company and they began to speak of him as if he were no longer present. He was astonished at this, and again touching the ring he turned the collet outwards and reappeared; he made several trials of the ring, and always with the same result—when he turned the collet inwards he became invisible, when outwards he reappeared. Whereupon he contrived to be chosen one of the messengers who were sent to the court; whereas soon as he arrived he seduced the queen, and with her help conspired against the king and slew him, and took the kingdom. Suppose now that there were two such magic rings, and the just put on one of them and the unjust the other; no man can be imagined to be of such an iron nature that he would stand fast in justice. No man would keep his hands off what was not his own when he could safely take what he liked out of the market, or go into houses and lie with any one at his pleasure, or kill or release from prison whom he would, and in all respects be like a God among men. Then the actions of the just would be as the actions of the unjust; they would both come at last to the same point. And this we may truly affirm to be a great proof that a man is just, not willingly or because he thinks that justice is any good to him individually, but of necessity, for wherever anyone thinks that he can safely be unjust, there he is unjust. For all men believe in their hearts that injustice is far more profitable to the individual than justice, and he who argues as I have been supposing, will say that they are right. If you could imagine any one obtaining this power of becoming invisible, and never doing any wrong or touching what was another's, he would be thought by the lookers-on to be a most wretched idiot, although they would praise him to one another's faces, and keep up appearances with one another from a fear that they too might suffer injustice. Enough of this.

Now, if we are to form a real judgment of the life of the just and unjust, we must isolate them; there is no other way; and how is the isolation to be effected? I answer: Let the unjust man be entirely unjust, and the just man entirely just; nothing is to be taken away from either of them, and both are to be perfectly furnished for the work of their respective lives. First, let the unjust be like other distinguished masters of craft; like the skilful pilot or physician, who knows intuitively his own powers and keeps within their limits, and who, if he fails at any point, is able to recover himself. So let the unjust make his unjust attempts in the right way, and lie hidden if he means to be great in his injustice: (he who is found out is nobody:) for the highest reach of injustice is, to be deemed just when you are not. Therefore I say that in the perfectly unjust man we must assume the most perfect injustice; there is to be no deduction, but we must allow him, while doing the most unjust acts, to have acquired the greatest reputation for justice. If he have taken a false step he must be able to recover himself; he must be one who can speak with effect, if any of his deeds come to light, and who can force his way where force is required by his courage and strength, and command of money and friends. And at his side let us place the just man in his nobleness and simplicity, wishing, as Aeschylus says, to be and not to seem good. There must be no seeming, for if he seem to be just he will be honoured and rewarded, and then we shall not know whether he is just for the sake of justice or for the sake of honours and rewards; therefore, let him be clothed in justice only, and have no other covering; and he must be imagined in a state of life the opposite of the former. Let him be the best of men, and let him be thought the worst; then he will have been put to the proof; and we shall see whether he will be affected by the fear of infamy and its consequences. And let him continue thus to the hour of death; being just and seeming to be unjust. When both have reached the uttermost extreme, the one of justice and the other of injustice, let judgment be given which of them is the happier of the two.

Heavens! my dear Glaucon, I said, how energetically you polish them up for the decision, first one and then the other, as if they were two statues.

I do my best, he said. And now that we know what they are like there is no difficulty in tracing out the sort of life which awaits either of them. This I will proceed to describe; but as you may think the description a little too coarse, I ask you to suppose, Socrates, that the words which follow are not mine.—Let me put them into the mouths of the eulogists of injustice: They will tell you that the just man who is thought unjust will be scourged, racked, bound—will have his eyes burnt out; and, at last, after suffering every kind of evil, he will be impaled: Then he will understand that he ought to seem only, and not to be, just; the words of Aeschylus may be more truly spoken of the unjust than of the just. For the unjust is pursuing a reality;

he does not live with a view to appearances—he wants to be really unjust and not to seem only:—

> 'His mind has a soil deep and fertile, Out of which spring his prudent counsels.'

In the first place, he is thought just, and therefore bears rule in the city; he can marry whom he will, and give in marriage to whom he will; also he can trade and deal where he likes, and always to his own advantage, because he has no misgivings about injustice; and at every contest, whether in public or private, he gets the better of his antagonists, and gains at their expense, and is rich, and out of his gains he can benefit his friends, and harm his enemies; moreover, he can offer sacrifices, and dedicate gifts to the gods abundantly and magnificently, and can honour the gods or any man whom he wants to honour in a far better style than the just, and therefore he is likely to be dearer than they are to the gods. And thus, Socrates, gods and men are said to unite in making the life of the unjust better than the life of the just.

I was going to say something in answer to Glaucon, when Adeimantus, his brother, interposed: Socrates, he said, you do not suppose that there is nothing more to be urged?

Why, what else is there? I answered.

The strongest point of all has not been even mentioned, he replied.

Well, then, according to the proverb, 'Let brother help brother'—if he fails in any part do you assist him; although I must confess that Glaucon has already said quite enough to lay me in the dust, and take from me the power of helping justice.

Nonsense, he replied. But let me add something more: There is another side to Glaucon's argument about the praise and censure of justice and injustice, which is equally required in order to bring out what I believe to be his meaning. Parents and tutors are always telling their sons and their wards that they are to be just; but why? not for the sake of justice, but for the sake of character and reputation; in the hope of obtaining for him who is reputed just some of those offices, marriages, and the like which Glaucon has enumerated among the advantages accruing to the unjust from the reputation of justice. More, however, is made of appearances by this class of persons than by the others; for they throw in the good opinion of the gods, and will tell you of a shower of benefits which the heavens, as they say, rain upon the pious; and this accords with the testimony of the noble Hesiod and Homer, the first of whom says,

> 'That the gods make the oaks of the just — To bear acorns at their summit, and bees in the middle; And the sheep are bowed down with the weight of their fleeces and many other blessings of a like kind are provided for them'.

And Homer has a very similar strain; for he speaks of one whose fame is—

> 'As the fame of some blameless king who, like a god, Maintains justice; to whom the black earth brings forth Wheat and barley, whose trees are bowed with fruit, And his sheep never fail to bear, and the sea gives him fish.'

Still grander are the gifts of heaven which Musaeus and his son vouchsafe to the just; they take them down into the world below, where they have the saints lying on couches at a feast, everlastingly drunk, crowned with garlands; their idea seems to be that an immortality of drunkenness is the highest meed of virtue. Some extend their rewards yet further; the posterity, as they say, of the faithful and just shall survive to the third and fourth generation. This is the style in which they praise justice. But about the wicked there is another strain; they bury them in a slough in Hades, and make them carry water in a sieve; also while they are yet living they bring them to infamy, and inflict upon them the punishments which Glaucon described as the portion of the just who are reputed to be unjust; nothing else does their invention supply. Such is their manner of praising the one and censuring the other.

Once more, Socrates, I will ask you to consider another way of speaking about justice and injustice, which is not confined to the poets, but is found in prose writers. The universal voice of mankind is always declaring that justice and virtue are honourable, but grievous and toilsome; and that the pleasures of vice and injustice are easy of attainment and are only censured by law and opinion. They say also that honesty is for the most part less profitable than dishonesty; and they are quite ready to call wicked men happy, and to honour them both in public and private when they are rich or in any other way influential, while they despise and overlook those who may be weak and poor, even though acknowledging them to be better than the others. But most extraordinary of all is their mode of speaking about virtue and the gods: they say that the gods apportion calamity and misery to many good men, and good and happiness to the wicked. And mendicant prophets go to rich men's doors and persuade them that they have a power committed to them by the gods of making an atonement for a man's own or his ancestor's sins by sacrifices or charms, with rejoicings and feasts; and they promise to harm an enemy, whether just or unjust, at a small cost; with magic arts and incantations binding heaven, as they say, to execute their will. And the poets are the authorities to whom they appeal, now smoothing the path of vice with the words of Hesiod;—

> 'Vice may be had in abundance without trouble; the way is smooth and her dwelling-place is near. But before virtue the gods have set toil,'

and a tedious and uphill road: then citing Homer as a witness that the gods may be influenced by men; for he also says:—

> 'The gods, too, may be turned from their purpose; and men pray to them and avert their wrath by sacrifices and soothing entreaties, and by libations and the odour of fat, when they have sinned and transgressed.'

And they produce a host of books written by Musaeus and Orpheus, who were children of the Moon and the Muses—that is what they say—according to which they perform their ritual, and persuade not only individuals, but whole cities, that expiations and atonements for sin may be made by sacrifices and amusements which fill a vacant hour, and are equally at the service of the living and the dead; the latter sort they call mysteries, and they redeem us from the pains of hell, but if we neglect them no one knows what awaits us.

He proceeded: And now when the young hear all this said about virtue and vice, and the way in which gods and men regard them, how are their minds likely to be affected, my dear Socrates,—those of them, I mean, who are quick-witted, and, like bees on the wing, light on every flower, and from all that they hear are prone to draw conclusions as to what manner of persons they should be and in what way they should walk if they would make the best of life? Probably the youth will say to himself in the words of Pindar—

> 'Can I by justice or by crooked ways of deceit ascend a loftier tower which may be a fortress to me all my days?'

For what men say is that, if I am really just and am not also thought just profit there is none, but the pain and loss on the other hand are unmistakable. But if, though unjust, I acquire the reputation of justice, a heavenly life is promised to me. Since then, as philosophers prove, appearance tyrannizes over truth and is lord of happiness, to appearance I must devote myself. I will describe around me a picture and shadow of virtue to be the vestibule and exterior of my house; behind I will trail the subtle and crafty fox, as Archilochus, greatest of sages, recommends. But I hear someone exclaiming that the concealment of wickedness is often difficult; to which I answer, nothing great is easy. Nevertheless, the argument indicates this, if we would be happy, to be the path along which we should proceed. With a view to concealment we will establish secret brotherhoods and political clubs. And there are professors of rhetoric who teach the art of persuading courts and assemblies; and so, partly by persuasion and partly by force, I shall make unlawful gains and not be punished. Still I hear a voice saying that the gods cannot be deceived, neither can they be compelled. But what if there are no gods? or, suppose them to have no care of human things—why in either case should we mind about concealment? And even if there are gods, and they do care about us, yet we know of them only from tradition and the genealogies of the poets; and these are the very persons who say that they may be influenced and turned by 'sacrifices and soothing entreaties and by offerings.' Let us be consistent then, and believe both or neither. If the poets speak truly, why then we had better be unjust, and offer of the fruits of injustice; for if we are just, although we may escape the vengeance of heaven, we shall lose the gains of injustice; but, if we are unjust, we shall keep the gains, and by our sinning and praying, and praying and sinning, the gods will be propitiated, and we shall not be punished. 'But there is a world below in which either we or our posterity will suffer for our unjust deeds.' Yes, my friend, will be the reflection, but there are mysteries and atoning deities, and these have great power. That is what mighty cities declare; and the children of the gods, who were their poets and prophets, bear a like testimony.

On what principle, then, shall we any longer choose justice rather than the worst injustice? when, if we only unite the latter with a deceitful regard to appearances, we shall fare to our mind both with gods and men, in life and after death, as the most numerous and the highest authorities tell us. Knowing all this, Socrates, how can a man who has any superiority of mind or person or rank or wealth, be willing to honour justice; or indeed to refrain from laughing when he hears justice praised? And even if there should be someone who is able to disprove the truth of my words, and who is satisfied that justice is best, still he is not angry with the unjust, but is very ready to forgive them, because he also knows that men are not just of their own free will; unless, peradventure, there be some one whom the divinity within him may have inspired with a hatred of injustice, or who has attained knowledge of the truth—but no other man. He only blames injustice who, owing to cowardice or age or some weakness, has not the power of being unjust. And this is proved by the fact that when he obtains the power, he immediately becomes unjust as far as he can be.

The cause of all this, Socrates, was indicated by us at the beginning of the argument, when my brother and I told you how astonished we were to find that of all the professing panegyrists of justice—beginning with the ancient heroes of whom any memorial has been preserved to us, and ending with the men of our own time—no one has ever blamed injustice or praised justice except with a view to the glories, honours, and benefits which flow from them. No one has ever adequately described either in verse or prose the true essential nature of either of them abiding in the soul, and invisible to any human or divine eye; or shown that of all the things of a man's soul which he has within him, justice is the greatest good, and injustice the greatest evil. Had this been the universal strain, had you sought to persuade us of this from our youth upwards, we should not have been on the watch to keep one another from doing wrong, but every one would have been his own watchman, because afraid, if he did wrong, of harbouring in himself the greatest of evils. I dare say that Thrasymachus and others would seriously hold the language which I have been merely repeating, and words even stronger than these about justice and injustice, grossly, as I conceive, perverting their true nature. But I speak in this vehement manner, as I must frankly confess to you, because I want to hear from you the opposite side; and I would ask you to show not only the superiority which justice has over injustice, but what effect they have on the possessor of them which makes the one to be a good and the other an evil to him. And please, as Glaucon requested of you, to exclude reputations; for unless you take away from each of them his true reputation and add on the false, we shall say that you do not praise justice, but the appearance of it; we shall think that you are only exhorting us to keep injustice dark, and that you really agree with Thrasymachus in thinking that justice is another's good and the interest of the stronger, and that injustice is a man's own profit and interest, though injurious to the weaker. Now as you have admitted that justice is one of that highest class of goods which are desired indeed for their results, but in a far greater degree for their own sakes—like sight or hearing or knowledge or health, or any other real and natural and not merely conventional good—I would ask you in your praise of justice to regard one point only: I mean the essential good and evil which justice and injustice work in the possessors of them. Let others praise justice and censure injustice, magnifying the rewards and honours of the one and abusing the other; that is a manner of arguing which, coming from them, I am ready to tolerate, but from you who have spent your whole life in the consideration of this question, unless I hear the contrary from your own lips, I expect something better. And therefore, I say, not only prove to us that justice is better than injustice, but show what they either of them do to the possessor of them, which makes the one to be a good and the other an evil, whether seen or unseen by gods and men.

I had always admired the genius of Glaucon and Adeimantus, but on hearing these words I was quite delighted, and said: Sons of an illustrious father, that was not a bad beginning of the Elegiac verses which the admirer of Glaucon made in honour of you after you had distinguished yourselves at the battle of Megara:—

> 'Sons of Ariston,' he sang, 'divine offspring of an illustrious hero.'

The epithet is very appropriate, for there is something truly divine in being able to argue as you have done for the superiority of injustice, and remaining unconvinced by your own arguments. And I do believe that you are not convinced—this I infer from your general character, for had I judged only from your speeches I should have mistrusted you. But now, the greater my confidence in you, the greater is my difficulty in knowing what to say. For I am in a strait between two; on the one hand I feel that I am unequal to the task; and my inability is brought home to me by the fact that you were not satisfied with the answer which I made to Thrasymachus, proving, as I thought, the superiority which justice has over injustice. And yet I cannot refuse to help, while breath and speech remain to me; I am afraid that there would be an impiety in being present when justice is evil spoken of and not lifting up a hand in her defence. And therefore I had best give such help as I can.

Glaucon and the rest entreated me by all means not to let the question drop, but to proceed in the investigation. They wanted to arrive at the truth, first, about the nature of justice and injustice, and secondly, about their relative advantages. I told them, what I really thought, that the enquiry would be of a serious nature, and would require very good eyes. Seeing then, I said, that we are no great wits, I think that we had better adopt a method which I may illustrate thus; suppose that a short-sighted person had been asked by some one to read small letters from a distance; and it occurred to some one else that they might be found in another place which was larger and in which the letters were larger—if they were the same and he could read the larger letters first, and then proceed to the lesser—this would have been thought a rare piece of good fortune.

Very true, said Adeimantus; but how does the illustration apply to our enquiry?

I will tell you, I replied; justice, which is the subject of our enquiry, is, as you know, sometimes spoken of as the virtue of an individual, and sometimes as the virtue of a State.

True, he replied.

And is not a State larger than an individual?

It is.

Then in the larger the quantity of justice is likely to be larger and more easily discernible. I propose therefore that we enquire into the nature of justice and injustice, first as they appear in the State, and secondly in the individual, proceeding from the greater to the lesser and comparing them.

That, he said, is an excellent proposal.

And if we imagine the State in process of creation, we shall see the justice and injustice of the State in process of creation also.

I dare say.

When the State is completed there may be a hope that the object of our search will be more easily discovered.

Yes, far more easily.

But ought we to attempt to construct one? I said; for to do so, as I am inclined to think, will be a very serious task. Reflect, therefore.

I have reflected, said Adeimantus, and am anxious that you should proceed.

A State, I said, arises, as I conceive, out of the needs of mankind; no one is self-sufficing, but all of us have many wants. Can any other origin of a State be imagined?

There can be no other.

Then, as we have many wants, and many persons are needed to supply them, one takes a helper for one purpose and another for another; and when these partners and helpers are gathered together in one habitation the body of inhabitants is termed a State.

True, he said.

And they exchange with one another, and one gives, and another receives, under the idea that the exchange will be for their good.

Very true.

Then, I said, let us begin and create in idea a State; and yet the true creator is necessity, who is the mother of our invention.

Of course, he replied.

Now the first and greatest of necessities is food, which is the condition of life and existence.

Certainly.

The second is a dwelling, and the third clothing and the like.

True.

And now let us see how our city will be able to supply this great demand: We may suppose that one man is a husbandman, another a builder, some one else a weaver—shall we add to them a shoemaker, or perhaps some other purveyor to our bodily wants?

Quite right.

The barest notion of a State must include four or five men.

Clearly.

And how will they proceed? Will each bring the result of his labours into a common stock?—the individual husbandman, for example, producing for four, and labouring four times as long and as much as he need in the provision of food with which he supplies others as well as himself; or will he have nothing to do with others and not be at the trouble of producing for them, but provide for himself alone a fourth of the food in a fourth of the time, and in the remaining three fourths of his time be employed in making a house or a coat or a pair of shoes, having no partnership with others, but supplying himself all his own wants?

Adeimantus thought that he should aim at producing food only and not at producing everything.

Probably, I replied, that would be the better way; and when I hear you say this, I am myself reminded that we are not all alike; there are diversities of natures among us which are adapted to different occupations.

Very true.

And will you have a work better done when the workman has many occupations, or when he has only one?

When he has only one.

Further, there can be no doubt that a work is spoilt when not done at the right time?

No doubt.

For business is not disposed to wait until the doer of the business is at leisure; but the doer must follow up what he is doing, and make the business his first object.

He must.

And if so, we must infer that all things are produced more plentifully and easily and of a better quality when one man does one thing which is natural to him and does it at the right time, and leaves other things.

Undoubtedly.

Then more than four citizens will be required; for the husbandman will not make his own plough or mattock, or other implements of agriculture, if they are to be good for anything. Neither will the builder make his tools—and he too needs many; and in like manner the weaver and shoemaker.

True.

Then carpenters, and smiths, and many other artisans, will be sharers in our little State, which is already beginning to grow?

True.

Yet even if we add neatherds, shepherds, and other herdsmen, in order that our husbandmen may have oxen to plough with, and builders as well as husbandmen may have draught cattle, and curriers and weavers fleeces and hides,—still our State will not be very large.

That is true; yet neither will it be a very small State which contains all these.

Then, again, there is the situation of the city—to find a place where nothing need be imported is wellnigh impossible.

Impossible.

Then there must be another class of citizens who will bring the required supply from another city?

There must.

But if the trader goes empty-handed, having nothing which they require who would supply his need, he will come back empty-handed.

That is certain.

And therefore, what they produce at home must be not only enough for themselves, but such both in quantity and quality as to accommodate those from whom their wants are supplied.

Very true.

Then more husbandmen and more artisans will be required?

They will.

Not to mention the importers and exporters, who are called merchants?

Yes.

Then we shall want merchants?

We shall.

And if merchandise is to be carried over the sea, skilful sailors will also be needed, and in considerable numbers?

Yes, in considerable numbers.

Then, again, within the city, how will they exchange their productions? To secure such an exchange was, as you will remember, one of our principal objects when we formed them into a society and constituted a State.

Clearly they will buy and sell.

Then they will need a market-place, and a money-token for purposes of exchange.

Certainly.

Suppose now that a husbandman, or an artisan, brings some production to market, and he comes at a time when there is no one to exchange with him,—is he to leave his calling and sit idle in the marketplace?

Not at all; he will find people there who, seeing the want, undertake the office of salesmen. In well-ordered states they are commonly those who are the weakest in bodily strength, and therefore of little use for any other purpose; their duty is to be in the market, and to give money in exchange for goods to those who desire to sell and to take money from those who desire to buy.

This want, then, creates a class of retail-traders in our State. Is not 'retailer' the term which is applied to those who sit in the marketplace engaged in buying and selling, while those who wander from one city to another are called merchants?

Yes, he said.

And there is another class of servants, who are intellectually hardly on the level of companionship; still they have plenty of bodily strength for labour, which accordingly they sell, and are called, if I do not mistake, hirelings, hire being the name which is given to the price of their labour.

True.

Then hirelings will help to make up our population?

Yes.

And now, Adeimantus, is our State matured and perfected?

I think so.

Where, then, is justice, and where is injustice, and in what part of the State did they spring up?

Probably in the dealings of these citizens with one another. I cannot imagine that they are more likely to be found any where else.

I dare say that you are right in your suggestion, I said; we had better think the matter out, and not shrink from the enquiry.

Let us then consider, first of all, what will be their way of life, now that we have thus established them. Will they not produce corn, and wine, and clothes, and shoes, and build houses for themselves? And when they are housed, they will work, in summer, commonly, stripped and barefoot, but in winter substantially clothed and shod. They will feed on barley-meal and flour of wheat, baking and kneading them, making noble cakes and loaves; these they will serve up on a mat of reeds or on clean leaves, themselves reclining the while upon beds strewn with yew or myrtle. And they and their children will feast, drinking of the wine which they have made, wearing garlands on their heads, and hymning the praises of the gods, in happy converse with one another. And they will take care that their families do not exceed their means; having an eye to poverty or war.

But, said Glaucon, interposing, you have not given them a relish to their meal.

True, I replied, I had forgotten; of course they must have a relish—salt, and olives, and cheese, and they will boil roots and herbs such as country people prepare; for a dessert we shall give them figs, and peas, and beans; and they will roast myrtle-berries and acorns at the fire, drinking in moderation. And with such a diet they may be expected to live in peace and health to a good old age, and bequeath a similar life to their children after them.

Yes, Socrates, he said, and if you were providing for a city of pigs, how else would you feed the beasts?

But what would you have, Glaucon? I replied.

Why, he said, you should give them the ordinary conveniences of life. People who are to be comfortable are accustomed to lie on sofas, and dine off tables, and they should have sauces and sweets in the modern style.

Yes, I said, now I understand: the question which you would have me consider is, not only how a State, but how a luxurious State is created; and possibly there is no harm in this, for in such a State we shall be more likely to see how justice and injustice originate. In my opinion the true and healthy constitution of the State is the one which I have described. But if you wish also to see a State at fever-heat, I have no objection. For I suspect that many will not be satisfied with the simpler way of life. They will be for adding sofas, and tables, and other furniture; also dainties, and perfumes, and incense, and courtesans, and cakes, all these not of one sort only, but in every variety; we must go beyond the necessaries of which I was at first speaking, such as houses, and clothes, and shoes: the arts of the painter and the embroiderer will have to be set in motion, and gold and ivory and all sorts of materials must be procured.

True, he said.

Then we must enlarge our borders; for the original healthy State is no longer sufficient. Now will the city have to fill and swell with a multitude of callings which are not required by any natural want; such as the whole tribe of hunters and actors, of whom one large class have to do with forms and colours; another will be the votaries of music—poets and their attendant train of rhapsodists, players, dancers, contractors; also makers of divers kinds of articles, including women's dresses. And we shall want more servants. Will not tutors be also in request, and nurses wet and dry, tirewomen and barbers, as well as confectioners and cooks; and swineherds, too, who were not needed and therefore had no place in the former edition of our State, but are needed now? They must not be forgotten: and there will be animals of many other kinds, if people eat them.

Certainly.

And living in this way we shall have much greater need of physicians than before?

Much greater.

And the country which was enough to support the original inhabitants will be too small now, and not enough?

Quite true.

Then a slice of our neighbours' land will be wanted by us for pasture and tillage, and they will want a slice of ours, if, like ourselves, they exceed the limit of necessity, and give themselves up to the unlimited accumulation of wealth?

That, Socrates, will be inevitable.

And so we shall go to war, Glaucon. Shall we not?

Most certainly, he replied.

Then without determining as yet whether war does good or harm, thus much we may affirm, that now we have discovered war to be derived from causes which are also the causes of almost all the evils in States, private as well as public.

Undoubtedly.

And our State must once more enlarge; and this time the enlargement will be nothing short of a whole army, which will have to go out and fight with the invaders for all that we have, as well as for the things and persons whom we were describing above.

Why? he said; are they not capable of defending themselves?

No, I said; not if we were right in the principle which was acknowledged by all of us when we were framing the State: the principle, as you will remember, was that one man cannot practise many arts with success.

Very true, he said.

But is not war an art?

Certainly.

And an art requiring as much attention as shoemaking?

Quite true.

And the shoemaker was not allowed by us to be a husbandman, or a weaver, or a builder—in order that we might have our shoes well made; but to him and to every other worker was assigned one work for which he was by nature fitted, and at that he was to continue working all his life long and at no other; he was not to let opportunities slip, and then he would become a good workman. Now nothing can be more important than that the work of a soldier should be well done. But is war an art so easily acquired that a man may be a warrior who is also a husbandman, or shoemaker, or other artisan; although no one in the world would be a good dice or draught player who merely took up the game as a recreation, and had not from his earliest years devoted himself to this and nothing else? No tools will make a man a skilled workman, or master of defence, nor be of any use to him who has not learned how to handle them, and has never bestowed any attention upon them. How then will he who takes up a shield or other implement of war become a good fighter all in a day, whether with heavy-armed or any other kind of troops?

Yes, he said, the tools which would teach men their own use would be beyond price.

And the higher the duties of the guardian, I said, the more time, and skill, and art, and application will be needed by him?

No doubt, he replied.

Will he not also require natural aptitude for his calling?

Certainly.

Then it will be our duty to select, if we can, natures which are fitted for the task of guarding the city?

It will.

And the selection will be no easy matter, I said; but we must be brave and do our best.

We must.

Is not the noble youth very like a well-bred dog in respect of guarding and watching?

What do you mean?

I mean that both of them ought to be quick to see, and swift to overtake the enemy when they see him; and strong too if, when they have caught him, they have to fight with him.

All these qualities, he replied, will certainly be required by them.

Well, and your guardian must be brave if he is to fight well?

Certainly.

And is he likely to be brave who has no spirit, whether horse or dog or any other animal? Have you never observed how invincible and unconquerable is spirit and how the presence of it makes the soul of any creature to be absolutely fearless and indomitable?

I have.

Then now we have a clear notion of the bodily qualities which are required in the guardian.

True.

And also of the mental ones; his soul is to be full of spirit?

Yes.

But are not these spirited natures apt to be savage with one another, and with everybody else?

A difficulty by no means easy to overcome, he replied.

Whereas, I said, they ought to be dangerous to their enemies, and gentle to their friends; if not, they will destroy themselves without waiting for their enemies to destroy them.

True, he said.

What is to be done then? I said; how shall we find a gentle nature which has also a great spirit, for the one is the contradiction of the other?

True.

He will not be a good guardian who is wanting in either of these two qualities; and yet the combination of them appears to be impossible; and hence we must infer that to be a good guardian is impossible.

I am afraid that what you say is true, he replied.

Here feeling perplexed I began to think over what had preceded.—My friend, I said, no wonder that we are in a perplexity; for we have lost sight of the image which we had before us.

What do you mean? he said.

I mean to say that there do exist natures gifted with those opposite qualities.

And where do you find them?

Many animals, I replied, furnish examples of them; our friend the dog is a very good one: you know that well-bred dogs are perfectly gentle to their familiars and acquaintances, and the reverse to strangers.

Yes, I know.

Then there is nothing impossible or out of the order of nature in our finding a guardian who has a similar combination of qualities?

Certainly not.

Would not he who is fitted to be a guardian, besides the spirited nature, need to have the qualities of a philosopher?

I do not apprehend your meaning.

The trait of which I am speaking, I replied, may be also seen in the dog, and is remarkable in the animal.

What trait?

Why, a dog, whenever he sees a stranger, is angry; when an acquaintance, he welcomes him, although the one has never done him any harm, nor the other any good. Did this never strike you as curious?

The matter never struck me before; but I quite recognise the truth of your remark.

And surely this instinct of the dog is very charming;—your dog is a true philosopher.

Why?

Why, because he distinguishes the face of a friend and of an enemy only by the criterion of knowing and not knowing. And must not an animal be a lover of learning who determines what he likes and dislikes by the test of knowledge and ignorance?

Most assuredly.

And is not the love of learning the love of wisdom, which is philosophy?

They are the same, he replied.

And may we not say confidently of man also, that he who is likely to be gentle to his friends and acquaintances, must by nature be a lover of wisdom and knowledge?

That we may safely affirm.

Then he who is to be a really good and noble guardian of the State will require to unite in himself philosophy and spirit and swiftness and strength?

Undoubtedly.

Then we have found the desired natures; and now that we have found them, how are they to be reared and educated? Is not this an enquiry which may be expected to throw light on the greater enquiry which is our final end—How do justice and injustice grow up in States? for we do not want either to omit what is to the point or to draw out the argument to an inconvenient length.

Adeimantus thought that the enquiry would be of great service to us.

Then, I said, my dear friend, the task must not be given up, even if somewhat long.

Certainly not.

Come then, and let us pass a leisure hour in story-telling, and our story shall be the education of our heroes.

By all means.

And what shall be their education? Can we find a better than the traditional sort?—and this has two divisions, gymnastic for the body, and music for the soul.

True.

Shall we begin education with music, and go on to gymnastic afterwards?

By all means.

And when you speak of music, do you include literature or not?

I do.

And literature may be either true or false?

Yes.

And the young should be trained in both kinds, and we begin with the false?

I do not understand your meaning, he said.

You know, I said, that we begin by telling children stories which, though not wholly destitute of truth, are in the main fictitious; and these stories are told them when they are not of an age to learn gymnastics.

Very true.

That was my meaning when I said that we must teach music before gymnastics.

Quite right, he said.

You know also that the beginning is the most important part of any work, especially in the case of a young and tender thing; for that is the time at which the character is being formed and the desired impression is more readily taken.

Quite true.

And shall we just carelessly allow children to hear any casual tales which may be devised by casual persons, and to receive into their minds ideas for the most part the very opposite of those which we should wish them to have when they are grown up?

We cannot.

Then the first thing will be to establish a censorship of the writers of fiction, and let the censors receive any tale of fiction which is good, and reject the bad; and we will desire mothers and nurses to tell their children the authorised ones only. Let them fashion the mind with such tales, even more fondly than they mould the body with their hands; but most of those which are now in use must be discarded.

Of what tales are you speaking? he said.

You may find a model of the lesser in the greater, I said; for they are necessarily of the same type, and there is the same spirit in both of them.

Very likely, he replied; but I do not as yet know what you would term the greater.

Those, I said, which are narrated by Homer and Hesiod, and the rest of the poets, who have ever been the great storytellers of mankind.

But which stories do you mean, he said; and what fault do you find with them?

A fault which is most serious, I said; the fault of telling a lie, and, what is more, a bad lie.

But when is this fault committed?

Whenever an erroneous representation is made of the nature of gods and heroes,—as when a painter paints a portrait not having the shadow of a likeness to the original.

Yes, he said, that sort of thing is certainly very blameable; but what are the stories which you mean?

First of all, I said, there was that greatest of all lies in high places, which the poet told about Uranus, and which was a bad lie too,—I mean what Hesiod says that Uranus did, and how Cronus retaliated on him. The doings of Cronus, and the sufferings which in turn his son inflicted upon him, even if they were true, ought certainly not to be lightly told to young and thoughtless persons; if possible, they had better be buried in silence. But if there is an absolute necessity for their mention, a chosen few might hear them in a mystery, and they should sacrifice not a common (Eleusinian) pig, but some huge and unprocurable victim; and then the number of the hearers will be very few indeed.

Why, yes, said he, those stories are extremely objectionable.

Yes, Adeimantus, they are stories not to be repeated in our State; the young man should not be told that in committing the worst of crimes he is far from doing anything outrageous; and that even if he chastises his father when he does wrong, in whatever manner, he will only be following the example of the first and greatest among the gods.

I entirely agree with you, he said; in my opinion those stories are quite unfit to be repeated.

Neither, if we mean our future guardians to regard the habit of quarrelling among themselves as of all things the basest, should any word be said to them of the wars in heaven, and of the plots and fightings of the gods against one another, for they are not true. No, we shall never mention the battles of the giants, or let them be embroidered on garments; and we shall be silent about the innumerable other quarrels of gods and heroes with their friends and relatives. If they would only believe us we would tell them that quarrelling is unholy, and that never up to this time has there been any quarrel between citizens; this is what old men and old women should begin by telling children; and when they grow up, the poets also should be told to compose for them in a similar spirit. But the narrative of Hephaestus binding Here his mother, or how on another occasion Zeus sent him flying for taking her part when she was being beaten, and all the battles of the gods in Homer—these tales must not be admitted into our State, whether they are supposed to have an allegorical meaning or not. For a young person cannot judge what is allegorical and what is literal; anything that he receives into his mind at that age is likely to become indelible and unalterable; and therefore it is most important that the tales which the young first hear should be models of virtuous thoughts.

There you are right, he replied; but if any one asks where are such models to be found and of what tales are you speaking—how shall we answer him?

I said to him, You and I, Adeimantus, at this moment are not poets, but founders of a State: now the founders of a State ought to know the general forms in which poets should cast their tales, and the limits which must be observed by them, but to make the tales is not their business.

Very true, he said; but what are these forms of theology which you mean?

Something of this kind, I replied:—God is always to be represented as he truly is, whatever be the sort of poetry, epic, lyric or tragic, in which the representation is given.

Right.

And is he not truly good? and must he not be represented as such?

Certainly.

And no good thing is hurtful?

No, indeed.

And that which is not hurtful hurts not?

Certainly not.

And that which hurts not does no evil?

No.

And can that which does no evil be a cause of evil?

Impossible.

And the good is advantageous?

Yes.

And therefore the cause of well-being?

Yes.

It follows therefore that the good is not the cause of all things, but of the good only?

Assuredly.

Then God, if he be good, is not the author of all things, as the many assert, but he is the cause of a few things only, and not of most things that occur to men. For few are the goods of human life, and many are the evils, and the good is to be attributed to God alone; of the evils the causes are to be sought elsewhere, and not in him.

That appears to me to be most true, he said.

Then we must not listen to Homer or to any other poet who is guilty of the folly of saying that two casks

> 'Lie at the threshold of Zeus, full of lots, one of good, the other of evil lots,'

and that he to whom Zeus gives a mixture of the two

> 'Sometimes meets with evil fortune, at other times with good;'

but that he to whom is given the cup of unmingled ill,

> 'Him wild hunger drives o'er the beauteous earth.'

And again—

> 'Zeus, who is the dispenser of good and evil to us.'

And if any one asserts that the violation of oaths and treaties, which was really the work of Pandarus, was brought about by Athene and Zeus, or that the strife and contention of the gods was instigated by Themis and Zeus, he shall not have our approval; neither will we allow our young men to hear the words of Aeschylus, that

> 'God plants guilt among men when he desires utterly to destroy a house.'

And if a poet writes of the sufferings of Niobe—the subject of the tragedy in which these iambic verses occur—or of the house of Pelops, or of the Trojan war or on any similar theme, either we must not permit him to say that these are the works of God, or if they are of God, he must devise some explanation of them such as we are seeking; he must say that God did what was just and right, and they were the better for being punished; but that those who are punished are miserable, and that God is the author of their misery—the poet is not to be permitted to say; though he may say that the wicked are miserable because they require to be punished, and are benefited by receiving punishment from God; but that God being good is the author of evil to any one is to be strenuously denied, and not to be said or sung or heard in verse or prose by any one whether old or young in any well-ordered commonwealth. Such a fiction is suicidal, ruinous, impious.

I agree with you, he replied, and am ready to give my assent to the law.

Let this then be one of our rules and principles concerning the gods, to which our poets and reciters will be expected to conform,—that God is not the author of all things, but of good only.

That will do, he said.

And what do you think of a second principle? Shall I ask you whether God is a magician, and of a nature to appear insidiously now in one shape, and now in another—sometimes himself changing and passing into many forms, sometimes deceiving us with the semblance of such transformations; or is he one and the same immutably fixed in his own proper image?

I cannot answer you, he said, without more thought.

Well, I said; but if we suppose a change in anything, that change must be effected either by the thing itself, or by some other thing?

Most certainly.

And things which are at their best are also least liable to be altered or discomposed; for example, when healthiest and strongest, the human frame is least liable to be affected by meats and drinks, and the plant which is in the fullest vigour also suffers least from winds or the heat of the sun or any similar causes.

Of course.

And will not the bravest and wisest soul be least confused or deranged by any external influence?

True.

And the same principle, as I should suppose, applies to all composite things—furniture, houses, garments: when good and well made, they are least altered by time and circumstances.

Very true.

Then everything which is good, whether made by art or nature, or both, is least liable to suffer change from without?

True.

But surely God and the things of God are in every way perfect?

Of course they are.

Then he can hardly be compelled by external influence to take many shapes?

He cannot.

But may he not change and transform himself?

Clearly, he said, that must be the case if he is changed at all.

And will he then change himself for the better and fairer, or for the worse and more unsightly?

If he change at all he can only change for the worse, for we cannot suppose him to be deficient either in virtue or beauty.

Very true, Adeimantus; but then, would any one, whether God or man, desire to make himself worse?

Impossible.

Then it is impossible that God should ever be willing to change; being, as is supposed, the fairest and best that is conceivable, every God remains absolutely and for ever in his own form.

That necessarily follows, he said, in my judgment.

Then, I said, my dear friend, let none of the poets tell us that

> 'The gods, taking the disguise of strangers from other lands, walk up and down cities in all sorts of forms;'

and let no one slander Proteus and Thetis, neither let anyone, either in tragedy or in any other kind of poetry, introduce Here disguised in the likeness of a priestess asking an alms

> 'For the life-giving daughters of Inachus the river of Argos;'

—let us have no more lies of that sort. Neither must we have mothers under the influence of the poets scaring their children with a bad version of these myths—telling how certain gods, as they say, 'Go about by night in the likeness of so many strangers and in divers forms;' but let them take heed lest they make cowards of their children, and at the same time speak blasphemy against the gods.

Heaven forbid, he said.

But although the gods are themselves unchangeable, still by witchcraft and deception they may make us think that they appear in various forms?

Perhaps, he replied.

Well, but can you imagine that God will be willing to lie, whether in word or deed, or to put forth a phantom of himself?

I cannot say, he replied.

Do you not know, I said, that the true lie, if such an expression may be allowed, is hated of gods and men?

What do you mean? he said.

I mean that no one is willingly deceived in that which is the truest and highest part of himself, or about the truest and highest matters; there, above all, he is most afraid of a lie having possession of him.

Still, he said, I do not comprehend you.

The reason is, I replied, that you attribute some profound meaning to my words; but I am only saying that deception, or being deceived or uninformed about the highest realities in the highest part of themselves, which is the soul, and in that part of them to have and to hold the lie, is what mankind least like;—that, I say, is what they utterly detest.

There is nothing more hateful to them.

And, as I was just now remarking, this ignorance in the soul of him who is deceived may be called the true lie; for the lie in words is only a kind of imitation and shadowy image of a previous affection of the soul, not pure unadulterated falsehood. Am I not right?

Perfectly right.

The true lie is hated not only by the gods, but also by men?

Yes.

Whereas the lie in words is in certain cases useful and not hateful; in dealing with enemies—that would be an instance; or again, when those whom we call our friends in a fit of madness or illusion are going to do some harm, then it is useful and is a sort of medicine or preventive; also in the tales of mythology, of which we were just now speaking—because we do not know the truth about ancient times, we make falsehood as much like truth as we can, and so turn it to account.

Very true, he said.

But can any of these reasons apply to God? Can we suppose that he is ignorant of antiquity, and therefore has recourse to invention?

That would be ridiculous, he said.

Then the lying poet has no place in our idea of God?

I should say not.

Or perhaps he may tell a lie because he is afraid of enemies?

That is inconceivable.

But he may have friends who are senseless or mad?

But no mad or senseless person can be a friend of God.

Then no motive can be imagined why God should lie?

None whatever.

Then the superhuman and divine is absolutely incapable of falsehood?

Yes.

Then is God perfectly simple and true both in word and deed; he changes not; he deceives not, either by sign or word, by dream or waking vision.

Your thoughts, he said, are the reflection of my own.

You agree with me then, I said, that this is the second type or form in which we should write and speak about divine things. The gods are not magicians who transform themselves, neither do they deceive mankind in any way.

I grant that.

Then, although we are admirers of Homer, we do not admire the lying dream which Zeus sends to Agamemnon; neither will we praise the verses of Aeschylus in which Thetis says that Apollo at her nuptials

> 'Was celebrating in song her fair progeny whose days were to be long, and to know no sickness. And when he had spoken of my lot as in all things blessed of heaven he raised a note of triumph and cheered my soul. And I thought that the word of Phoebus, being divine and full of prophecy, would not fail. And now he himself who uttered the strain, he who was present at the banquet, and who said this—he it is who has slain my son.'

These are the kind of sentiments about the gods which will arouse our anger; and he who utters them shall be refused a chorus; neither shall we allow teachers to make use of them in the instruction of the young, meaning, as we do, that our guardians, as far as men can be, should be true worshippers of the gods and like them.

I entirely agree, he said, in these principles, and promise to make them my laws.

Project Gutenberg
Last Updated: June 22, 2016.
https://www.gutenberg.org/files/1497/1497-h/1497-h.htm#link2H_4_0005

Appendix 2: The Allegory of the Cave

THE REPUBLIC
By PLATO
Translated by Benjamin Jowett

Persons of the Dialogue
Socrates, who is the narrator.
Glaucon.
Adeimantus.
Polemarchus.
Cephalus.
Thrasymachus.
Cleitophon.
And others who are mute auditors.

Book VII

And now, I said, let me show in a figure how far our nature is enlightened or unenlightened:—Behold! human beings living in a underground den, which has a mouth open towards the light and reaching all along the den; here they have been from their childhood, and have their legs and necks chained so that they cannot move, and can only see before them, being prevented by the chains from turning round their heads. Above and behind them a fire is blazing at a distance, and between the fire and the prisoners there is a raised way; and you will see, if you look, a low wall built along the way, like the screen which marionette players have in front of them, over which they show the puppets.

I see.

And do you see, I said, men passing along the wall carrying all sorts of vessels, and statues and figures of animals made of wood and stone and various materials, which appear over the wall? Some of them are talking, others silent.

You have shown me a strange image, and they are strange prisoners.

Like ourselves, I replied; and they see only their own shadows, or the shadows of one another, which the fire throws on the opposite wall of the cave?

True, he said; how could they see anything but the shadows if they were never allowed to move their heads?

And of the objects which are being carried in like manner they would only see the shadows?

Yes, he said.

And if they were able to converse with one another, would they not suppose that they were naming what was actually before them?

Very true.

And suppose further that the prison had an echo which came from the other side, would they not be sure to fancy when one of the passers-by spoke that the voice which they heard came from the passing shadow?

No question, he replied.

To them, I said, the truth would be literally nothing but the shadows of the images.

That is certain.

And now look again, and see what will naturally follow if the prisoners are released and disabused of their error. At first, when any of them is liberated and compelled suddenly to stand up and turn his neck round and walk and look towards the light, he will suffer sharp pains; the glare will distress him, and he will be unable to see the realities of which in his former state he had seen the shadows; and then conceive some one saying to him, that what he saw before was an illusion, but that now, when he is approaching nearer to being and his eye is turned towards more real existence, he has a clearer vision,—what will be his reply? And you may further imagine that his instructor is pointing to the objects as they pass and requiring him to name them,—will he not be perplexed? Will he not fancy that the shadows which he formerly saw are truer than the objects which are now shown to him?

Far truer.

And if he is compelled to look straight at the light, will he not have a pain in his eyes which will make him turn away to take refuge in the objects of vision which he can see, and which he will conceive to be in reality clearer than the things which are now being shown to him?

True, he said.

And suppose once more, that he is reluctantly dragged up a steep and rugged ascent, and held fast until he is forced into the presence of the sun himself, is he not likely to be pained and irritated? When he approaches the light his eyes will be dazzled, and he will not be able to see anything at all of what are now called realities.

Not all in a moment, he said.

He will require to grow accustomed to the sight of the upper world. And first he will see the shadows best, next the reflections of men and other objects in the water, and then the objects themselves; then he will gaze upon the light of the moon and the stars and the spangled heaven; and he will see the sky and the stars by night better than the sun or the light of the sun by day?

Certainly.

Last of all he will be able to see the sun, and not mere reflections of him in the water, but he will see him in his own proper place, and not in another; and he will contemplate him as he is.

Certainly.

He will then proceed to argue that this is he who gives the season and the years, and is the guardian of all that is in the visible world, and in a certain way the cause of all things which he and his fellows have been accustomed to behold?

Clearly, he said, he would first see the sun and then reason about him.

And when he remembered his old habitation, and the wisdom of the den and his fellow-prisoners, do you not suppose that he would felicitate himself on the change, and pity them?

Certainly, he would.

And if they were in the habit of conferring honours among themselves on those who were quickest to observe the passing shadows and to remark which of them went before, and which followed after, and which were together; and who were therefore best able to draw conclusions as to the future, do you think that he would care for such honours and glories, or envy the possessors of them? Would he not say with Homer,

> 'Better to be the poor servant of a poor master,'

and to endure anything, rather than think as they do and live after their manner?

Yes, he said, I think that he would rather suffer anything than entertain these false notions and live in this miserable manner.

Imagine once more, I said, such an one coming suddenly out of the sun to be replaced in his old situation; would he not be certain to have his eyes full of darkness?

To be sure, he said.

And if there were a contest, and he had to compete in measuring the shadows with the prisoners who had never moved out of the den, while his sight was still weak, and before his eyes had become steady (and the time which would be needed to acquire this new habit of sight might be very considerable), would he not be ridiculous? Men would say of him that up he went and down he came without his eyes; and that it was better not even to think of ascending; and if any one tried to loose another and lead him up to the light, let them only catch the offender, and they would put him to death.

No question, he said.

This entire allegory, I said, you may now append, dear Glaucon, to the previous argument; the prison-house is the world of sight, the light of the fire is the sun, and you will not misapprehend me if you interpret the journey upwards to be the ascent of the soul into the intellectual world according to my poor belief, which, at your desire, I have expressed—whether rightly or wrongly God knows. But, whether true or false, my opinion is that in the world of knowledge the idea of good appears last of all, and is seen only with an effort; and, when seen, is also inferred to be the universal author of all things beautiful and right, parent of light and of the lord of light in this visible world, and the immediate source of reason and truth in the intellectual; and that this is the power upon which he who would act rationally either in public or private life must have his eye fixed.

I agree, he said, as far as I am able to understand you.

Moreover, I said, you must not wonder that those who attain to this beatific vision are unwilling to descend to human affairs; for their souls are ever hastening into the upper world where they desire to dwell; which desire of theirs is very natural, if our allegory may be trusted.

Yes, very natural.

And is there anything surprising in one who passes from divine contemplations to the evil state of man, misbehaving himself in a ridiculous manner; if, while his eyes are blinking and before he has become accustomed to the surrounding darkness, he is compelled to fight in courts of law, or in other places, about the images or the shadows of images of justice, and is endeavouring to meet the conceptions of those who have never yet seen absolute justice?

Anything but surprising, he replied.

Anyone who has common sense will remember that the bewilderments of the eyes are of two kinds, and arise from two causes, either from coming out of the light or from going into the light, which is true of the mind's eye, quite as much as of the bodily eye; and he who remembers this when he sees any one whose vision is perplexed and weak, will not be too ready to laugh; he will first ask whether that soul of man has come out of the brighter life, and is unable to see because unaccustomed to the dark, or having turned from darkness to the day is dazzled by excess of light. And he will count the one happy in his condition and state of being, and he will pity the other; or, if he have a mind to laugh at the soul which comes from below into the light, there will be more reason in this than in the laugh which greets him who returns from above out of the light into the den.

That, he said, is a very just distinction.

But then, if I am right, certain professors of education must be wrong when they say that they can put a knowledge into the soul which was not there before, like sight into blind eyes.

They undoubtedly say this, he replied.

Whereas, our argument shows that the power and capacity of learning exists in the soul already; and that just as the eye was unable to turn from darkness to light without the whole body, so too the instrument of knowledge can only by the movement of the whole soul be turned from the world of becoming into that of being, and learn by degrees to endure the sight of being, and of the brightest and best of being, or in other words, of the good.

Very true.

And must there not be some art which will effect conversion in the easiest and quickest manner; not implanting the faculty of sight, for that exists already, but has been turned in the wrong direction, and is looking away from the truth?

Yes, he said, such an art may be presumed.

And whereas the other so-called virtues of the soul seem to be akin to bodily qualities, for even when they are not originally innate they can be implanted later by habit and exercise, the virtue of wisdom more than anything else contains a divine element which always remains, and by this conversion is rendered useful and profitable; or, on the other hand, hurtful and useless. Did you never observe the narrow intelligence flashing from the keen eye of a clever rogue—how eager he is, how clearly his paltry soul sees the way to his end; he is the reverse of blind, but his keen eye-sight is forced into the service of evil, and he is mischievous in proportion to his cleverness?

Very true, he said.

But what if there had been a circumcision of such natures in the days of their youth; and they had been severed from those sensual pleasures, such as eating and drinking, which, like leaden weights, were attached to them at their birth, and which drag them down and turn the vision of their souls upon the things that are below—if, I say, they had been released from these impediments and turned in the opposite direction, the very same faculty in them would have seen the truth as keenly as they see what their eyes are turned to now.

Very likely.

Yes, I said; and there is another thing which is likely, or rather a necessary inference from what has preceded, that neither the uneducated and uninformed of the truth, nor yet those who never make an end of their education, will be able ministers of State; not the former, because they have no single aim of duty which is the rule of all their actions, private as well as public; nor the latter, because they will not act at all except upon compulsion, fancying that they are already dwelling apart in the islands of the blest.

Very true, he replied.

Then, I said, the business of us who are the founders of the State will be to compel the best minds to attain that knowledge which we have already shown to be the greatest of all—they must continue to ascend until they arrive at the good; but when they have ascended and seen enough we must not allow them to do as they do now.

What do you mean?

I mean that they remain in the upper world: but this must not be allowed; they must be made to descend again among the prisoners in the den, and partake of their labours and honours, whether they are worth having or not.

But is not this unjust? he said; ought we to give them a worse life, when they might have a better?

You have again forgotten, my friend, I said, the intention of the legislator, who did not aim at making any one class in the State happy above the rest; the happiness was to be in the whole State, and he held the citizens together by persuasion and necessity, making them benefactors of the State, and therefore benefactors of one another; to this end he created them, not to please themselves, but to be his instruments in binding up the State.

True, he said, I had forgotten.

Observe, Glaucon, that there will be no injustice in compelling our philosophers to have a care and providence of others; we shall explain to them that in other States, men of their class are not obliged to share in the toils of politics: and this is reasonable, for they grow up at their own sweet will, and the government would rather not have them. Being self-taught, they cannot be expected to show any gratitude for a culture which they have never received. But we have brought you into the world to be rulers of the hive, kings of yourselves and of the other citizens, and have educated you far better and more perfectly than they have been educated, and you are better able to share in the double duty. Wherefore each of you, when his turn comes, must go down to the general underground abode, and get the habit of seeing in the dark. When you have acquired the habit, you will see 10,000 times better than the inhabitants of the den, and you will know what the several images are, and what they represent, because you have seen the beautiful and just and good in their truth. And thus our State, which is also yours, will be a reality, and not a dream only, and will be administered in a spirit unlike that of other States, in which men fight with one another about shadows only and are distracted in the struggle for power, which in their eyes is a great good. Whereas the truth is that the State in which the rulers are most reluctant to govern is always the best and most quietly governed, and the State in which they are most eager, the worst.

Quite true, he replied.

And will our pupils, when they hear this, refuse to take their turn at the toils of State, when they are allowed to spend the greater part of their time with one another in the heavenly light?

Impossible, he answered; for they are just men, and the commands which we impose upon them are just; there can be no doubt that every one of them will take office as a stern necessity, and not after the fashion of our present rulers of State.

Yes, my friend, I said; and there lies the point. You must contrive for your future rulers another and a better life than that of a ruler, and then you may have a well-ordered State; for only in the State which offers this, will they rule who are truly rich, not in silver and gold, but in virtue and wisdom, which are the true blessings of life. Whereas if they go to the administration of public affairs, poor and hungering after their own private advantage, thinking that hence they are to snatch the chief good, order there can never be; for they will be fighting about office, and the civil and domestic broils which thus arise will be the ruin of the rulers themselves and of the whole State.

Most true, he replied.

And the only life which looks down upon the life of political ambition is that of true philosophy. Do you know of any other?

Indeed, I do not, he said.

And those who govern ought not to be lovers of the task? For, if they are, there will be rival lovers, and they will fight.

No question.

Who then are those whom we shall compel to be guardians? Surely they will be the men who are wisest about affairs of State, and by whom the State is best administered, and who at the same time have other honours and another and a better life than that of politics?

They are the men, and I will choose them, he replied.

And now shall we consider in what way such guardians will be produced, and how they are to be brought from darkness to light,—as some are said to have ascended from the world below to the gods?

By all means, he replied.

The process, I said, is not the turning over of an oyster-shell (In allusion to a game in which two parties fled or pursued according as an oyster-shell which was thrown into the air fell with the dark or light side uppermost.), but the turning round of a soul passing from a day which is little better than night to the true day of being, that is, the ascent from below, which we affirm to be true philosophy?

Quite so.

And should we not enquire what sort of knowledge has the power of effecting such a change?

Certainly.

What sort of knowledge is there which would draw the soul from becoming to being? And another consideration has just occurred to me: You will remember that our young men are to be warrior athletes?

Yes, that was said.

Then this new kind of knowledge must have an additional quality?

What quality?

Usefulness in war.

Yes, if possible.

There were two parts in our former scheme of education, were there not?

Just so.

There was gymnastic which presided over the growth and decay of the body, and may therefore be regarded as having to do with generation and corruption?

True.

Then that is not the knowledge which we are seeking to discover?

No.

But what do you say of music, which also entered to a certain extent into our former scheme?

Music, he said, as you will remember, was the counterpart of gymnastic, and trained the guardians by the influences of habit, by harmony making them harmonious, by rhythm rhythmical, but not giving them science; and the words, whether fabulous or possibly true, had kindred elements of rhythm and harmony in them. But in music there was nothing which tended to that good which you are now seeking.

You are most accurate, I said, in your recollection; in music there certainly was nothing of the kind. But what branch of knowledge is there, my dear Glaucon, which is of the desired nature; since all the useful arts were reckoned mean by us?

Undoubtedly; and yet if music and gymnastic are excluded, and the arts are also excluded, what remains?

Well, I said, there may be nothing left of our special subjects; and then we shall have to take something which is not special, but of universal application.

What may that be?

A something which all arts and sciences and intelligences use in common, and which every one first has to learn among the elements of education.

What is that?

The little matter of distinguishing one, two, and three—in a word, number and calculation:—do not all arts and sciences necessarily partake of them?

Yes.

Then the art of war partakes of them?

To be sure.

Then Palamedes, whenever he appears in tragedy, proves Agamemnon ridiculously unfit to be a general. Did you never remark how he declares that he had invented number, and had numbered the ships and set in array the ranks of the army at Troy; which implies that they had never been numbered before, and Agamemnon must be supposed literally to have been incapable of counting his own feet—how could he if he was ignorant of number? And if that is true, what sort of general must he have been?

I should say a very strange one, if this was as you say.

Can we deny that a warrior should have a knowledge of arithmetic?

Certainly he should, if he is to have the smallest understanding of military tactics, or indeed, I should rather say, if he is to be a man at all.

I should like to know whether you have the same notion which I have of this study?

What is your notion?

It appears to me to be a study of the kind which we are seeking, and which leads naturally to reflection, but never to have been rightly used; for the true use of it is simply to draw the soul towards being.

Will you explain your meaning? he said.

I will try, I said; and I wish you would share the enquiry with me, and say 'yes' or 'no' when I attempt to distinguish in my own mind what branches of knowledge have this attracting power, in order that we may have clearer proof that arithmetic is, as I suspect, one of them.

Explain, he said.

I mean to say that objects of sense are of two kinds; some of them do not invite thought because the sense is an adequate judge of them; while in the case of other objects sense is so untrustworthy that further enquiry is imperatively demanded.

You are clearly referring, he said, to the manner in which the senses are imposed upon by distance, and by painting in light and shade.

No, I said, that is not at all my meaning.

Then what is your meaning?

When speaking of uninviting objects, I mean those which do not pass from one sensation to the opposite; inviting objects are those which do; in this latter case the sense coming upon the object, whether at a distance or near, gives no more vivid idea of anything in particular than of its opposite. An illustration will make my meaning clearer:—here are three fingers—a little finger, a second finger, and a middle finger.

Very good.

You may suppose that they are seen quite close: And here comes the point.

What is it?

Each of them equally appears a finger, whether seen in the middle or at the extremity, whether white or black, or thick or thin—it makes no difference; a finger is a finger all the same. In these cases a man is not compelled to ask of thought the question what is a finger? for the sight never intimates to the mind that a finger is other than a finger.

True.

And therefore, I said, as we might expect, there is nothing here which invites or excites intelligence.

There is not, he said.

But is this equally true of the greatness and smallness of the fingers? Can sight adequately perceive them? and is no difference made by the circumstance that one of the fingers is in the middle and another at the extremity? And in like manner does the touch adequately perceive the qualities of thickness or thinness, of softness or hardness? And so of the other senses; do they give perfect intimations of such matters? Is not their mode of operation on this wise—the sense which is concerned with the quality of hardness is necessarily concerned also with the quality of softness, and only intimates to the soul that the same thing is felt to be both hard and soft?

You are quite right, he said.

And must not the soul be perplexed at this intimation which the sense gives of a hard which is also soft? What, again, is the meaning of light and heavy, if that which is light is also heavy, and that which is heavy, light?

Yes, he said, these intimations which the soul receives are very curious and require to be explained.

Yes, I said, and in these perplexities the soul naturally summons to her aid calculation and intelligence, that she may see whether the several objects announced to her are one or two.

True.

And if they turn out to be two, is not each of them one and different?

Certainly.

And if each is one, and both are two, she will conceive the two as in a state of division, for if there were undivided they could only be conceived of as one?

True.

The eye certainly did see both small and great, but only in a confused manner; they were not distinguished.

Yes.

Whereas the thinking mind, intending to light up the chaos, was compelled to reverse the process, and look at small and great as separate and not confused.

Very true.

Was not this the beginning of the enquiry 'What is great?' and 'What is small?'

Exactly so.

And thus arose the distinction of the visible and the intelligible.

Most true.

This was what I meant when I spoke of impressions which invited the intellect, or the reverse—those which are simultaneous with opposite impressions, invite thought; those which are not simultaneous do not.

I understand, he said, and agree with you.

And to which class do unity and number belong?

I do not know, he replied.

Think a little and you will see that what has preceded will supply the answer; for if simple unity could be adequately perceived by the sight or by any other sense, then, as we were saying in the case of the finger, there would be nothing to attract towards being; but when there is some contradiction always present, and one is the reverse of one and involves the conception of plurality, then thought begins to be aroused within us, and the soul perplexed and wanting to arrive at a decision asks 'What is absolute unity?' This is the way in which the study of the one has a power of drawing and converting the mind to the contemplation of true being.

And surely, he said, this occurs notably in the case of one; for we see the same thing to be both one and infinite in multitude?

Yes, I said; and this being true of one must be equally true of all number?

Certainly.

And all arithmetic and calculation have to do with number?

Yes.

And they appear to lead the mind towards truth?

Yes, in a very remarkable manner.

Then this is knowledge of the kind for which we are seeking, having a double use, military and philosophical; for the man of war must learn the art of number or he will not know how to array his troops, and the philosopher also, because he has to rise out of the sea of change and lay hold of true being, and therefore he must be an arithmetician.

That is true.

And our guardian is both warrior and philosopher?

Certainly.

Then this is a kind of knowledge which legislation may fitly prescribe; and we must endeavour to persuade those who are to be the principal men of our State to go and learn arithmetic, not as amateurs, but they must carry on the study until they see the nature of numbers with the mind only; nor again, like merchants or retail-traders, with a view to buying or selling, but for the sake of their military use, and of the soul herself; and because this will be the easiest way for her to pass from becoming to truth and being.

That is excellent, he said.

Yes, I said, and now having spoken of it, I must add how charming the science is! and in how many ways it conduces to our desired end, if pursued in the spirit of a philosopher, and not of a shopkeeper!

How do you mean?

I mean, as I was saying, that arithmetic has a very great and elevating effect, compelling the soul to reason about abstract number, and rebelling against the introduction of visible or tangible objects into the argument. You know how steadily the masters of the art repel and ridicule any one who attempts to divide absolute unity when he is calculating, and if you divide, they multiply (Meaning either (1) that they integrate the number because they deny the possibility of fractions; or (2) that division is regarded by them as a process of multiplication, for the fractions of one continue to be units.), taking care that one shall continue one and not become lost in fractions.

That is very true.

Now, suppose a person were to say to them: O my friends, what are these wonderful numbers about which you are reasoning, in which, as you say, there is a unity such as you demand, and each unit is equal, invariable, indivisible,—what would they answer?

They would answer, as I should conceive, that they were speaking of those numbers which can only be realized in thought.

Then you see that this knowledge may be truly called necessary, necessitating as it clearly does the use of the pure intelligence in the attainment of pure truth?

Yes; that is a marked characteristic of it.

And have you further observed, that those who have a natural talent for calculation are generally quick at every other kind of knowledge; and even the dull, if they have had an arithmetical training, although they may derive no other advantage from it, always become much quicker than they would otherwise have been.

Very true, he said.

And indeed, you will not easily find a more difficult study, and not many as difficult.

You will not.

And, for all these reasons, arithmetic is a kind of knowledge in which the best natures should be trained, and which must not be given up.

I agree.

Let this then be made one of our subjects of education. And next, shall we enquire whether the kindred science also concerns us?

You mean geometry?

Exactly so.

Clearly, he said, we are concerned with that part of geometry which relates to war; for in pitching a camp, or taking up a position, or closing or extending the lines of an army, or any other military manoeuvre, whether in actual battle or on a march, it will make all the difference whether a general is or is not a geometrician.

Yes, I said, but for that purpose a very little of either geometry or calculation will be enough; the question relates rather to the greater and more advanced part of geometry—whether that tends in any degree to make more easy the vision of the idea of good; and thither, as I was saying, all things tend which compel the soul to turn her gaze towards that place, where is the full perfection of being, which she ought, by all means, to behold.

True, he said.

Then if geometry compels us to view being, it concerns us; if becoming only, it does not concern us?

Yes, that is what we assert.

Yet anybody who has the least acquaintance with geometry will not deny that such a conception of the science is in flat contradiction to the ordinary language of geometricians.

How so?

They have in view practice only, and are always speaking, in a narrow and ridiculous manner, of squaring and extending and applying and the like—they confuse the necessities of geometry with those of daily life; whereas knowledge is the real object of the whole science.

Certainly, he said.

Then must not a further admission be made?

What admission?

That the knowledge at which geometry aims is knowledge of the eternal, and not of aught perishing and transient.

That, he replied, may be readily allowed, and is true.

Then, my noble friend, geometry will draw the soul towards truth, and create the spirit of philosophy, and raise up that which is now unhappily allowed to fall down.

Nothing will be more likely to have such an effect.

Then nothing should be more sternly laid down than that the inhabitants of your fair city should by all means learn geometry. Moreover the science has indirect effects, which are not small.

Of what kind? he said.

There are the military advantages of which you spoke, I said; and in all departments of knowledge, as experience proves, any one who has studied geometry is infinitely quicker of apprehension than one who has not.

Yes indeed, he said, there is an infinite difference between them.

Then shall we propose this as a second branch of knowledge which our youth will study?

Let us do so, he replied.

And suppose we make astronomy the third—what do you say?

I am strongly inclined to it, he said; the observation of the seasons and of months and years is as essential to the general as it is to the farmer or sailor.

I am amused, I said, at your fear of the world, which makes you guard against the appearance of insisting upon useless studies; and I quite admit the difficulty of believing that in every man there is an eye of the soul which, when by other pursuits lost and dimmed, is by these purified and re-illumined; and is more precious far than 10,000 bodily eyes, for by it alone is truth seen. Now there are two classes of persons: one class of those who will agree with you and will take your words as a revelation; another class to whom they will be utterly unmeaning, and who will naturally deem them to be idle tales, for they see no sort of profit which is to be obtained from them. And therefore you had better decide at once with which of the two you are proposing to argue. You will very likely say with neither, and that your chief aim in carrying on the argument is your own improvement; at the same time you do not grudge to others any benefit which they may receive.

I think that I should prefer to carry on the argument mainly on my own behalf.

Then take a step backward, for we have gone wrong in the order of the sciences.

What was the mistake? he said.

After plane geometry, I said, we proceeded at once to solids in revolution, instead of taking solids in themselves; whereas after the second dimension the third, which is concerned with cubes and dimensions of depth, ought to have followed.

That is true, Socrates; but so little seems to be known as yet about these subjects.

Why, yes, I said, and for two reasons:—in the first place, no government patronises them; this leads to a want of energy in the pursuit of them, and they are difficult; in the second place, students cannot learn them unless they have a director. But then a director can hardly be found, and even if he could, as matters now stand, the students, who are very conceited, would not attend to him. That, however, would be otherwise if the whole State became the director of these studies and gave honour to them; then disciples would want to come, and there would be continuous and earnest search, and discoveries would be made; since even now, disregarded as they are by the world, and maimed of their fair proportions, and although none of their votaries can tell the use of them, still these studies force their way by their natural charm, and very likely, if they had the help of the State, they would some day emerge into light.

Yes, he said, there is a remarkable charm in them. But I do not clearly understand the change in the order. First you began with a geometry of plane surfaces?

Yes, I said.

And you placed astronomy next, and then you made a step backward?

Yes, and I have delayed you by my hurry; the ludicrous state of solid geometry, which, in natural order, should have followed, made me pass over this branch and go on to astronomy, or motion of solids.

True, he said.

Then assuming that the science now omitted would come into existence if encouraged by the State, let us go on to astronomy, which will be fourth.

The right order, he replied. And now, Socrates, as you rebuked the vulgar manner in which I praised astronomy before, my praise shall be given in your own spirit. For every one, as I think, must see that astronomy compels the soul to look upwards and leads us from this world to another.

Everyone but myself, I said; to everyone else this may be clear, but not to me.

And what then would you say?

I should rather say that those who elevate astronomy into philosophy appear to me to make us look downwards and not upwards.

What do you mean? he asked.

You, I replied, have in your mind a truly sublime conception of our knowledge of the things above. And I dare say that if a person were to throw his head back and study the fretted ceiling, you would still think that his mind was the percipient, and not his eyes. And you are very likely right, and I may be a simpleton: but, in my opinion, that knowledge only which is of being and of the unseen can make the soul look upwards, and whether a man gapes at the heavens or blinks on the ground, seeking to learn some particular of sense, I would deny that he can learn, for nothing of that sort is matter of science; his soul is looking downwards, not upwards, whether his way to knowledge is by water or by land, whether he floats, or only lies on his back.

I acknowledge, he said, the justice of your rebuke. Still, I should like to ascertain how astronomy can be learned in any manner more conducive to that knowledge of which we are speaking?

I will tell you, I said: The starry heaven which we behold is wrought upon a visible ground, and therefore, although the fairest and most perfect of visible things, must necessarily be deemed inferior far to the true motions of absolute swiftness and absolute slowness, which are relative to each other, and carry with them that which is contained in them, in the true number and in every true figure. Now, these are to be apprehended by reason and intelligence, but not by sight.

True, he replied.

The spangled heavens should be used as a pattern and with a view to that higher knowledge; their beauty is like the beauty of figures or pictures excellently wrought by the hand of Daedalus, or some other great artist, which we may chance to behold; any geometrician who saw them would appreciate the exquisiteness of their workmanship, but he would never dream of thinking that in them he could find the true equal or the true double, or the truth of any other proportion.

No, he replied, such an idea would be ridiculous.

And will not a true astronomer have the same feeling when he looks at the movements of the stars? Will he not think that heaven and the things in heaven are framed by the Creator of them in the most perfect manner? But he will never imagine that the proportions of night and day, or of both to the month, or of the month to the year, or of the stars to these and to one another, and any other things that are material and visible can also be eternal and subject to no deviation—that would be absurd; and it is equally absurd to take so much pains in investigating their exact truth.

I quite agree, though I never thought of this before.

Then, I said, in astronomy, as in geometry, we should employ problems, and let the heavens alone if we would approach the subject in the right way and so make the natural gift of reason to be of any real use.

That, he said, is a work infinitely beyond our present astronomers.

Yes, I said; and there are many other things which must also have a similar extension given to them, if our legislation is to be of any value. But can you tell me of any other suitable study?

No, he said, not without thinking.

Motion, I said, has many forms, and not one only; two of them are obvious enough even to wits no better than ours; and there are others, as I imagine, which may be left to wiser persons.

But where are the two?

There is a second, I said, which is the counterpart of the one already named.

And what may that be?

The second, I said, would seem relatively to the ears to be what the first is to the eyes; for I conceive that as the eyes are designed to look up at the stars, so are the ears to hear harmonious motions; and these are sister sciences—as the Pythagoreans say, and we, Glaucon, agree with them?

Yes, he replied.

But this, I said, is a laborious study, and therefore we had better go and learn of them; and they will tell us whether there are any other applications of these sciences. At the same time, we must not lose sight of our own higher object.

What is that?

There is a perfection which all knowledge ought to reach, and which our pupils ought also to attain, and not to fall short of, as I was saying that they did in astronomy. For in the science of harmony, as you probably know, the same thing happens. The teachers of harmony compare the sounds and consonances which are heard only, and their labour, like that of the astronomers, is in vain.

Yes, by heaven! he said; and 'tis as good as a play to hear them talking about their condensed notes, as they call them; they put their ears close alongside of the strings like persons catching a sound from their neighbour's wall—one set of them declaring that they distinguish an intermediate note and have found the least interval which should be the unit of measurement; the others insisting that the two sounds have passed into the same—either party setting their ears before their understanding.

You mean, I said, those gentlemen who tease and torture the strings and rack them on the pegs of the instrument: I might carry on the metaphor and speak after their manner of the blows which the plectrum gives, and make accusations against the strings, both of backwardness and forwardness to sound; but this would be tedious, and therefore I will only say that these are not the men, and that I am referring to the Pythagoreans, of whom I was just now proposing to enquire about harmony. For they too are in error, like the astronomers; they investigate the numbers of the harmonies which are heard, but they never attain to problems—that is to say, they never reach the natural harmonies of number, or reflect why some numbers are harmonious and others not.

That, he said, is a thing of more than mortal knowledge.

A thing, I replied, which I would rather call useful; that is, if sought after with a view to the beautiful and good; but if pursued in any other spirit, useless.

Very true, he said.

Now, when all these studies reach the point of inter-communion and connection with one another, and come to be considered in their mutual affinities, then, I think, but not till then, will the pursuit of them have a value for our objects; otherwise there is no profit in them.

I suspect so; but you are speaking, Socrates, of a vast work.

What do you mean? I said; the prelude or what? Do you not know that all this is but the prelude to the actual strain which we have to learn? For you surely would not regard the skilled mathematician as a dialectician?

Assuredly not, he said; I have hardly ever known a mathematician who was capable of reasoning.

But do you imagine that men who are unable to give and take a reason will have the knowledge which we require of them?

Neither can this be supposed.

And so, Glaucon, I said, we have at last arrived at the hymn of dialectic. This is that strain which is of the intellect only, but which the faculty of sight will nevertheless be found to imitate; for sight, as you may remember, was imagined by us after a while to behold the real animals and stars, and last of all the sun himself. And so with dialectic; when a person starts on the discovery of the absolute by the light of reason only, and without any assistance of sense, and perseveres until by pure intelligence he arrives at the perception of the absolute good, he at last finds himself at the end of the intellectual world, as in the case of sight at the end of the visible.

Exactly, he said.

Then this is the progress which you call dialectic?

True.

But the release of the prisoners from chains, and their translation from the shadows to the images and to the light, and the ascent from the underground den to the sun, while in his presence they are vainly trying to look on animals and plants and the light of the sun, but are able to perceive even with their weak eyes the images in the water (which are divine), and are the shadows of true existence (not shadows of images cast by a light of fire, which compared with the sun is only an image)—this power of elevating the highest principle in the soul to the contemplation of that which is best in existence, with which we may compare the raising of that faculty which is the very light of the body to the sight of that which is brightest in the material and visible world—this power is given, as I was saying, by all that study and pursuit of the arts which has been described.

I agree in what you are saying, he replied, which may be hard to believe, yet, from another point of view, is harder still to deny. This, however, is not a theme to be treated of in passing only, but will have to be discussed again and again. And so, whether our conclusion be true or false, let us assume all this, and proceed at once from the prelude or preamble to the chief strain (A play upon the Greek word, which means both 'law' and 'strain.'), and describe that in like manner. Say, then, what is the nature and what are the divisions of dialectic, and what are the paths which lead thither; for these paths will also lead to our final rest.

Dear Glaucon, I said, you will not be able to follow me here, though I would do my best, and you should behold not an image only but the absolute truth, according to my notion. Whether what I told you would or would not have been a reality I cannot venture to say; but you would have seen something like reality; of that I am confident.

Doubtless, he replied.

But I must also remind you, that the power of dialectic alone can reveal this, and only to one who is a disciple of the previous sciences.

Of that assertion you may be as confident as of the last.

And assuredly no one will argue that there is any other method of comprehending by any regular process all true existence or of ascertaining what each thing is in its own nature; for the arts in general are concerned with the desires or opinions of men, or are cultivated with a view to production and construction, or for the preservation of such productions and constructions; and as to the mathematical sciences which, as we were saying, have some apprehension of true being—geometry and the like—they only dream about being, but never can they behold the waking reality so long as they leave the hypotheses which they use unexamined, and are unable to give an account of them. For when a man knows not his own first principle, and when the conclusion and intermediate steps are also constructed out of he knows not what, how can he imagine that such a fabric of convention can ever become science?

Impossible, he said.

Then dialectic, and dialectic alone, goes directly to the first principle and is the only science which does away with hypotheses in order to make her ground secure; the eye of the soul, which is literally buried in an outlandish slough, is by her gentle aid lifted upwards; and she uses as handmaids and helpers in the work of conversion, the sciences which we have been discussing. Custom terms them sciences, but they ought to have some other name, implying greater clearness than opinion and less clearness than science: and this, in our previous sketch, was called understanding. But why should we dispute about names when we have realities of such importance to consider?

Why indeed, he said, when any name will do which expresses the thought of the mind with clearness?

At any rate, we are satisfied, as before, to have four divisions; two for intellect and two for opinion, and to call the first division science, the second understanding, the third belief, and the fourth perception of shadows, opinion being concerned with becoming, and intellect with being; and so to make a proportion:—.

As being is to becoming, so is pure intellect to opinion. And as intellect is to opinion, so is science to belief, and understanding to the perception of shadows.

But let us defer the further correlation and subdivision of the subjects of opinion and of intellect, for it will be a long enquiry, many times longer than this has been.

As far as I understand, he said, I agree.

And do you also agree, I said, in describing the dialectician as one who attains a conception of the essence of each thing? And he who does not possess and is therefore unable to impart this conception, in whatever degree he fails, may in that degree also be said to fail in intelligence? Will you admit so much?

Yes, he said; how can I deny it?

And you would say the same of the conception of the good? Until the person is able to abstract and define rationally the idea of good, and unless he can run the gauntlet of all objections, and is ready to disprove them, not by appeals to opinion, but to absolute truth, never faltering at any step of the argument—unless he can do all this, you would say that he knows neither the idea of good nor any other good; he apprehends only a shadow, if anything at all, which is given by opinion and not by science;—dreaming and slumbering in this life, before he is well awake here, he arrives at the world below, and has his final quietus.

In all that I should most certainly agree with you.

And surely you would not have the children of your ideal State, whom you are nurturing and educating—if the ideal ever becomes a reality—you would not allow the future rulers to be like posts (Literally 'lines,' probably the starting-point of a race-course.), having no reason in them, and yet to be set in authority over the highest matters?

Certainly not.

Then you will make a law that they shall have such an education as will enable them to attain the greatest skill in asking and answering questions?

Yes, he said, you and I together will make it.

Dialectic, then, as you will agree, is the coping-stone of the sciences, and is set over them; no other science can be placed higher—the nature of knowledge can no further go?

I agree, he said.

But to whom we are to assign these studies, and in what way they are to be assigned, are questions which remain to be considered.

Yes, clearly.

You remember, I said, how the rulers were chosen before?

Certainly, he said.

The same natures must still be chosen, and the preference again given to the surest and the bravest, and, if possible, to the fairest; and, having noble and generous tempers, they should also have the natural gifts which will facilitate their education.

And what are these?

Such gifts as keenness and ready powers of acquisition; for the mind more often faints from the severity of study than from the severity of gymnastics: the toil is more entirely the mind's own, and is not shared with the body.

Very true, he replied.

Further, he of whom we are in search should have a good memory, and be an unwearied solid man who is a lover of labour in any line; or he will never be able to endure the great amount of bodily exercise and to go through all the intellectual discipline and study which we require of him.

Certainly, he said; he must have natural gifts.

The mistake at present is, that those who study philosophy have no vocation, and this, as I was before saying, is the reason why she has fallen into disrepute: her true sons should take her by the hand and not bastards.

What do you mean?

In the first place, her votary should not have a lame or halting industry—I mean, that he should not be half industrious and half idle: as, for example, when a man is a lover of gymnastic and hunting, and all other bodily exercises, but a hater rather than a lover of the labour of learning or listening or enquiring. Or the occupation to which he devotes himself may be of an opposite kind, and he may have the other sort of lameness.

Certainly, he said.

And as to truth, I said, is not a soul equally to be deemed halt and lame which hates voluntary falsehood and is extremely indignant at herself and others when they tell lies, but is patient of involuntary falsehood, and does not mind wallowing like a swinish beast in the mire of ignorance, and has no shame at being detected?

To be sure.

And, again, in respect of temperance, courage, magnificence, and every other virtue, should we not carefully distinguish between the true son and the bastard? for where there is no discernment of such qualities states and individuals unconsciously err; and the state makes a ruler, and the individual a friend, of one who, being defective in some part of virtue, is in a figure lame or a bastard.

That is very true, he said.

All these things, then, will have to be carefully considered by us; and if only those whom we introduce to this vast system of education and training are sound in body and mind, justice herself will have nothing to say against us, and we shall be the saviours of the constitution and of the State; but, if our pupils are men of another stamp, the reverse will happen, and we shall pour a still greater flood of ridicule on philosophy than she has to endure at present.

That would not be creditable.

Certainly not, I said; and yet perhaps, in thus turning jest into earnest I am equally ridiculous.

In what respect?

I had forgotten, I said, that we were not serious, and spoke with too much excitement. For when I saw philosophy so undeservedly trampled under foot of men I could not help feeling a sort of indignation at the authors of her disgrace: and my anger made me too vehement.

Indeed! I was listening, and did not think so.

But I, who am the speaker, felt that I was. And now let me remind you that, although in our former selection we chose old men, we must not do so in this. Solon was under a delusion when he said that a man when he grows old may learn many things—for he can no more learn much than he can run much; youth is the time for any extraordinary toil.

Of course.

And, therefore, calculation and geometry and all the other elements of instruction, which are a preparation for dialectic, should be presented to the mind in childhood; not, however, under any notion of forcing our system of education.

Why not?

Because a freeman ought not to be a slave in the acquisition of knowledge of any kind. Bodily exercise, when compulsory, does no harm to the body; but knowledge which is acquired under compulsion obtains no hold on the mind.

Very true.

Then, my good friend, I said, do not use compulsion, but let early education be a sort of amusement; you will then be better able to find out the natural bent.

That is a very rational notion, he said.

Do you remember that the children, too, were to be taken to see the battle on horseback; and that if there were no danger they were to be brought close up and, like young hounds, have a taste of blood given them?

Yes, I remember.

The same practice may be followed, I said, in all these things—labours, lessons, dangers—and he who is most at home in all of them ought to be enrolled in a select number.

At what age?

At the age when the necessary gymnastics are over: the period whether of 2 or 3 years which passes in this sort of training is useless for any other purpose; for sleep and exercise are unpropitious to learning; and the trial of who is first in gymnastic exercises is one of the most important tests to which our youth are subjected.

Certainly, he replied.

After that time those who are selected from the class of 20 years old will be promoted to higher honour, and the sciences which they learned without any order in their early education will now be brought together, and they will be able to see the natural relationship of them to one another and to true being.

Yes, he said, that is the only kind of knowledge which takes lasting root.

Yes, I said; and the capacity for such knowledge is the great criterion of dialectical talent: the comprehensive mind is always the dialectical.

I agree with you, he said.

These, I said, are the points which you must consider; and those who have most of this comprehension, and who are most steadfast in their learning, and in their military and other appointed duties, when they have arrived at the age of 30 have to be chosen by you out of the select class, and elevated to higher honour; and you will have to prove them by the help of dialectic, in order to learn which of them is able to give up the use of sight and the other senses, and in company with truth to attain absolute being: And here, my friend, great caution is required.

Why great caution?

Do you not remark, I said, how great is the evil which dialectic has introduced?

What evil? he said.

The students of the art are filled with lawlessness.

Quite true, he said.

Do you think that there is anything so very unnatural or inexcusable in their case? or will you make allowance for them?

In what way make allowance?

I want you, I said, by way of parallel, to imagine a supposititious son who is brought up in great wealth; he is one of a great and numerous family, and has many flatterers. When he grows up to manhood, he learns that his alleged are not his real parents; but who the real are he is unable to discover. Can you guess how he will be likely to behave towards his flatterers and his supposed parents, first of all during the period when he is ignorant of the false relation, and then again when he knows? Or shall I guess for you?

If you please.

Then I should say, that while he is ignorant of the truth he will be likely to honour his father and his mother and his supposed relations more than the flatterers; he will be less inclined to neglect them when in need, or to do or say anything against them; and he will be less willing to disobey them in any important matter.

He will.

But when he has made the discovery, I should imagine that he would diminish his honour and regard for them, and would become more devoted to the flatterers; their influence over him would greatly increase; he would now live after their ways, and openly associate with them, and, unless he were of an unusually good disposition, he would trouble himself no more about his supposed parents or other relations.

Well, all that is very probable. But how is the image applicable to the disciples of philosophy?

In this way: you know that there are certain principles about justice and honour, which were taught us in childhood, and under their parental authority we have been brought up, obeying and honouring them.

That is true.

There are also opposite maxims and habits of pleasure which flatter and attract the soul, but do not influence those of us who have any sense of right, and they continue to obey and honour the maxims of their fathers.

True.

Now, when a man is in this state, and the questioning spirit asks what is fair or honourable, and he answers as the legislator has taught him, and then arguments many and diverse refute his words, until he is driven into believing that nothing is honourable any more than dishonourable, or just and good any more than the reverse, and so of all the notions which he most valued, do you think that he will still honour and obey them as before?

Impossible.

And when he ceases to think them honourable and natural as heretofore, and he fails to discover the true, can he be expected to pursue any life other than that which flatters his desires?

He cannot.

And from being a keeper of the law he is converted into a breaker of it?

Unquestionably.

Now all this is very natural in students of philosophy such as I have described, and also, as I was just now saying, most excusable.

Yes, he said; and, I may add, pitiable.

Therefore, that your feelings may not be moved to pity about our citizens who are now 30 years of age, every care must be taken in introducing them to dialectic.

Certainly.

There is a danger lest they should taste the dear delight too early; for youngsters, as you may have observed, when they first get the taste in their mouths, argue for amusement, and are always contradicting and refuting others in imitation of those who refute them; like puppy-dogs, they rejoice in pulling and tearing at all who come near them.

Yes, he said, there is nothing which they like better.

And when they have made many conquests and received defeats at the hands of many, they violently and speedily get into a way of not believing anything which they believed before, and hence, not only they, but philosophy and all that relates to it is apt to have a bad name with the rest of the world.

Too true, he said.

But when a man begins to get older, he will no longer be guilty of such insanity; he will imitate the dialectician who is seeking for truth, and not the eristic, who is contradicting for the sake of amusement; and the greater moderation of his character will increase instead of diminishing the honour of the pursuit.

Very true, he said.

And did we not make special provision for this, when we said that the disciples of philosophy were to be orderly and steadfast, not, as now, any chance aspirant or intruder?

Very true.

Suppose, I said, the study of philosophy to take the place of gymnastics and to be continued diligently and earnestly and exclusively for twice the number of years which were passed in bodily exercise—will that be enough?

Would you say six or 4 years? he asked.

Say 5 years, I replied; at the end of the time they must be sent down again into the den and compelled to hold any military or other office which young men are qualified to hold: in this way they will get their experience of life, and there will be an opportunity of trying whether, when they are drawn all manner of ways by temptation, they will stand firm or flinch.

And how long is this stage of their lives to last?

Fifteen years, I answered; and when they have reached 50 years of age, then let those who still survive and have distinguished themselves in every action of their lives and in every branch of knowledge come at last to their consummation: the time has now arrived at which they must raise the eye of the soul to the universal light which lightens all things, and behold the absolute good; for that is the pattern according to which they are to order the State and the lives of individuals, and the remainder of their own lives also; making philosophy their chief pursuit, but, when their turn comes, toiling also at politics and ruling for the public good, not as though they were performing some heroic action, but simply as a matter of duty; and when they have brought up in each generation others like themselves and left them in their place to be governors of the State, then they will depart to the Islands of the Blest and dwell there; and the city will give them public memorials and sacrifices and honour them, if the Pythian oracle consent, as demigods, but if not, as in any case blessed and divine.

You are a sculptor, Socrates, and have made statues of our governors faultless in beauty.

Yes, I said, Glaucon, and of our governesses too; for you must not suppose that what I have been saying applies to men only and not to women as far as their natures can go.

There you are right, he said, since we have made them to share in all things like the men.

Well, I said, and you would agree (would you not?) that what has been said about the State and the government is not a mere dream, and although difficult not impossible, but only possible in the way which has been supposed; that is to say, when the true philosopher kings are born in a State, one or more of them, despising the honours of this present world which they deem mean and worthless, esteeming above all things right and the honour that springs from right, and regarding justice as the greatest and most necessary of all things, whose ministers they are, and whose principles will be exalted by them when they set in order their own city?

How will they proceed?

They will begin by sending out into the country all the inhabitants of the city who are more than 10 years old, and will take possession of their children, who will be unaffected by the habits of their parents; these they will train in their own habits and laws, I mean in the laws which we have given them: and in this way the State and constitution of which we were speaking will soonest and most easily attain happiness, and the nation which has such a constitution will gain most.

Yes, that will be the best way. And I think, Socrates, that you have very well described how, if ever, such a constitution might come into being.

Enough then of the perfect State, and of the man who bears its image—there is no difficulty in seeing how we shall describe him.

There is no difficulty, he replied; and I agree with you in thinking that nothing more need be said.

From Project Gutenberg
Last Updated: June 22, 2016.
https://www.gutenberg.org/files/1497/1497-h/1497-h.htm#link2H_4_0010

Bibliography

ABC, Four Corners. 1987. *The moonlight state*. https://www.abc.net.au/4corners/the-moonlight-state%2D%2D-1987/2832198. Accessed 8 Apr 2020.

———. 2014. *Banking bad*, a joint Four Corners Fairfax investigation reported by Adele Ferguson and presented by Kerry O'Brien, May 5, 2014.

Applbaum, Arthur Isak. 1999. *Ethics for adversaries: The morality of roles in public and professional life*, 85–99. Princeton: Princeton University Press.

Barber, Dylan. 2012. Tweet for your supper: the new wave of cash-for-comment, *Crikey.Inq (Independent Inquiry Journalism)*, April 24, 2015. https://www.crikey.com.au/2012/04/24/tweet-for-your-supper-the-new-wave-of-cash-for-comment/ Accessed 26 Mar 2020.

BBC. 2012. *Q&A: News of the World phone-hacking scandal*, 4 August 2012. https://www.bbc.com/news/uk-11195407. Accessed 2 July 2020.

Bernstein, Carl, and Bob Woodward. 1974. *All the President's men: The greatest reporting story pf all time*. New York: Simon & Schuster Paperbacks.

Beyleveld, Deryck. 1991. *The dialectical necessity of morality: An analysis and Defense of Alan Gewirth's argument to the principle of generic consistency*. Chicago: University of Chicago Press.

Black, Jay. 2010. Who is a journalist? In *Journalism ethics: A philosophical approach*, ed. C. Meyers, 103–116. New York: Oxford University Press.

Boylan, Michael. 2000. *Basic ethics: Basic ethics in action*. Upper Saddle River: Prentice Hall.

Bradlee B. Jr. 2002. *Deputy managing editor*. Betrayal: The Crisis in the Catholic Church, by the investigative staff of The *Boston Globe*, May 10, 2002.

Bright, Martin, Ed. Vulliamy, and Peter Beaumont. 2003. Revealed: U.S. dirty tricks to win vote on Iraq War, *The Guardian*, 2 March 2003.

Burkenman, Oliver, and Richard Norton-Taylor. 2004. The spy who wouldn't keep a secret, *The Guardian,* 26 February 2004.

Businesswire. 2004. *Marqui pays bloggers in revolutionary marketing move; generates 244,000 Google hits in one week*, December 02, 2004. https://www.businesswire.com/news/home/20041202005541/en/Marqui-Pays-Bloggers-Revolutionary-Marketing-Move-Generates. Accessed 26 Mar 2020.

Butterworth, Liam. 2020. Coronavirus treatment spruiked by chef Pete Evans criticised by health associations, to be investigated by TGA, *ABC News*, April 12, 2020.

Cadwalladr, Carole. 2018. 'I made Steve Bannon's psychological warfare tool': meet the data war whistleblower, *The Guardian,* March 18, 2018.

Ceva, Emanuela, and Maria Paola Ferretti. 2017. Political corruption. *Philosophy Compass* 7 (2): 1–10.

E. H. Spence, *Media Corruption in the Age of Information*, Library of Public Policy and Public Administration 15, https://doi.org/10.1007/978-3-030-61612-0

Cooper, Adam. 2020. More alleged victims of George Pell to have abuse claims aired on ABC, *The Sydney Morning Herald and The Age*, April 2, 2020. https://www.smh.com.au/national/new-allegations-of-child-sexual-abuse-by-pell-emerge-20200402-p54gbs.html. Accessed 2 Apr 2020.

Daily Express. 2004. *Al Qaeda scouts found ½ mile from PM's home*, August 16, 2004.

Davey, Melissa. 2015. 'None of it's true': Wellness blogger Belle Gibson admits she never had cancer, *The Guardian*, April 22, 2015.

Davies, Michael. 1998. *Encyclopedia of applied ethics* (Academic Press, Volume 1, A-D, page 590).

Davies, Nick. 2014. *Hack attack: How the truth caught up with Rupert Murdoch*. New York: Farrar, Status and Giroux.

Descartes, Rene. 2018. *Meditations on first philosophy* (ed. and trans. John Cottingham). Cambridge: Cambridge University Press. Online version by Jonathan Bennett (2017). https://www.earlymoderntexts.com/assets/pdfs/descartes1641.pdf: Accessed 3 July 2020.

Dretske, Fred. 1999. *Knowledge and the flow of information*. Stanford: CSLI Publications.

Drozdiak, Natalia and Sam Schenchner. 2017. Google slapped with $US2.7 billion EU fine over search results, *The Wall Street Journal*, June 27, 2017.

Dyson, George. 2012. *Turing's cathedral: The origins of the digital universe*, 308. New York: Pantheon.

Eco, Umberto. 1989. *The open work*. Translated by Anna Cancogni. Cambridge, MA: Harvard University Press.

Eco Umberto. 1989. *The open work* (trans. Anna Cancogni). Cambridge, MA: Harvard University Press.

Eliot, Thomas Stearns. 1934. *Choruses from The Rock*.

Elliott, Deni, and Edward Spence. 2018. *Ethics for a digital era*. Oxford: Wiley-Blackwell.

Farsetta, Diane, and Daniel Price. 2006. "Fake TV News: Widespread and Undisclosed" Centre for Media and Democracy. http://www.prwatch.org/fakenews/execsummary. 6, April.

Ferguson, Adele. 2014. Banking Bad, a joint *Four Corners Fairfax* investigation reported by Adele Ferguson and presented by Kerry O'Brien, May 5, 2014.

———. 2019. *Banking bad: Whistleblowers. Corporate cover-ups. One journalist's fight for the truth*. Sydney: ABC Books.

Floridi, Luciano. 2005. Is semantic information meaningful data? *Philosophy and Phenomenological Research* 70 (2).

Foroohar, Rana. 2019. *Don't be evil: The case against big tech*. London: Allen Lane, Random House.

Francis, Hannah. 2015. Cash-for-posts: The murky ethics of social media stardom, *The Sydney Morning Herald*, November 7, 2015. https://www.smh.com.au/technology/cash-for-posts-the-murky-ethics-of-social-media-stardom-20151105-gkrs29.html Accessed 26 Mar 2020.

Fukuyama, Francis. 1996. *Trust: The social virtues and the creation of prosperity*. London: Penguins Books.

Galloway, Scott. 2017. *The four: The hidden DNA of Amazon, Apple, Facebook and Google*. London: Bantam Press.

Garside, Juliette. 2017. Malta car bomb kills Panama Papers journalist, *The Guardian*, October 17, 2017.

———. 2019a. Maltese businessman charged over murder of investigative journalist, *The Guardian*, December 1, 2019.

———. 2019b. How a dog called Peter sparked Malta's political crisis, *The Guardian*, November 30, 2019.

Gauthier, David. 1986. *Morals by agreement*. Oxford: Oxford Scholarship Online, 2003. https://www.oxfordscholarship.com/view/10.1093/0198249926.001.0001/acprof-9780198249924. Accessed 3 July 2020.

Gewirth, Alan. 1978. *Reason and morality*. Chicago: University of Chicago Press.

———. 1986. Professional ethics: The separatist thesis. *Ethics* 96: 282–300.

———. 1991. Can any final ends be rational. *Ethics* 102. (October 1991).

———. 1996. *The community of rights*. Chicago: University of Chicago Press.

———. 1998. *Self-fulfillment*. Princeton, NJ: Princeton University Press.

Gorniak-Kocikowska, Krystyna. 1996. The computer revolution and the problem of global ethics. *Science and Engineering Ethics*. April 1996.

Greenwald, Robert. 2004. *Outfoxed: Rupert Murdoch's War on Journalism*, Documentary film. https://en.wikipedia.org/wiki/Outfoxed. Accessed 25 Mar 2020.

Hamilton, Janice. 2002. Inquiry highlights cover-up by the major parties, *The Guardian*, November 6, 2002.

Helbing, D., B. S. Frey, G. Gigerennzer, E. Hafen, M. Hagner, Y. Hofsstertter, J. Vn den Hoven, R. V. Zicari, and A. Zwitter. 2017. Will democracy survive big data and artificial intelligence? *Scientific American*, February 25, 2017. https://www.scientificamerican.com/article/will-democracy-survive-big-data-and-artificicial-intelligence/.

Helmore, Edward. 2020. Facebook commitment to free speech will 'piss people off' Zuckerbrg says, *The Guardian*, February 2, 2020.

Hern, Alex. 2019. Facebook agrees to pay fine over Cambridge Analytica scandal, *The Guardian*, October 30, 2019.

History.com Editors. 2020a. *The Pentagon papers*. https://www.history.com/topics/vietnam-war/pentagon-papers. Accessed 17 Feb 2020.

———. 2020b. *Watergate*. https://www.history.com/topics/1970s/watergate. Accessed 14 Feb 2020.

Hobbes, Thomas. 1651. *Leviathan*. http://www.gutenberg.org/ebooks/3207. Accessed 3 July 2020.

Hui, Jin. and Spence, Edward. 2016. Internet addiction and well-being: Daoist and stoic reflections. *Dao: A Journal of Contemporary Philosophy*. Springer.

Hunter, Fergus. 2019. Consumer watchdog takes legal action against Google for 'misleading' conduct, *The Sydney Morning Herald and The Age*, October 29, 2019.

Hunter, Fergus, and Zoe Samios. 2020. 'Systemic failures': Facebook facing legal action over Cambridge Analytica Scandal, *The Sydney Morning Herald and The Age*, March 9, 2020.

International Federation of Journalists. 1986. *Declaration of principles on the conduct of journalists*. Accessed 23 Jan 2009. https://www.ifj.org/who/rules-and-policy/global-charter-of-ethics-for-journalists.html. Accessed 1 Apr 2020.

Johnston, Jane and Zawawi, Clara. (eds). 2004. Media relations. In *Public relations theory and practice* (2nd edn.). Allen and Unwin.

Kang, Cecillia. 2019. F.T.C approves Facebook fine of about 5 billion, *The New York Times*, July 12, 2019.

Kant, Immanuel. 1785. *Groundwork for the metaphysics of morals*. http://www.gutenberg.org/ebooks/5682. Accessed 3 July 2020.

Kymlicka, Will. 1990. *Contemporary political philosophy: An introduction*. Oxford: Clarendon Press.

Lessig, Lawrence. 2013. "Institutional corruptions", *Edward J. Safra Working Papers 1*.

Lipset, Seymour Martin, and Gabriel Salman Lenz. 2000. Corruption, culture and markets. In *Culture matters: How values shape human Progress*, ed. Lawrence E. Harrison and Samuel P. Huntington. New York: Basic Books.

Locke, John. 1689. *Two treatises of civil government*. http://www.gutenberg.org/ebooks/7370. Accessed 3 July 2020.

Lynch, Michael P. 2016. *The Internet of us: Knowing and understanding less in the age of big data*, Penguin Random House.

McMahon, Barbara. 2006. Italian football in shock as Juventus manager tries to kill himself on eve of corruption hearings, *The Guardian*, June 28, 2006.

Media and Entertainment Arts Alliance (MEAA). 2020a. *Journalism Code of Ethics, Australia (2020)*. https://www.meaa.org/meaa-media/code-of-ethics/ Accessed 29 Mar 2020.

———. 2020b. *Code of Ethics*, Australia. https://www.meaa.org/meaa-media/code-of-ethics/. Accessed 29 Mar 2020.

Meyers, Christopher. 2010. *Journalism ethics: A philosophical approach*. New York: Oxford University Press.

Milkman, Oliver. 2019. Defiant Mark Zuckerberg defends Facebook policy to allow false ads. *The Guardian*, December 2, 2019.

Mill, John Stuart. 1863. *Utilitarianism*. http://www.gutenberg.org/ebooks/11224. Accessed 3 July 2020.

Miller, Seumas. 2018. *Corruption. Stanford encyclopedia of philosophy*. (Winter 2018 Edition), Edward N. Zalta (ed.).

Miller, Seumas, Peter Roberts, and Edward Spence. 2005. *Corruption and anti-corruption: An applied philosophical approach*. Upper Saddle River: Pearson/Prentice Hall.

Milmo, Dan. 2006. Net advertising 'to overtake national newspapers', *The Guardian*, May 31, 2006.

Mims, Christopher. 2018. Who has more of your personal data than Facebook? *The Australian and Wall St Journal*, April 23, 2018.

Mirkinson, Jack. 2004. 60 years ago, Edward R. Murrow Took Down Joseph McCarthy, *The Huffington Post,* March 11, 2004. https://www.huffingtonpost.com.au/entry/edward-murrow-joseph-mccarthy-60-years-later_n_4936308?ri18n=true. Accessed 8 Apr 2020.

Monaghan, Angela. 2010. Apple fined record 1.1bn by French competition regulator, *The Guardian,* March 17, 2020.

Oltermann, Philip. 2019. The inside story of Germany's biggest scandal since the Hitler diaries. *The Guardian*, December 9, 2019.

Pasquale, Frank. 2015. *The black box society: The secret algorithms that control money and information*. Cambridge, MA: Harvard University Press.

Plato. 1952. *The Republic*, *The dialogues of Plato*. Translated by Benjamin Jowett. Chicago: Encyclopedia Britannica Inc., Book II: 359–361.

Quinn, Aaron, and Edward Spence. 2007. Two dimensions of photo manipulation: Correction and corruption. *Australian Journal of Professional and Applied Ethics*.

Rankin, Jennifer. 2019. EU parliament calls on Malta PM to resign now over Caruana Galizia, *The Guardian*, December 19, 2019.

Rawls, John. 1971. *A theory of justice*. Cambridge, MA: Harvard University Press.

Robinson, Gregory. 2020. Eamon Holmes criticised for giving credence to Covid-19 5G conspiracy theory, *The Guardian*, April 14, 2020.

Rose, James. 2018. *Facebook and Google dominate online ads. Can alliances between news publishers compete? May 24, 2018*. https://www.poynter.org/business-work/2018/facebook-and-google-dominate-online-ads-can-alliances-between-news-publishers-compete/. Accessed 26 Mar 2020.

Rousseau, Jean-Jacques. 1762. *The social contract*. http://www.gutenberg.org/ebooks/46333. Accessed 3 July 2020.

SBS News. 2020. The government is fat-tracking a code of conduct to force Google and Facebook to pay for news content, *SBS News*, April 20, 2020. Accessed 20 Apr 2020.

Schwartz, Oscar. 2018. You thought fake news was bad? Deep fakes are where truth goes to die, *The Guardian,* November 12, 2018.

Searle, John. 1969. *Speech acts: An essay in the philosophy of language*. Cambridge: Cambridge University Press. esp. pp. 33–42, 50–53.

Simmons, Peter, and Edward Spence. 2006. The practice and ethics of media release journalism. *Australian Journalism Review* 28 (1) July 2006.

Snider, Mike, and Edward C. Baig. 2019. Facebook fined $5 billion by FTC, must update and adopt new privacy, security measures, USA *Today*, July 24, 2019.

Spence, Edward. 2006. *Ethics within reason: A Neo-Gewirthian approach*. Lanham: Lexington Books (a division of Rowman and Littlefield).

———. 2007. Positive rights and the cosmopolitan community: Right-centred foundations for global ethics. *Journal of Global Ethics* 3 (02) July/August 2007.

———. 2008. Corruption in the Media. *International Journal of Applied Philosophy* 22 (2 – Fall): 231–241.

———. 2009. A universal model for the normative evaluation of internet information. *Ethics and Information Technology* 11 (4): 243–253.

———. 2009a. The epistemology and ethics of media markets in the age of information. In *Business intelligence meets moral intelligence*, ed. Yvonne Thorhauer and Stefan Blachfellner. *International Review of Information Ethics* (IRIE) Vol. 10 (February 2009), Issue No. 010, 45–52.

———. 2010. Information ethics without metaphysics: A Neo-Gewirthian approach. *International Journal of Technology and Human Interaction* 6 (1): 1–14.

———. 2010a. The epistemology and ethics of internet information: A Neo-Gewirthian approach. *Journal of Information, Communication and Ethics in Society* 8 (1).

———. 2011. Is technology good for us? A Eudaimonic meta-model for evaluating the contributive competence of technologies for a good life. *NanoEthics* 5: 335–343.

———. 2011a. Information, knowledge and wisdom: Groundwork for the normative evaluation of digital information and its relation to the good life. *Ethics and Information Technology* 13 (3): 261–275.

———. 2011b. IT Savvy, but stupid. *Australasian Science;* May 2011; 32, 4.

———. 2013a. Wisdom and Well-being in a technological age. *Synesis: A Journal of Science, Technology, Ethics, and Policy* 2013.

———. 2013b. Wisdom and wellbeing in a technological age. *Synesis: A Journal of Science, Technology, Ethics, and Policy.*

———. 2014. The advertising of happiness and the branding of values. In *Business ethics*, ed. Michael Boylan, 2nd ed. Pearson/Prentice Hall: Upper Saddle River.

———. 2017. Corruption in the media. In *The handbook of business and corruption: Cross-sectoral experiences*, ed. Michael S. Aßländer and Sarah Hudson, 453–480. Emerald Group Publishing.

———. 2018. Harm in media marketing: The branding of values. In *The handbook of media ethics*, ed. Patrick Plaisance, 237–225. Walter de Gruyter GmbH.

———. 2020. The sixth estate: Media corruption in the age of information. *Journal of Information, Communication and Ethics in Society*. Emerald Publishing Limited, 1477996X.

Spence, Edward, Van Heekeren, and Brett. 2005. *Advertising ethics*. Upper Saddle River: Pearson/ Prentice Hall.

Spence, Edward, Andrew Alexandra, Aaron Quinn, and Anne Dunn. 2011. *Media, markets and morals*. Oxford: Wiley- Blackwell.

Stauber, John, and Sheldon Rampton. 1995. *Toxic sludge is good for you: Lies, damn lies and the public relations industry*. Maine: Common Courage Press, Monroe.

Taylor, Tegan. 2018. The 1918 influenza pandemic affected the whole world. Could it happen again? *ABC News*, April 13, 2020. https://www.abc.net.au/news/health/2018-04-13/flu-pandemic-1918-what-happened-and-could-it-happen-again/9601986. Accessed 16 Apr 2020.

Taylor, Josh. 2020. Facebook and Google to be forced to share advertising revenue with Australian media companies, *The Guardian*, April 20, 2020.

The Newsroom. 2014. "Reporter who exposed the phone-hacking scandal", *Yorkshire Post*, 15 October 2014.

Thompson, Dennis F. 2013. "Two concepts of corruption: Individual and institutional", *Edward J. Safra Working Papers* 16.

Toppo, Greg. 2005. Education Dept. paid commentator to promote law. *USA Today,* July 1.

Tucker, Eric, and Barbara Ortutay. 2020. *Facebook removes Trump ads with symbols once used by Nazis*. Australia: ABC News. June 19, 2020.

Tufekci, Zeynep. 2018a. Facebook's surveillance machine, *The New York Times*, March 19, 2018.

———. 2018b. You Tube, The great radicalizer, The *New York Times*, March 10, 2018.

Tunzelmann, Alex von. 2015. Good Night, and Good Luck: attack on McCarthyism simplifies but satisfies, *The Guardian*, March 30, 2015. https://www.theguardian.com/film/filmblog/2015/mar/30/ggod-night-and-good-luck-george-clooney-edward-murrow-reel-history. Accessed 8 Apr 2020.

van Dijck, José, Thomas Poell, and Martijn de Waal. 2018. *The platform society: Public values in a connected world*. Oxford: Oxford University Press.

Warren, Mark E. 2004. What does corruption mean in a democracy. *American Journal of Political Science* 48 (2): 328–343.

———. 2006. Political corruption as duplicitous exclusion. *PS: Political Science and Politics* 39 (4): 803–807.

Webb, Amy. 2019. *The big nine: How the tech titans and their thinking machines could warp humanity*. Hatchet: Books.

Wikipedia. 2020a. *Frank Serpico*. https://en.wikipedia.org/wiki/Frank_Serpico. Accessed 17 Mar 2020.

———. 2020b. *Panama papers*. https://en.wikipedia.org/wiki/Panama_Papers. Accessed 12 Feb 2020.

Zuboff, Shoshana. 2019. *The age of surveillance capitalism*. London: Profile Books Ltd.

Zucchino, David. 2004. Army stage-managed fall of Hussein Statue. *Los Angeles Times*, July 3, 2004.

Zuckerberg, Mark. 2019. Four ideas to regulate the internet, *Facebook*, March 30, 2019.

———. 2020. Big tech needs more regulation, *Financial Times*, February 18, 2020.

Index

E. H. Spence, *Media Corruption in the Age of Information*, Library of Public Policy and Public Administration 15, https://doi.org/10.1007/978-3-030-61612-0

D

J

K

L

The manufacturer's authorised representative in the EU is Springer Nature Customer Service Centre GmbH, Europaplatz 3, 69115 Heidelberg, Germany. If you have any concerns regarding our products, please contact ProductSafety@springernature.com

Printed and bound by CPI Group (UK) Ltd, Croydon, CR0 4YY
30/09/2026
02225497-0008